REAL WORLD
CLIENT/SERVER

Other Titles of Interest From Maximum Press

See back page for more information

REAL WORLD CLIENT/SERVER

Steve Krantz

MAXIMUM PRESS
605 Silverthorn Rd
Gulf Breeze, FL 32561
(904)934-0819

Library of Congress Cataloging-in-Publication Data

Krantz, Steve, 1947–
    Real world client server: learn how to successfully migrate to client/server computing from someone who's actually done it! / by Steve Krantz.
        p.   cm.
        ISBN 0-9633214-7-1
        1. Client/server computing.   I. Title.
QA76.9.C55K75   1995   94-37726
004'.36—dc20   CIP

Printed in the United States of America

95 96 10 9 8 7 6 5 4 3 2 1

To my wife Joan (beautiful, warm, and caring).
To my son Jeffrey (the Computer Genius).
To my son Paul (who will support me when I am old!).
Thanks for putting up with me!

Trademarks

1-2-3 is a registered trademark of the Lotus Development Corporation.

3090 is a trademark of the International Business Machines Corporation.

ADSTAR is a registered trademark of the International Business Machines Corporation.

Advanced Peer-to-Peer Networking is a registered trademark of the International Business Machines Corporation.

AFP is a trademark of the International Business Machines Corporation.

AIX is a registered trademark of the International Business Machines Corporation.

AIX/6000 is a registered trademark of the International Business Machines Corporation.

Ami Pro is a trademark of the Lotus Development Corporation.

Andrew File System is a trademark of Transarc Corporation.

Appletalk is a registered trademark of Apple Computer, Inc.

APPN is a registered trademark of the International Business Machines Corporation.

AT is a registered trademark of the International Business Machines Corporation.

Berkeley Software Distribution is a trademark of the University of California at Berkeley.

BookMaster is a registered trademark of the International Business Machines Corporation.

BSD is a trademark of the University of California at Berkeley.

CallUp is a trademark of the International Business Machines Corporation.

CA-SuperProject is a registered trademark of Computer Associates International, Inc.

cc:Mail is a registered trademark of cc:Mail Inc.

CORBA is a trademark of the Object Management Group.

C Set ++ is a trademark of the International Business Machines Corporation.

Database 2 is a trademark of the International Business Machines Corporation.

DB2 is a registered trademark of the International Business Machines Corporation.

DB2/2 is a trademark of the International Business Machines Corporation.

DCE is a trademark of the Open Software Foundation, Inc.

DECnet is a registered trademark of Digital Equipment Corporation.

Distributed Database Connection Services/2 is a trademark of the International Business Machines Corporation.

ES/9000 is a trademark of the International Business Machines Corporation.

Ethernet is a trademark of the Xerox Corporation.

Freelance Graphics is a trademark of the Lotus Development Corporation.

IBM is a registered trademark of the International Business Machines Corporation.

Intel is a registered trademark of the Intel Corporation.

ISSC is a registered trademark of the International Business Machines Corporation.

LANstreamer is a trademark of the International Business Machines Corporation.

LaserJet is a registered trademark of the Hewlett-Packard Company.

Lotus is a registered trademark of the Lotus Development Corporation.

Lotus Notes is a registered trademark of the Lotus Development Corporation

Lotus SmartSuite is a registered trademark of Lotus Development Corporation.

Micro Channel is a registered trademark of the International Business Machines Corporation.

Microsoft is a registered trademark of the Microsoft Corporation.

Motif is a trademark of the Open Software Foundation, Inc.

MVS/ESA is a trademark of the International Business Machines Corporation.

NetDoor is a trademark of the International Business Machines Corporation.

NetView is a registered trademark of the International Business Machines Corporation.

NetWare is a registered trademark of the Novell Corporation.

Network File System is a trademark of Sunsoft, Inc.

NFS is a registered trademark of Sun Microsystems Inc.

OfficeVision is a registered trademark of the International Business Machines Corporation.

OfficeVision/VM is a trademark of the International Business Machines Corporation.

OMG is a registered trademark of the Object Management Group.

ONC is a trademark of Sun Microsystems Inc.

Operating System/2 is a registered trademark of the International Business Machines Corporation.

OS/2 is a registered trademark of the International Business Machines Corporation.

OSF is a trademark of the Open Software Foundation, Inc.

Pennant is a trademark of the International Business Machines Corporation.

Pennant Systems is a trademark of the International Business Machines Corporation.

Pentium is a registered trademark of the Intel Corporation.

Person to Person is a trademark of the International Business Machines Corporation.

Personal Computer AT is a trademark of the International Business Machines Corporation.

Personal System/2 is a registered trademark of the International Business Machines Corporation.

ThinkPad is a registered trademark of the International Business Machines Corporation.

Time and Place is a trademark of the International Business Machines Corporation.

UNIX is a registered trademark of Unix System Laboratories, Inc.

ValuePoint is a trademark of the International Business Machines Corporation.

VM/ESA is a registered trademark of the International Business Machines Corporation.

Windows is a trademark of the Microsoft Corporation.

WIN-OS/2 is a trademark of the International Business Machines Corporation.

Workplace Shell is a registered trademark of the International Business Machines Corporation.

XGA is a registered trademark of the International Business Machines Corporation.

X/Open is a trademark of X/Open Company, Ltd.

Xyplex is a registered trademark of Xyplex Inc

Disclaimer

The purchase of computer software or hardware is an important and costly business decision. While the author and publisher of this book have made reasonable efforts to ensure the accuracy and timeliness of the information contained herein, the author and publisher assume no liability with respect to loss or damage caused or alleged to be caused by reliance on any information contained herein and disclaim any and all warranties, expressed or implied, as to the accuracy or reliability of said information.

This book is not intended to replace the manufacturers' product documentation or personnel in determining the specifications and capabilities of the products mentioned in this book. The manufacturers product documentation should always be consulted, as the specifications and capabilities of computer hardware and software products are subject to frequent modification. The reader is solely responsible for the choice of computer hardware and software. All configurations and applications of computer hardware and software should be reviewed with the manufacturers' representatives prior to choosing or using any computer hardware and software. This book is not sponsored or endorsed by IBM, and the author and publisher are neither affiliated with IBM nor acting as IBM agents.

Prologue

There is no background music in real life.

The purpose of this book is to explain how to migrate a medium-sized or large company to client/server computing, drawing heavily on the recent IBM Boca Raton migration experience. It is fundamentally a technical book, but has been written in an approachable style. New terms are printed in bold the first time they appear. In almost every case, they are defined immediately in the text or in the near 500-term Glossary of Terms (Appendix B). The author deeply appreciates how hard it is to grasp the all of what fits under the client/server umbrella! I am learning new terms almost every day.

CIOs of medium-sized and large corporations should find this book a valuable reference. It explains the client/server landscape and provides the details of an actual large-scale migration. Ditto for industry analysts, consultants, and technical professionals. Deep-knowledge, networking heavy techs will, on the other hand, find this light reading. However, it might fill in some gaps regarding the broad sweep of the client/server computing field.

IBM users, watchers, and employees should enjoy this book because it is not only generally informative, but it tells a great IBM story. Bottom-line, IBM Boca Raton has built a solid, reliable client/server environment on a large scale using primarily IBM products. Moreover, this tells a great OS/2 story—OS/2 is a winner. It is the standard operating system in IBM Boca Raton for PCs. AIX on RISC System/6000s is the standard for workstations.

The Client/Server Evolution

As mainframe technology evolved, networking technology emerged, providing businesses with corporate networks. The benefits of distributed computing and data centralization became apparent as corporate networks were increasingly deployed. But the limitations of traditional terminals and multiuser mainframe computing needed to be overcome to enable businesses to improve productivity.

The personal computer brought computing power to everyone's desktop. Standalone applications with improvements in human factors and performance typified the early PC scene (e.g., spreadsheet applications). In addition, the PC was employed by many large corporate users as a terminal, to enable continued use of mainframe applications.

As local area networking (LAN) technology evolved during the 1980s, application programs matured on the PC as well. This maturation resulted in client/server computing. Client/server computing is a computing model in which client systems (usually intelligent PCs and workstations) run user applications. The applications use a combination of their resources and a portion of the storage and computing resources of one or more server systems (e.g. high-performance PCs) to perform useful work. The application portion on the client requests server resources by communicating over a network. The results are nothing less than a revolution in information technology (IT), which is sweeping the world.

Today's typical medium or large corporation already has a substantial investment in computer hardware and software—one or more networked mid-sized computers or mainframes and an assortment of PCs and workstations, some of which are part of isolated local area networks. Leaders of these companies are trying to sort out how best to participate in this revolution. This book will provide some help. Here we will explore client/server computing, help you plot your migration strategy, and share the migration of a large percentage of IBM Boca Raton's employees (over 2,700 users) to client/server computing.

Following is a brief description of the contents:

Chapter 1: Client/Server Computing and Business Reengineering

This chapter introduces the client/server computing model and explains why it is the most important trend in information technology today.

Next, we explore the relationship of client/server computing to the major trends that are affecting most businesses today, including business process reengineering, empowered teams, and quality management. A Business Reengineering Model is defined. The impact of these trends are discussed with respect to the changes observed at the IBM development site at Boca Raton, Florida over the past ten years, leading up to its successful client/server migration in 1993–1994. Next, a recommended information technology strategy is presented, based on the IBM Boca Raton strategy developed at the beginning of the migration. The chapter winds up with an approach to business case development, necessary to justify the large expenditures required for a client/server migration.

Chapter 2: Migration Management

This is the "how to do it" chapter from an information technology management perspective, giving structure to the chapters that follow. The majority of the chapter describes a phased methodology to transform a business from mid-range or mainframe-centric computing to client/server computing. The chapter ends with a perspective on overall project management and how to evolve from migration management to ongoing information technology management.

Chapter 3: Selecting Application Programs

Application programs are of paramount importance in any type of computing environment because they "are the computer system" as far as the users are concerned. For this reason, the selection of reliable, effective, and easy-to-use application programs is vital to any computing solution (client/server or not). This chapter will help you evaluate your particular application program needs and select the appropriate application programs to meet those needs. It will show how an application program selection process was used in the IBM Boca Raton migration and discuss the importance of proper application program management. The chapter winds up with some critical success factors.

Chapter 4: Client Rollout

The client rollout is a major component of any client/server migration. Each individual user's requirements must be considered when deciding the clients to be replaced or upgraded. Careful planning must be performed prior to and during a client rollout to guarantee user satisfaction. This chapter details the IBM Boca Raton experience during a large-scale client rollout in 1993–1994, with a look back at the relatively small-scale client migrations in the 1991–1992 timeframe. It will focus on each of these client migrations in turn, detailing requirements, the transition to client/server computing, future considerations, and some critical success factors.

Chapter 5: The Server Farm

The organized collection of servers necessary to support a large number of clients requires careful planning, staged acquisition, and staged installation. This chapter will discuss the overall requirements for server systems, how this evolved on the IBM Boca site, future considerations, and some critical success factors.

Chapter 6: Network Infrastructure

This chapter defines the complex client/server network, lists the major requirements, details the important components, and describes the IBM Boca Raton network. Next, network management requirements, activities, and tools are described. The IBM Boca Raton approach is detailed, and the future of client/server networks is explored. The chapter winds up with a few closing thoughts and the network administrator's pledge.

Chapter 7: Communications, Education, and Support

This chapter will first discuss the communications process necessary to win the hearts and minds of users migrating to client/server computing.

The development of a just-in-time user education process will be presented. Next, user support for the client/server environment will be explored, including Help Desk and Tools. The chapter winds up with critical success factors.

Chapter 8: Measuring Results

This chapter recommends the set of measurements you should use to control your client/server migration. The IBM Boca Raton results provide examples. Some overall critical success factors are discussed.

Appendices

Appendix A: Products and Tools   All products and internally developed tools used in the IBM Boca Raton Client/Server Network are listed with a brief description of each.

Appendix B: Glossary of Terms   A nearly 500-word client/server glossary is included.

Appendix C: Pro Forma Client/Server Financial Spreadsheet

Appendix D: Client Migration Questionnaire   The actual on-line form filled out by each IBM Boca Raton user to gather migration requirements.

Appendix E: Sample Service-Level Agreements

Foreword

Lotus Consulting enjoyed supporting Steve's team as it undertook a major migration from mainframe technology to client/server systems. In this book, Steve has provided a comprehensive tutorial of how, over a 14-month period, his team converted IBM's Boca Raton site from centralized IBM mainframe tools to a flexible set of client/server tools. It was a real pleasure to work together, and to see Steve's team develop strong, independent, client/server and Lotus Notes expertise.

The opening chapter introduces an important Business Reengineering Model, which clearly and simply relates global competition to the powerful transformations occurring in many businesses, including empowered teams, rightsizing, and client/server computing. Using this model, Steve's team balanced its focus both on deploying new technology—groupware—*and* the cultural transformation this technology requires. Succeeding chapters cover methodology, applications, clients, servers, and the network in an orderly fashion. Each chapter provides the basics, describes actual experiences, and looks toward the future in a reader-friendly fashion.

The emerging technologies which underlie the success of client/server computing are described with insight, from the OS/2 GUI desktop and groupware with Lotus Notes to RAID disk storage and ATM. Those of you interested in extending your knowledge in client/server computing and Lotus Notes deployment should make this book a part of your reference library.

As participants in Steve's project, Lotus Consulting team members admire the Boca Raton group's commitment to managing not just technology, but also the essentials of cultural transformation. We also wish our friends in Boca Raton the best in all their future endeavors.

Peter Brennan
Regional Managing Director, The Americas
Lotus Consulting

Acknowledging the Teams

Network Team

- Bob Slossberg, Nelson Hernandez, Paul Hill, and Al Madsen—the bedrock of Boca. Because of their skill and dedication, the Boca Raton site has one of the best networks in IBM.

Standard Tools Team

- Moises Behar, a.k.a. the Magician, problem solver extraordinaire, and Application Review Board Chairman.

Client Rollout Team

- Sal Abady and Dan Slutsky—Sal and Dan exceeded all expectations with their meticulous, ever-improving process to rollout thousands of PC clients. Hats are off!

- Michelle Davis, Debbie Burton, and Walter A. Sotillo (a.k.a. Mr. Print), Al Zahacefski.

Finance Team

- Jeff Hathaway—Green eye-shade and all, Jeff kept everyone on their toes finding all the buried information technology dollars (and bones).

Applications Development Team

- Dave Lasdon (a.k.a. the Doctor of Squeezology).
- Diane Lomatch (a.k.a. Grandma Query).
- Bill Ordway, Bea Fernandez, and Sue Weber.
- Lynda Reed—whenever the CIO team needed to get something done for applications, requiring coordination and communication, they turned to her.

Communications/Education Team

- Barbara Brown—made education go with skill and dynamics.
- Ann Lamberti, Ellen Del Greco, Nadine Smith, and Pete Sabio.

Server Administration Team

- Linda Campbell—the Server Queen, the mistress of all she surveyed!

- Dave Quarles—Lotus Notes Engineer extraordinaire!

- Tim Fischer, Kevin Knight, Vivian Fitzsimmons, Tom Chalmers, Mike Kennedy, Julie Acosta, Lou Giambalvo, Uri Chamish, Dierdre Donnelly, and Laney Siegel

User Support Team

- Brian Conley—ISSC RTP. Leader of the Help Desk.

- Maren Nelson—POS Tools. Whenever someone with good judgment was needed, the CIO team turned to her.

- Chuck O'Halloran—POS Tools.

Leadership

- Jan Jackman—The IBM Boca Raton site's first CIO. A wonderful lady who got everything started.

- Ed Kloster—The IBM Boca Raton site's current CIO. Allowed everyone to become an empowered team.

- Steve Krantz—Project Leader. The author, yours truly.

- Charlie Gumula—An extra-special acknowledgment is in order for Charlie Gumula, a.k.a. Murphy's Master, the ISSC project leader. I dubbed him that after nearly a year of working side by side with him and seeing how wonderfully effective he was in resolving problems. His calm maturity, wisdom, and good nature made the complex rollout a success. He tackled each problem one by one with the patience that comes with great experience. It was a privilege to work with him in every respect.

- Charlie Emond and Joann Collins-Smee—the original ISSC business executives.

- George Kopa—the current ISSC business executive, a "bud" among "buds."

- Doug Foster—ISSC team manager.

- Larry Taylor—POS Tools. Sartorially eclectic, Larry earned every arrow, as most pioneers do!

- Lorene Schlegel—POS Tools Manager.

- Phil Zofcin—manager and moneybags. Loaned me the dough I needed to pay for those consultants!

- Palmer Newman—PC Co. architect. He incisively contributed much to the strategy.

The Extended Team

- Al Gojuangco—the best chartsman east of the Mississippi.

- Tonya Spoonamore—the CIO team's dedicated secretary.

- Albert Schneider—PC Co. Somers, who shared with the teams all his goodies at the beginning!

- Tony Lostaglio—PC Co. RTP, who educated the CIO team when they were completely in the dark!

- Peggy Chowning—PC Co. RTP.

- Harry Bennett—IBM LAN Business Solutions. Stomped the site, writing Notes applications as he went!

- John Deel—IBM LAN Business Solutions.

- Bill Morris—Lotus Consulting. I must credit Bill Morris for inspiring me to set up the highly successful focus group sessions with key site areas. This was the springboard for creation of several important Lotus Notes groupware applications, which helped to cement IBM Boca's client/server success.

- David Carno, Al McAlpine, Rob McAuley, George Parker—Lotus Consulting.

- Debbie Bothwell—ISSC SER.

Special Acknowledgments

- Jim Hoskins—my editor, publisher, and friend. He taught me everything I didn't know about writing a book—which was considerable! His support, good nature, and dedication are deeply appreciated. (Kamel and Nunzio feel the same way!)
- Lois Dimpfel, Marie Thompson, Dennis Bancks, Kathy McAndrews, Doug Knickerbocker, Bob Thorpe, Bob Chernow, Keith Silva, Mike Cohen, and Mark Weber—thanks for the interviews!

Maximum Press is an accredited member of the IBM Independent/International Vendor League.

Table of Contents

Chapter 2:
Migration Management 29

Chapter 3:
Selecting Application Programs   53

Chapter 4:
Client Rollout   88

Chapter 6:
Network Infrastructure   163

1

Client/Server Computing and Business Reengineering

Networks make it possible for organizations to abandon the top-down management structure—that is, where a lot of information was held at the top—and move on to a flatter, more responsive structure where information is shared and widely available.

[DERFLER, 1993]

This chapter introduces the client/server computing model and explains why it is the most important trend in information technology today. Next, we explore the relationship of client/server computing to the major trends that are affecting most businesses today, including business process reengineering, empowered teams, and quality management. A Business Reengineering Model is defined. The impact of these trends is discussed with respect to the changes observed at the IBM development site at Boca Raton, Florida over the past ten years, leading up to its successful client/server migration in 1993–1994. Next, a recommended information technology strategy is presented, based on the IBM Boca Raton strategy developed at the beginning of the migration. The chapter winds up with an approach to business case development, necessary to justify the large expenditures required for a client/server migration.

1

Client/Server Computing Defined

Client/server computing is a computer architecture based on **client** systems (systems requesting services—usually **personal computers** or simply PCs) communicating over a high-speed network (often a **local area network** or simply a **LAN**) with **server** systems. Servers are computer systems (sometimes just more powerful PCs) that offer some resource to other computers (the clients) in the network. In the client/server environment, the programming on the server interacts with the programming on the client in order to do work for the users. For example, the functions provided by a calendar management application program would be split between the client and the server. The client portion of the application typically includes the user interface and requests services from the server. The server portion of the application might store the calendar information for many users and responds to request from clients for data or processing of that information. Figure 1.1 illustrates this. To the user, the processing appears to be a single, unified task.

Client/server computing gives any user the ability to easily access any authorized application, data, computer system (server), or other resource

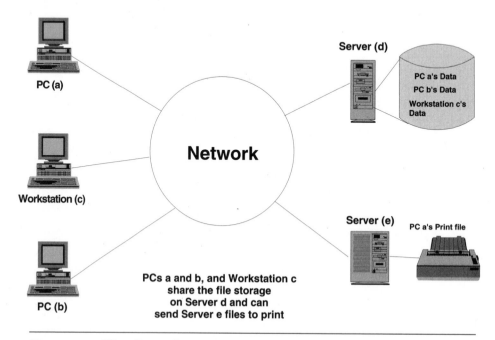

Figure 1.1   Client/Server Computing

(e.g., a printer) throughout an enterprise or between enterprises. It spans multiple computing **platforms** (a platform is a base product, system, or design upon which other products, systems, or designs rely) and heterogeneous networks (a network is a data communications system that interconnects computer systems). It includes the latest advances in PCs, workstations (such as an IBM RS/6000 system or high-powered PC used to do design or development activities), specially designed servers, general- purpose mid-range and mainframe computers, databases, and more.

Because of the strong productivity and efficiency gains offered by client/server computing, a consulting study commissioned this year by IBM estimates that 84 percent of U.S. businesses polled favor a move to client/server computing within the next few years. A recent study done by IBM indicated that more than 50 percent of the Fortune 1,000 companies are already using client/server computing, and of those not using it, more than 50 percent intended to be using it within two years.

Client/server computing is a significant change in computing methodology. It is as fundamental as the shift from batch/unit record processing of the 1950s to on-line interactive processing of the 1960s and 1970s. With the advent of the minicomputer in the 1970s, individual departments were able to begin computing outside the realm of the information systems department or the "glass house." This trend was accelerated in the 1980s as PCs were increasingly deployed by businesses large and small.

Figure 1.2 provides a snapshot of the past three decades of computer system and network evolution leading up the development of client/server computing.

Mainframe-centric and minicomputer-centric networks dominated the 1970s. In this environment, users employed dumb terminals to instruct these host systems over the network. It also became common to interconnect mainframes and minicomputers to create large-scale distributed systems over computer networks.

The 1980s brought PCs, workstations, and LANs. PCs were quickly linked to the large-scale distributed systems, but primarily to emulate the dumb terminal, where the local PC computing capability was not exploited. From their beginning, powerful workstations running engineering/scientific applications used LANs to share data among users. Little by little, users began installing LANs to interconnect a few PCs so they could share printers and exchange data files and messages. PC LAN programs and entirely new LAN operating systems were developed. They made LAN resources, such as server disk storage and printers, appear as

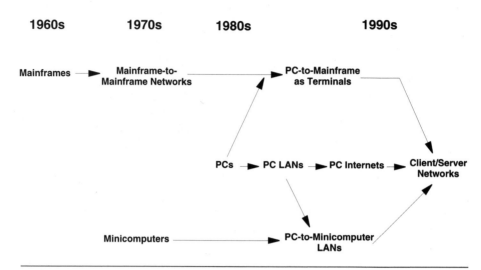

Figure 1.2 Evolution of Computer Networks

if they were part of the user's PC. More significantly, performance of these network-attached devices could be made to appear fast or faster than resident devices! This was the birth of client/server computing.

The breakthrough in technology which made client/server practical was the introduction of very-high-speed LAN networks in the 1980s. Very-high-speed is a relative term. Early token-ring LANs operating at 4 Mbps (million bits per second) were dramatically faster than traditional networks communicating at up to 56 Kbps (thousand bits per second). Such speeds as 56 Kbps are still common in wide area networks (WANs). Advances in communication technology for local area networks and wide area networks have allowed connectivity among users and departments. This has led to increasing demands for better access to information stored on mainframe computers. Add to this the significant advances in operating system software (such as OS/2) and application programs with greater ease of use, and you have employees achieving higher levels of productivity without having to become computer experts.

Continuing developments through the early 1990s have accelerated the trend to complex client/server networks. Hierarchical, host-centric networks are giving way to heterogeneous, flat networks, where clients select from a suite of server systems, from floor-standing PC servers to water-cooled mainframes. The internetworking components have undergone a similar revolution in performance and design (Chapter 6, "Network Infrastructure," provides details).

This fundamental shift in computing away from exclusively mainframe-centric or minicomputer-based computing to client/server computing is based on both technological and business environment changes. First we will compare both approaches to computing on a technological basis. Let's walk through Figure 1.3's side-by-side analysis.

System architecture means the principles of design used for the computing system involved. The mainframe's architecture is typically proprietary, specifying a single type of computer system from a single vendor. Client/server computing architecture is based on standards defined by standards setting bodies, such as **ISO** or **IEEE** (see Glossary for definitions), or de facto standards defined by individual vendors or consortiums of several vendors. This is an advantage for client/server computing as it affords the user more flexibility in purchasing from several competing vendors.

Network architecture specifies how systems are to be interconnected in a network. Mainframe-centric network architectures define the mainframe as the master system, with all other systems or clients as slaves. This makes the network easier to manage (the mainframe is in control), but less flexible when changes are required to the network. Client/server

Attribute	Mainframe-Centric	Client/Server
System Architecture	Proprietary standards. Single platform.	Industry standards (Open). Flexible, multiple platforms
Network Architecture	Hierarchical, master-slave	Flat, peer-to-peer
User's Perspective	Organization solutions	Individual, group solutions
Processing	Centralized	Distributed
Scalability	Limited, in large increments	Extensive, in small increments
Clients	Dumb, no processing	Intelligent, shares processing with servers
Servers	Single-platform, performs all processing	Multiple platforms. Best-fit-of-technology.
Information Forms	Text, numerics primarily. Graphics, image.	Text, numerics, graphics, image, multimedia
Management, Security	Mature	Immature, incomplete
Application advantages	Large scale: batch processing, transaction processing, database.	Interactive. Groupware. Distributed database and processing.

Figure 1.3 Mainframe-Centric vs. Client/Server Computing

systems are typically interconnected in flat, distributed networks, with no one system in control. This makes them harder to manage, but more flexible when new systems or clients are added to the network.

From the user's perspective, the mainframe is monolithic, providing one-size-fits-all application solutions. Client/server computing offers individualized or group-based solutions (e.g., applications and LANs), a clear advantage.

Processing is completely centralized on the mainframe. Although mainframes are extremely reliable, based on years of incremental improvements, when one goes down, everybody in the organization is affected. Processing is distributed in the client/server environment across multiple, independent systems. Although servers are individually less reliable than a top-flight mainframe, if a server system crashes it only affects a limited percentage of the users.

Scalability means the ability to incrementally increase processing capacity as needs warrant. Mainframe processing power can be scaled up for a specific system, in big increments. This is important for a large, monolithic application process that cannot be distributed (e.g., large-scale simulation). In a client/server environment, scalability is fairly limited for an individual system, but if processing can be distributed, then additional capacity can be achieved by purchasing additional server systems. The right conclusion is that each approach offers scalability based on its particular application strength (discussed later in this chapter).

The traditional client for a mainframe is the dumb terminal (sometimes called a dependent display terminal or a nonprogrammable terminal), which performs no independent processing. The client in a client/server environment is an intelligent system that shares the processing with one or more servers. There are clear advantages to an intelligent client, particularly in the area of high-quality, high-performance user interface.

As servers to a set of dumb clients, mainframes offer a single platform that performs all processing. A server in a client/server environment can be selected from multiple platforms (e.g., PC or RS/6000 systems), applying the "best fit of technology" to the problem. To be fair to the mainframe, its role as a server is evolving to where it can share processing with an intelligent client; that is, it can act as a true server in the client/server sense. For example, there is an explosion of application builder tools that offer an intelligent, graphic user interface (GUI) on the client PC, which can request data from a remote mainframe database—see "Decision Support" in Chapter 3, "Selecting Application Programs," for additional details.

Looking at information forms, a client/server environment offers more flexibility than the mainframe-centric environment. The most salient example is the handling of multimedia information, which demands an intelligent client capable of transforming digital sound and digital video data into their auditory and visual versions.

Management and security is clearly superior in the mainframe-centric environment. There are mature, time-tested procedures and tools available, for example IBM's NetView, to manage the environment. A similar observation is true for preserving security. Although a blizzard of new products appear almost daily, client/server network management and security is by no means a mature discipline. There are holes, redundant tools, and pitfalls. Chapter 6 provides more details.

It is vital to understand the application strengths of each environment. The mainframe is unbeatable at handling large-scale batch processing (e.g., payroll processing for a large corporation or a weather system simulation); it is unbeatable in handling a large central database for a multiuser query application; and it is unbeatable for large-scale transaction processing, such as an airlines reservations system. Client/server is best for user-intensive, interactive applications, such as computer-aided design or **CAD**. It supports information sharing (or groupware) superbly for teams of people with work to do. For distributed databases and distributed processes, where multiple people in multiple places wish to process information, but don't need up-to-the-minute accurate information (up to the hour is fine), client/server computing is dynamite (see the discussion of Lotus Notes in Chapter 3).

So, the mainframe is *not* dead, just the mainframe-centric computing environment. Mainframes just need to be integrated into the client/server computing paradigm (model) where their great advantages can best be applied. An excellent vision of this integration is provided by Vaskevitch [1993]. He defines three concentric rings of data with an inner core: The outer ring of data is on user PCs, the middle ring of data is on servers, and the inner core of corporate data is on mainframes or mid-range computing systems (see Figure 1.4). Until recently, this model lacked the middle ring. Servers in Vaskevitch's model contain local copies of the data from the inner core, which is thus made accessible across the client/server environment. Users can easily query and update the local server data. Periodically, the server data can then be "uploaded" to the corporate database for other processing. This client/server model combines the best of large mainframes or mid-range computing systems with the best of smaller, local servers and clients.

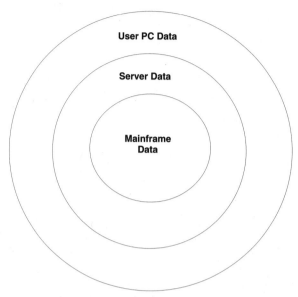

Adapted with permission of the publisher from an illustration which appears in *Client/Server Strategies* by David Vaskevitch. Text and art copyright © 1993 by David Vaskevitch. Published by IDG Books Worldwide, Inc. All rights reserved.

Figure 1.4   Enterprise Data Model

Client/Server Positives

With powerful, graphical personal computers on the desks of users in a client/server environment, application vendors have dramatically improved the user interface section of their applications. They have standardized the look and feel by using the underlying framework of the operating system graphics support. OS/2 applications use the features of the Presentation Manager interface, for example. This makes users productive quickly because applications are consistent and easier to learn. Because user interfaces are more intuitive, applications can be picked up for use, put down for lengthy periods, and then reused with virtually no loss of skill.

Personal and team applications are supported effectively in the client/server environment, greatly improving user productivity. Personal applications include word processors, spreadsheets, and business graphics applications. Team applications include electronic mail and groupware, a new type of information-sharing application. New, powerful application development tools make it easy to use an intelligent client as a means to readily access server data and enterprise data on a mainframe, thereby turning the mainframe into a server. See Chapter 3 for details.

Intelligent, high-performance client systems can support graphic, easy-to-use interfaces. Multimedia data is supported, adding the dimension of image (e.g., photographs), audio, and video to applications. Chapter 4, "Client Rollout," supplies more details.

Servers in a client/server environment can be selected from multiple platforms, implying the "best fit of technology" to most problems. Additional server capacity can be achieved by purchasing additional, relatively inexpensive systems. Chapter 5, "The Server Farm," provides a complete discussion of the server environment.

Well-designed client/server networks can easily support the addition of more clients and servers—they are flexible. They can seamlessly interoperate across local and remote areas using today's networking technology, expanding the scope of information sharing (see Chapter 6).

Client/server computing can be built with industry-standard components (PCs, servers, applications, operating systems, network communication protocols). This gives the user more flexibility in purchasing from several competing vendors. It is sometimes more cost-effective to have many small computers working together than to have one large computer of equivalent power. See "Information Technology Finances" later in this chapter.

Client/Server Negatives

Some of the technologies employed in client/server computing are relatively new. A few are immature and risky. Without careful planning and a solid migration methodology, failure is a possibility. Chapter 2, "Migration Management," supplies a proven approach.

Client/server network management is very difficult and requires highly skilled support staffs. This was cited by over 50 percent of the respondents of a late 1992 survey as a key drawback [Sentry, 1992]. The May 23, 1994, issue of *Computerworld* cited it as one of the top ten barriers to client/server implementation based on their survey of computing users. Establishing a secure network is another major barrier to adopting this computing approach. Management of security data is almost impossible to centralize (applications have their own implementations), and complex networks can spring leaks without careful planning and installation. Chapter 6 provides more details on how to effectively manage the complex client/server computing environment with the required security.

It may be difficult to cost-justify a major client/server migration. Depending on the current infrastructure, your organization may have to replace its networking components, upgrade its PCs, and buy new servers just to get started. A medium-sized or large enterprise may choose to live with the status quo rather than spend several million dollars of precious capital to replace its Information Technology infrastructure. "Information Technology Finance" later in this chapter offers an approach.

If the financial justification barrier is surmounted, migration to client/server computing requires committed management from the top down and committed users from the bottom up. Each must learn a new way of performing their daily office activities. Chapter 7, "Communication, Education, and Support," offers a way to make this happen.

A Business Reengineering Model

To gain insight in the business environment changes, we must go back to the major impact of W. Deming and his plan for reinvigorating modern business. Deming has become famous in recent years for his influence in reinvigorating Japan's major industries in the 1950s and 1960s. His *Out of the Crisis,* published in 1982, documented his ideas.

Deming thought of production as a system where a never-ending improvement of quality continues cyclically resulting in lower and lower cost. The steps are:

1. Design the product.

2. Make it; test it in the production line and in the laboratory.

3. Put it on the market.

4. Test it in service; find out what the user thinks of it and why the nonuser has not bought it.

He defined 14 points for management, which emphasized constancy of purpose, building quality in, cost minimization, and, most important, teamwork. "People in research, design, sales, and production must work as a team, to foresee problems of production and in use that may be encountered with the product or service" [Deming, 1982]. Deming's approach was adopted in the 1950s by Japan to revolutionize their industries, leading to a dramatic shift in the balance of global competition. Based on Deming's process model, we can visualize a simple cycle of process leading to team formation, resulting in improved quality and lower cost, ultimately leading to improved profit, which can be invested in yet better processes (see Figure 1.5).

Deming set in motion a separate cycle, the Information Sharing Cycle (see Figure 1.6), spun from his teamwork insight. Major corporations (IBM among them) have recognized the value of this insight. They are flattening their hierarchical organizations and creating interdisciplinary, empowered teams. An empowered team is a team of workers able to make any and all decisions necessary to accomplish their mission, with full accountability for the results. Empowered teams need to share information effectively. Information sharing is best accomplished with **groupware** applications, which are supported most effectively with a **client/server** computing environment. Groupware is a new classification of application software that allows users to conveniently share data across a network. An example is a database on a shared server system where each member of a team can conveniently place files for each member of the team to see. Another example of groupware is where a business process is controlled in a step-by-step fashion by a software application, communicating information to all participants in the process via electronic mail. Advances in client/server computing, in turn, improve the productivity of empowered teams, and the cycle continues. Tapscott and Caston, in their 1993 book *Paradigm Shift,* describe this as the "enabling effect of Information Technology." Workgroup computing (another term

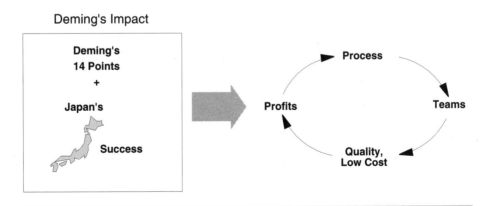

Figure 1.5 Process to Profits Cycle

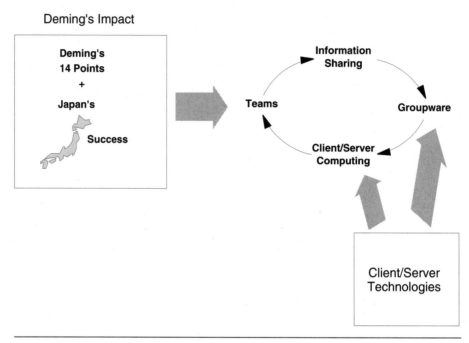

Figure 1.6 Information Sharing Cycle

for groupware) enables a high-performance team to perform effectively as a result of the newly redesigned business process [Tapscott, 1993]. This is one of the key insights for the success of the client/server computing model.

The success of client/server technology in small companies and as splinter (or renegade) projects in large companies (with mainframe-centric computing environments) has spawned a separate Rightsizing Cycle (Figure 1.7). These successes (productivity gains and savings) spur additional investments in client/server technology, which in turn cause more large businesses to **rightsize** their **information technology (IT)** infrastructure (the computing and networking systems used by a business to process and store its information). To rightsize means to move to a best-fit-of-technology computing environment, where a mix of PCs, workstations, PC servers, workstation servers, minicomputers, and mainframes interoperate in a client/server computing network.

If we look at the fierce global marketplace competition facing the leader of a large business, we can put all three cycles together to define **business reengineering** and the substantial changes that are occurring.

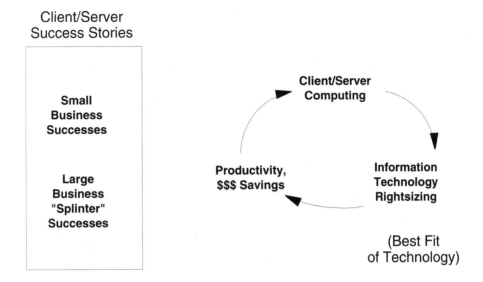

Figure 1.7 Rightsizing Cycle

Figure 1.8, the Business Reengineering Model, illustrates that the astute business leader is grabbing onto our three cycles, now interlinked, to gain leverage for his company. With redefined processes built around empowered teams, he gains quality, cost control, and, hopefully, renewed profits (Process to Profits Cycle). He buys into client/server computing to enhance the information-sharing capacity of his now-flattened, team-oriented organization (Information Sharing Cycle). His client/server investment leads to a rightsized information technology infrastructure, further improving productivity and savings (the Rightsizing Cycle).

IBM's Reality

The industry-sweeping System/360 concepts have propelled IBM to huge success since the mid-1960s. Mainframes running multiuser operating systems in centralized computing centers became the preferred approach for large corporate computing. In the 1970s, IBM broadened its product line by producing highly successful minicomputer systems such as the

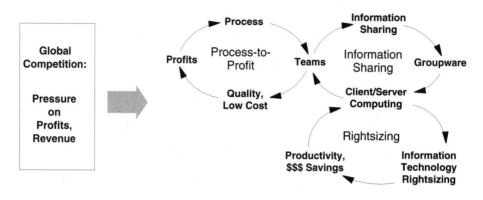

Figure 1.8   A Business Reengineering Model

System/34 and Series/1. In the 1980s, the IBM Personal Computer set the industry standard for personal computers.

Established in 1967, the IBM Boca Raton site is best known for being the birthplace of the IBM Personal Computer introduced in 1981. Subsequent major accomplishments, such as the IBM Personal Computer AT, the PS/2, and OS/2, defined standards for personal workstations and set the stage for today's evolution to client/server computing.

Throughout much of its existence, the IBM Boca Raton site has reflected the hierarchical, mainframe-centric information technology. Traditional management practices, much revered throughout the world, were unquestioned tenets of behavior, reflected throughout the management and employee ranks.

Empowered Teams in IBM Boca Raton

Traditional IBM organizations featured first-line managers with technical, business, and personnel responsibility. A typical span of control for professional groups was around ten employees per manager. "Advocates and advanced practitioners of Business Process Re-engineering and Total Quality Management, employee empowerment, and self-managed teams have begun suggesting that the classical span of control may be too limited" [Vaskevitch, 1993]. As a result, a shift in responsibilities between managers and technical professionals has occurred. Managers have increased spans of control with a renewed emphasis on personnel management. Correspondingly, technical professionals have been given more autonomy, decision-making power, and accountability in the organization, a process called empowerment.

At the IBM Boca Raton site, there were three major process reengineering projects undertaken over the past three years: in the OS/2 development organization, in the PC Company, and in information technology across the site. In each case, empowered teams coupled with information technology tools were the key ingredients. Following is an overview of each project.

OS/2 Development Process Reengineering in IBM Boca Raton

The OS/2 development organization has been through two major transitions in its development processes since its beginnings in the mid-1980s. Through 1991, the traditional waterfall model of software development was rigidly followed (Figure 1.9). Planners developed requirements and

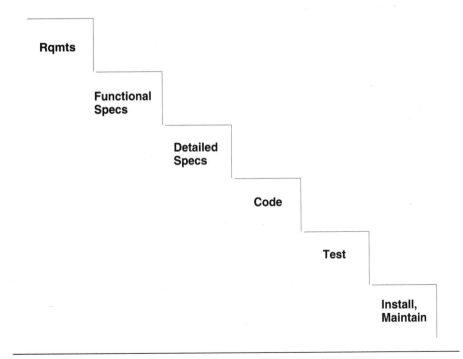

Figure 1.9 Waterfall Model

handed them to high-level designers. The high-level designers completed the design and handed off to low-level designers who wrote the code and performed unit testing. The code was handed off to independent test organizations for component-level and system-level testing. When complete, the code was released and maintenance would commence. Full specifications, design workbooks and formal reviews punctuated the process. It was slow, but thorough.

This traditional approach clashed loudly with the more free-wheeling Microsoft developers who were codeveloping the first few OS/2 releases (through OS/2 1.3). By the late 1980s, Microsoft went its own way to develop Windows, while the OS/2 developers were creating OS/2 2.0, a full-fledged 32-bit version of the operating system. According to Lois Dimpfel, former director of OS/2 development in IBM Boca Raton, they "needed to do something dramatically different" with OS/2 2.0. Their processes, unfortunately, did not allow them to be timely to market with new features and functions to meet user needs. They were geared to meet just the IBM industrial-strength needs. In early 1991, the OS/2 2.0 plan could be delivered, but it was not competitive with Windows 3.0, already in the marketplace. Specifically lacking was the user-friendly interface that came later with the OS/2 Workplace Shell, or drag-and-drop GUI (graphic user interface) interface. The developers needed to support multiple DOS applications and support Windows applications better than Windows. The goal was to deliver 4 million lines of code with 400 programmers in one year! There was simply no process defined in IBM, or anywhere else, that could accomplish that. So, the developers threw out the old waterfall model. This was the first major process transition for the organization.

Waterfall to Chaos

Throwing out the rigid, traditional processes meant chaos at times. They had to rethink how to get from here to there. A few small, cross-functional teams were formed, combining development, design, and marketing. Some physically relocated into open rooms to improve communication. An iterative development process emerged where components of the operating system would be introduced, tested, and then changed iteratively to satisfy requirements. Another major change was the use of wide, public beta testing to test the code. Three major beta test versions were distributed to an estimated 300,000 users. In March 1992, OS/2 2.0

shipped. It was a major accomplishment, but completed almost 12 months later than promised.

Both iterative development and small teams achieved some measure of success, but the pervading process was no process at all. A major paradigm shift was needed. The programmers needed some framework to operate in. However, it had to guarantee them enough empowerment and flexibility to make decisions. This was a hard line to walk, for it was easy to put in too much process. Too much process forced people to do things a rigid way, tied the hands of people who didn't need the rigidity, and would slow things down too much.

Chaos to LIT

For the OS/2 2.1 development project (which shipped in June 1993), some things were different. Teams were formed by subsystems (e.g., the install subsystem, the kernel subsystem, the Workplace Shell subsystem). But there were still no formal development processes.

With little fanfare, in early 1993, however, two employees were assigned to focus on doing things better. They grabbed some key technical people (developers, designers, test, service) to form a Process Council. Its goal was to come up with the best process to maintain a fast development cycle while improving quality over the long haul. They determined that their root problem was lack of ownership of the overall product. There was little communication and no cooperation across organizations.

The Process Team decided that cross-functional teams assigned to key, identifiable features (called line items) of upcoming OS/2 releases would help solve the problem. Examples of line items are support for a new communication protocol, multiprocessor support, or a new device driver. They knew they needed buy-in from people, not organizations, so teams were formed by naming its members. Teams had members representing design, development, planning, information development (publications), testing, and other groups as required.

Next, the Process Team built a process, called the Line Item Tracking (LIT) process, around this simple approach. A LIT manager was named for each LIT team. A LIT team could handle more than one line item, if the items were naturally associated. A LIT application was developed to enable sharing of status information among the team members.

Since the Process Council introduced the LIT process, the organization has begun to change. The word *LIT* is on people's tongues. Success, as measured by stable code builds for testing purposes, is apparent. Another valuable result is that lack of resources can now be discovered much earlier in the process—an understaffed LIT team is the determining factor.

IBM PC Company Reengineering in Boca Raton

In 1991, the IBM PC Company's product volumes were in decline. Aside from serious pricing problems, IBM appeared to be unable to keep pace with the product introductions of competitors. An analysis of the competitors' development processes revealed that a **concurrent engineering** approach enabled them to maintain the product introduction pace necessary for success. Concurrent engineering is a development process that promotes simultaneous development of the components of a complex project through teamwork and sharing of information.

A new development paradigm was conceived by IBM's senior staff. The new development paradigm revised established organizations and processes to reduce elapsed development schedules substantially. At its core was the definition of classes of **subsystems** and **systems** around which tightly coupled processes could be built:

- Subsystems included processor complexes, storage subsystems, displays, keyboards, power supplies, and so on—the well-known parts that comprise a personal computer. A subsystem represented a new development project that would be included in a system (new personal computer) when it achieved technical readiness. Subsystem development was, at the business case level, decoupled from system development. The goal was to make long term investments in subsystem technologies with an eye toward system incorporation, but only direct coupling of subsystem to system when technical readiness was sure.

- Systems were classified as new, derivative, or refreshed. A new system was one that contained three or more new subsystems. A derivative system would contain at most one or two new subsystems. A refreshed system would not have any new subsystems (i.e., ones with a new design), only technologically refreshed ones (i.e., new chip technology or new printed circuit wiring). Tied to system classification were schedule guidelines—no more than 12 months for a new system, no more than 6 months for a derivative system, and no more than 3 months for a refreshed system. The subsystem contents of a system were determined by the readiness schedules of the subsystems—a key change in product planning thinking and processes.

Driving these new processes were empowered, cross-functional teams, with representatives from development, finance, manufacturing, marketing, and competitive analysis organizations. Behind the scenes, a process to capture and share planning information about the subsystems and systems among the team members was put in place. It used mainframe-based tools initially, but is migrating to a client/server environment this year (see "Selecting Application Programs, the PSPLAN Project" in Chapter 3. These changes helped the PC Company turn the tide by 1993 and return to profitability and increasing market share.

IBM Boca Raton Goes Client/Server

The decade of the 1980s brought a renewed interest by U.S. businessmen in improving the quality and competitiveness of their products. The recognition of Japan's great success in automobiles and electronics caused great fear of lost markets and profits. The urgings of leaders like Deming were a rallying cry for change. This led to the development of corporate programs under the umbrella term **Total Quality Management (TQM)**. TQM espoused many of Deming's recommendations of process reengineering, focus on quality and cost reduction, and empowered teams. The federal government established the Malcolm Baldrige National Quality Award in 1987 to inspire American businesses to adopt these practices and regain their competitiveness. As a result, in late 1989 IBM launched a corporate-wide Market Driven Quality program to improve product quality.

Baldrige Assessment: Recast Information Technology Investments

The decision to make a major investment in client/server computing was the result of a 1993 internal Baldrige Assessment in IBM Boca Raton. One of the three major findings of that assessment was that information assets were not being managed in a systematic way. Information technology dollars were not being used wisely. As a result, people were not getting the information they needed.

As a follow-on to performing the Baldrige Assessment, information technology processes were compared with other IBM sites and customers, as well as an analysis of information technology expenditures. The financial analysis showed that most of the expense was in Boca's mainframe systems, followed by PCs and technical workstations. Therefore, it was recommended that improvement activities be focused on the mainframes and PCs.

Despite the great success of the IBM PC and the industry-wide growth in LAN installations in the late 1980s, IBM Boca Raton continued to depend on mainframe-based applications for most of its internal information and data sharing. The OfficeVision/VM (OV/VM) application was the IBM internal standard software for e-mail and calendar functions with tens of thousands of users worldwide by the mid-1980s. Most site users employed IBM personal computers for terminal emulation for mainframe application access and standalone PC applications. Data from the standalone applications were shared through upload to a VM mainframe and then forwarded using file transfer facilities.

The Assessment Team also recommended that a Chief Information Officer (CIO) be appointed to be responsible for the changes necessary to bring the right information at the right time to the site's users. As a result, the Chief Information Officer position and organization was established on July 1, 1993. This marked the beginning of the challenging migration to client/server computing for the IBM Boca Raton site.

A Clear, Elevating Goal

Almost a year earlier, in September 1992, top management directed the Personal Systems line of business (which included major development sites in Boca Raton, Austin, and Raleigh) to create a collaborative client/server computing environment. Subsequently, Lotus Notes was selected as the strategic application for workgroup computing. Personal Systems headquarters (in Somers, New York) took immediate action and rolled Notes out to more than 400 professionals. The strategy was to migrate all Personal Systems businesses to client/server computing by the end of 1994.

A combination of forces and findings were driving IBM Boca Raton to client/server. The empowered teams and new processes driven by external competition in both the IBM PC Company and OS/2 Development ment organization would soon be aided by a robust, new client/server computing infrastructure and powerful, new groupware applications. The Process to Profits cycle would be linking up with the Information Sharing Cycle.

As the home of OS/2 and the IBM PC, the IBM Boca Raton site established its goal to have an operational client/server computing environment by the end of the third quarter of 1994. It was to support the functional operations and business information applications of most IBM Boca Raton operating units. The scope of the project encompassed the Boca Raton site, while maintaining interoperability with other IBM sites, and selected non-IBM companies. The CIO and her team was charged with creating the required Migration Plan.

The Migration Plan

The Migration Plan addressed the 1994 management challenge. The plan was simple:

- Use what we sell. This meant IBM products, and, in particular, IBM PC Company products and OS/2.

- Define and establish the IBM Boca Raton network; then migrate to it. This meant evaluating the existing network to determine if it could support a client/server environment. Enhance the network, if necessary, and use it as the basis of the client/server environment.

- Implement with standard tools. Choose industry-standard applications, protocols, and products. Seek agreement on a single suite of products to promote interoperability.

- Build the migration financial plan on the 3Q94 target. This meant that a solid business case was needed for the next year that would provide a complete environment.

- Manage the implementation to the 3Q94 operational goal. Plans and organization were required such that the 3Q94 goal was achievable.

- Manage the 1995 Plan to the overall goal of a 50 percent reduction in I/S expenses. This was achievable based upon the large reductions in expense observed in previous, small-scale client/server migrations in the computer-aided-design and software library areas (see Chapter 4).

Information Technology Strategy

The IBM Boca Raton Information Technology Strategy, which looked beyond the Migration Plan, was built during the 1994 client/server migration rollout. Logically, it is better to create a complete strategy before embarking on an important tactical plan, such as the Migration Plan. However, the CIO had to move quickly. So to achieve the goal, the risk was taken that strategic directions might have to change along the way.

The Information Technology Strategy created is general enough such that you can adapt it to serve your enterprise in its efforts to migrate to client/server computing. When developing your strategy, consider these seven components:

Business Paradigm.   Client/server computing fits best in businesses that have modified their business paradigm (or model) to use empowered teams executing groupware-enabled processes. Team-specific groupware applications should be developed to improve information sharing and workflow to support the business goals of the enterprise.

Information Technology Paradigm.   Client/server computing should be implemented with a best-fit-of-technology philosophy. The process to achieve best fit of technology is called rightsizing. It means that no one system will be the standard for delivering computer processing and information to the organization. You should use open industry standards throughout the computing environment, if possible (e.g., TCP/IP, and X.500, which are discussed in later chapters).

Information Technology Management.   You should establish a Chief Information Officer (CIO) who will control the information Technology environment for the benefit of the users. A long-term relationship with an information technology subcontractor for complete support should be established. In IBM Boca Raton's case, the subcontractor is the Integrated Systems Solutions Corporation (ISSC).

An Application Review Board, composed of user organization representatives should be set up to control investments in standard applications for business use.

Applications. You should invest in best-of-breed, standard client/server applications supporting the information, and information sharing requirements of your business's users. Common user interface attributes (i.e., common look and feel) and data interoperability are key. User application access should be via the client/server network to minimize installation and upgrade costs. Therefore applications should support **network licensing** for shared use. Also, applications should support standard industry interfaces for access to client/server network resources, such as OSF's Distributed Computing Environment (DCE). See Chapter 3 for additional details.

Network Infrastructure. You should establish a client/server network with PCs and workstations as clients and a heterogeneous suite of systems as servers (i.e., "best fit-of technology" servers) supporting industry-standard protocols and interfaces. The client/server network should be upgradable to be multimedia capable across the enterprise and be interoperable with other remote corporate sites, suppliers, and business partners. It must support central management for faults, configuration, accounting, performance, and security. See Chapter 6 for additional details.

Clients. High-performance, multimedia-capable, industry-standard personal systems should be used for office clients. Clients should be capable of supporting user application and information requirements, including multimedia applications. Client systems should provide ease of use (e.g., support a graphic user interface), high performance, and application access comparable to the best in the industry. For mobile client systems (e.g., notebooks) add "from anywhere in the world." Clients should have a standard configuration for ease of installation, upgrade, backup and remote management over the client/server network. A three-year replacement cycle to maintain competitiveness of user function should be planned. See Chapter 4 for additional details.

Servers. You should plan a heterogeneous, centrally managed suite of systems capable of supporting site user application and information requirements, including multimedia applications. Servers should be reliable, fault-tolerant, and support industry-standard interfaces for expansion. They should have standard configurations for ease of installation, upgrade, backup, and remote management over the client/server network. See Chapter 5 for additional details.

The network budget grows as the administrative support budget gets smaller—and the result is more productivity [Derfler, 1993].

Information Technology Finances

Migrating to client/server computing for a business with a substantial investment in mainframe systems and applications requires a major financial investment. A well-managed business will require a well-crafted business plan to demonstrate a financial return on investment, a significant productivity gain, or both.

The Information Technology Inventory

When planning your migration, your first activity should be getting your arms around all the current information technology assets (systems, software, network components, etc.) and expenses (software licenses, support, etc.). This means a complete inventory of PCs, workstations, servers, and network infrastructure. The PC and workstation inventory should include CPU, memory, hard disk storage, and operating system installed. This data will be used to project future upgrade requirements, and, hence, future cost.

Building a Model

First, create a spreadsheet financial model of current, total information technology expenses as soon as possible, in your planning process. When complete, this will be the base data from which future projections can be made. This should include the following major categories:

1. Office Client hardware, software, and support, if any.

2. Server hardware, software, and support, if any.

3. Network Infrastructure hardware, software, and support, if any.

4. Mainframe hardware, software, and support, if any.

5. Additional services (e.g., wide area network services), if any.

Make sure you include depreciation expense for hardware, software license fees, installation and maintenance fees, and support charges. Unique environments, such as computer-aided design (CAD), should be categorized separately and included in the total.

Next, project expenses out for the next four years, assuming that you maintain the status quo (i.e., no investment in a client/server migration). Factor in any manpower or business-related changes that you anticipate, so that the model reflects your current business plan. This should be done jointly with your current information technology supplier of service so that proper assumptions are made.

Next, based on your Information Technology Strategy, develop the capital and expense investment necessary to migrate your organization to client/server computing. This is a multistep process. Figure 1.10 (page 26) outlines a recommended approach for a large site, such as IBM Boca Raton.

1. Determine your major application requirements and select a standard application suite. Chapter 3 provides guidance here. These selections are critical, for they drive all succeeding investments. The application suite determines the minimal client system required, the type and number of servers required for your users, the network infrastructure required, and so on.

2. Determine your minimum **office and mobile client** system configurations. The office client is the system that most users have in their offices. The mobile client is the system that traveling or work-at-home users have. The delta between these requirements and your current inventory will dictate the upgrade investment required. Based on the number of new and upgraded systems required, you can then estimate capital and client rollout expenses. Chapter 4 offers guidance as to how to plan an office and mobile client rollout.

3. Based on the applications and number of users, the type and number of server systems required can be determined. Chapter 5 offers guidance for developing a robust server installation with adequate support.

4. Assessing the adequacy of your site network or deciding to invest

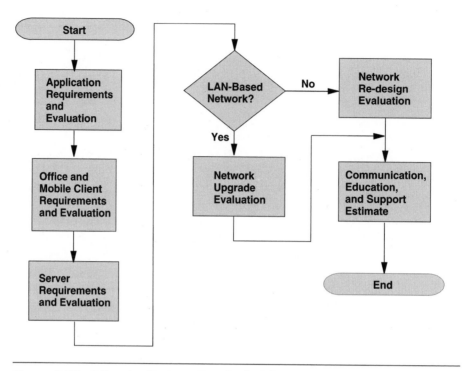

Figure 1.10 Migration Business Case Analysis Process

in a new one is a highly complex, and challenging effort. It is strongly recommended that, in addition to studying Chapter 6, networking experts be consulted to develop the required network design and investment required. This assessment should include internal and external networking requirements at the same time.

5. Estimate education, support and communication expenses required. This should be based on the number of users involved and their relative client/server skills.

Appendix C, "Pro Forma Client/Server Financial Spreadsheet," contains a suggested simplified table format to be used in the spreadsheet and an accompanying explanation of each of the tables. A similar Lotus 1-2-3 spreadsheet was used in IBM Boca Raton to project migration capital and expense dollars for purposes of business case justification.

Expect to spend up to 50 percent more in information technology expenses during the migration year for initial set up, support and license expenses. This will be in addition to any capital dollars required for new equipment (PCs, servers, network components). Once the migration year financial projection is complete, at least two succeeding years should be projected to evaluate potential savings or additional expenses. The IBM Boca Raton business case was based on a projection of client/server expenditures in the four succeeding postmigration years versus continuing to use an exclusively mainframe-centric environment. The projected savings provided an internal rate of return in excess of 28 percent, which was well above the required return for capital investments in IBM. It should be stated that the positive business case was greatly benefited by a previous large investment in 1989 and 1990 that upgraded the site network infrastructure to a token-ring LAN environment for mainframe connectivity. This minimized the capital investment required in 1994 and allowed success within the 14-month period allotted by top management.

Your business case may be quite different from that experienced in IBM Boca Raton. In fact, your estimate may fail to show any savings, and might show that client/server computing is more expensive than your current information technology environment. The current thinking of more than one industry consultant is that a client/server migration should not be done as a cost reduction but rather as a fallout of reengineering. However, it is strongly recommended that a complete business model be developed, if for no other reason than establishing an understanding of how your information technology dollars are being spent.

IBM Boca Raton Gets the Go Signal

In December 1993, the business case was approved. PC Company top management gave the go signal for the large capital and expense budget necessary to achieve these aggressive goals. This included new or upgraded PCs for seventy percent of the desktops, a major investment in PS/2 servers, a strengthened network infrastructure, and a client/server support organization to make it happen. A mere ten months later, in September 1994, the major migration was complete with over 2,700 client/server enabled users. The client/server vision (see Figure 1.11, page 28) had become a reality. A major portion of the IBM Boca Raton development site had migrated to a best-fit-of-technology, client/server computing environment.

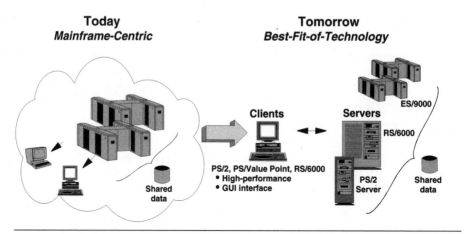

Figure 1.11 Client/Server Migration Vision

Setting the Stage

With your strategy and positive business case in hand, you next need to convince your financial gurus that without investing in a client/server computing environment your company will fall hopelessly behind its competitors in empowering its employees with productive, state-of-the-art tools. If you succeed, it is only the beginning.

This chapter has just set the stage to lead you through the many arduous decisions necessary to successfully migrate to a client/server computing environment. The following chapters fill in the technical details you must consider to complete the journey.

2

Migration Management

Successful client/server development requires new teamwork approaches and skill mix integrated with project management. Investment of time and money in disciplined project management will yield tangible pay back.

[IBM CONSULTING GROUP, 1994]

This is the "how to do it" chapter from an information technology management perspective, giving structure to the chapters that follow. The majority of the chapter describes a phased methodology to transform a business from mid-range or mainframe-centric computing to client/server computing. The chapter ends with a perspective on overall project management and how to evolve from migration management to ongoing information technology management.

Migration Methodology

Migrating to client/server computing from a host-centric base is a major challenge. It requires a commitment across the entire organization for change. New skills must be learned. The migration process is very much like a large development project where an overall methodology is critical to success.

A client/server project can be managed by breaking it into five phases—that's what was done in IBM Boca Raton. Phase 1 ("Getting Started") includes team formation, information gathering, and action plan definition. Phase 2 ("Build the Bedrock") establishes the network, client, and server infrastructures. Education courses are prepared, user support is organized, and user communication goes into full swing. Phase 3 ("The Rollout Engine") delivers client PCs in synchronization with education delivery, server setup, and support delivery. In Phase 4 ("Planting the Seeds of Productivity") groupware applications are developed for specific user areas. Applications are tailored to meet local needs and tools are deployed to encourage migration from the legacy environment. In Phase 5 ("Steady State") long-term processes are initiated, rollout activities and staffs are scaled down. Figure 2.1 depicts the time relationship of the phases graphically. Note that phase overlap and elapsed time will vary considerably based on resources available and the scale of the rollout. The IBM Boca Raton teams found it beneficial that Phases 1 through

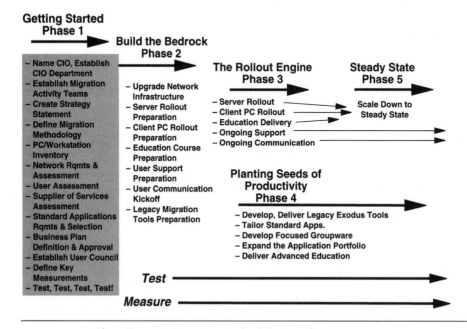

Figure 2.1   Client/Server Migration Methodology—Phase 1

3 occur sequentially with relatively little overlap. Phase 4 can occur at any time through the start of Phase 3, and probably never ends! Depending on the number of users and the state of the network (its readiness to support client/server computing, discussed in Chapter 6), a client/server migration may take from 12 to 24 months. For the record, the IBM Boca Raton rollout of over 2,700 users, utilizing this approach, took approximately 14 months.

Phase 1—Getting Started

Getting started is the hardest part of any major project. All the people involved are learning their roles and responsibilities. Interpersonal relationships are just being formed. The Phase 1 activities encompass basic personnel organization and information gathering which allow the actual migration to begin. These baseline activities include naming a Chief Information Officer (CIO); establishing a CIO department; establishing migration activity teams; creating a clear statement of strategy; defining a migration methodology, a PC/Workstation inventory, a network infrastructure assessment, a complete user assessment, a supplier of service assessment, standard application requirements, and a business plan; establishing a user council; and defining measurements. Now let's look at each of the steps listed in Figure 2.1 under "Phase 1—Getting Started."

Name a CIO and Establish a CIO Department

CIO stands for **Chief Information Officer**. The CIO is responsible the individual responsible for management of a business unit's information technology infrastructure, ongoing investments, and ongoing support. The CIO department is a staff organization empowered to carry out the CIO's mission. It should consist of strong leaders with critical skills, including:

Finance

Networking

Computer Systems Operations

Business Processes

Communications and Education

Application and Database Programming

Project Management

A computer science background (software or hardware) is desirable for all members. As an example, IBM Boca Raton's CIO department hired 12 people in 1994.

Technological change is very rapid for the client/server environment. By examining the extensive glossary at the end of this book, you can get a feel for the pace. There are over 450 definitions, of which perhaps 100 are new terms which emerged only in the past two years! Therefore, to be on the leading edge of this volatile environment, you should invest in a team of technologists to formulate investment plans in addition to the core CIO team. IBM Boca Raton has not made this investment, but is sharing plans with IBM's Austin site, which has.

Establish Migration Activity Teams

Empowered teams with proactive leadership can make a client/server migration fly. An empowered team is a team able to execute all required actions without approval from any other party. Such teams are effective because there are no process delays once a course of action is chosen. Teams should be made up of both CIO and information technology support staff.

You should form the following eight teams (depicted in Figure 2.2) to cover the bases:

1. **Network Team.** This team should focus on documenting the current network infrastructure, identifying new requirements, creating a comprehensive plan, and making things happen. It must be staffed with network administrators and planners who have the deep knowledge necessary to make the right decisions. This is an area where outside consultants may be required to join the team periodically. Chapter 6 goes into considerable detail regarding client/server networking and the IBM Boca Raton experience.

2. **Standard Tools Team.** This team should define a standard application suite for **office client** (a PC with e-mail, calendar, phone

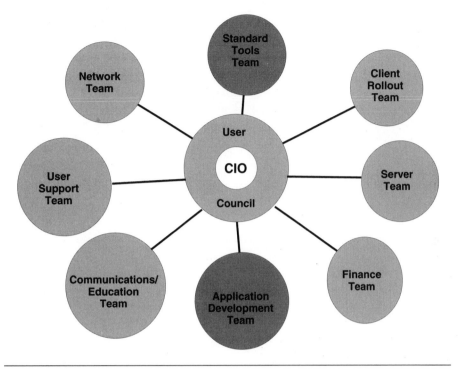

Figure 2.2 Client/Server Migration Activity Teams

directory, and, optionally, word processing, spreadsheet, and business graphics applications installed in an office), and **mobile client** (a client system with access to the enterprise network, but not present on-site) PCs based on user requirements. It should define the minimum PC hardware configuration to support the standard applications based on careful benchmark testing. It should also survey legacy (host-based) applications requirements to guarantee convergence. Additional details and the IBM Boca Raton experience are described in Chapters 3 and 4.

3. **Client Rollout Team.** This team should define and execute processes to deploy office and mobile clients. This involves hiring the required staff, setting up the required client configuration facilities, and working with users to upgrade or replace their PCs. Chapter 4 provides addition details and describes the IBM Boca Raton experience. This workgroup should be staffed with skilled coordinators and people with strong PC support skills.

4. **Finance Team.**   This team should create and sell the business case for client/server computing to upper management, negotiate contracts with suppliers of service, track to budget, and create long-range financial plans. Individuals with strong financial background and knowledge of information technology fit on this team. Chapter 1 provides details and the IBM Boca Raton experience.

5. **Applications Development Team.**   You should staff this team with application programmers. Its mission should be the creation of tools and groupware applications to meet specific user needs. Initially, hiring of outside consultants to jumpstart this team may be required. This was the case in IBM Boca Raton, where the CIO hired Lotus Consulting, IBM LAN Business Solutions (a group of client/server experts within IBM's Marketing and Services division), and ISSC (Integrated Systems Solutions Corporation, the IBM subsidiary that provides most information technology services inside IBM) to perform critical application development and customization. Chapter 3 provides several examples where key groupware applications built on Lotus Notes and other special-purpose tools improved user productivity and acceptance of the new environment.

6. **Communications/Education Team.**   You should staff this team with strong communicators and writers. Its mission should be development of an education delivery system for the new applications, synchronized with the client rollout. It should also be responsible for development and execution of a business-wide communication plan to win the hearts and minds of all site users and keep them regularly informed of migration progress. Chapter 7 supplies details and the IBM Boca Raton experience.

7. **Server Administration Team.**   This team is responsible for the acquisition, configuration, setup, and support of server systems. This includes installation of all application, operating system, and services software, as well as support of server data management, security, backup, and recovery. Server deployment needs to be carefully coordinated with the client rollout process. Staffing necessary skills is a major challenge in this area. In an installation with a large number of users, several key staff must be knowledgeable in server hardware, software, and applications. Chapter 5 provides details and the IBM Boca Raton experience.

8. **User Support Team.** This team is responsible for defining and executing a complete user support plan. It should include phone-based and hands-on support for user problems for all applications, PCs and workstations. Leadership must be flexible and proactive if a large migration is in progress, due to the tremendous user impact of new tools. Chapter 7 provides details and the IBM Boca Raton experience.

Figure 2.3 provides a sample staffing for each of the teams as employed in the IBM Boca Raton migration in 1994. The first column lists the CIO department members, who were IBM PC Company employees. The second column lists the Personal Operating System (POS) personnel from the internal tools group involved in the migration. POS is the acronym for the Personnel Operating System organization, which develops IBM DOS and OS/2 in Boca Raton. The third column details the staffing from ISSC, the primary supplier of services. The fourth column identifies the IBM Education and Training coordinator and course developers. The fifth column details contractors hired to assist in the migration

	CIO Dept	POS (OS/2, DOS Dev.)	ISSC (I/S Support)	IBM Educ. & Trng	Contractors	Total
Network Team			8		3	11
Standard Tools Team*	1					1
Client Team	3		6		23	32
Finance Team	1		1			2
Application Development Team	2	4	2		2	10
Communications & Education Team	3			1	1	5
Server Team	1		8		9	18
User Support Team		2	2		6	10
Project Leadership	1		1			2
Total	12	6	28	1	44	91

*The Standard Tools Team completed its work in January 1994 and was disbanded. It consisted of a team of six working members during its four months of activities. The remaining member in the CIO department became the chairman of the Application Review Board - see Chapter 3 for details.

Figure 2.3   IBM Boca Raton Support Personnel—1994

and, in some cases, ongoing information technology support. The advantage of hiring contractor personnel for specific teams was that their assignments were only for the duration of the migration. Not to be overlooked is the need for overall project leadership to coordinate team activity and make key overall migration decisions along the way. At the IBM Boca Raton site, the CIO department project leader (the author) and the ISSC supplier of services leader shared these responsibilities.

Creating a Strategy Statement

Your project leaders should create a strategy statement in the form of a presentation. This accomplishes three vital purposes. First, it establishes goals for all participants. Second, it helps win the hearts and minds of the user community (when effectively presented!). Most important, it gains executive support for the financial and people investments required. A more elaborate strategy document is useful for the long haul to benchmark results and keep things on track. It should be created in parallel with all five phases.

Note well that yesterday's strategy becomes tomorrow's policy. In IBM Boca Raton, two of the strategic goals were to support a single office application suite and reduce mainframe use where appropriate. These became policy as the migration wore on, requiring public communication and enforcement. Other examples of new policies were standard office client configuration, server disk space management, and mainframe (VM) usage. The IBM Boca Raton strategy is discussed in Chapter 1.

Define Migration Methodology

The project leaders should customize the migration methodology phases in this chapter to fit your business' requirements and produce an appropriate plan. The methodology presented here reflects the plans and improvements based on lessons learned in the IBM Boca Raton migration.

PC/Workstation Inventory

Performed by the Client Rollout Team, a complete PC/Workstation inventory to understand the magnitude of any client/server migration should be an initial activity. The results of the inventory will be the basis for many assumptions in the business case. For example, in IBM Boca Raton, the Client Rollout Team was able to assess how many current systems could support the standard application suite and which needed replacement or upgrade. This drove the PC capital investment target. The inventory should encompass all PC and workstation hardware and software, including any remotely located systems. A database should be established to house the information to become the base for ongoing asset management.

In IBM Boca Raton, the Client Rollout Team surveyed all user PCs with a diskette-based program that simplified most of the data gathering. This program created a standard text file with all required information. The team provided each department manager with a diskette to be used by every employee in the department and requested that they run the program by the requested deadline. They then followed up with each manager, gathered the diskettes, and imported the information into a Lotus Notes database.

The information gathered included operating system (level included), PC machine type, processor, coprocessor, total memory, total hard disk storage, display type and communication adapter. User identification, such as name and department, was included as well.

To maintain a current inventory, the Client Rollout Team included the IBM LAN Station Manager application, which automatically extracted necessary data and placed it in a central database, as part of the standard applications. See Chapters 3 and 6 for additional information.

Network Requirements and Assessment

Your Network team should complete a statement of requirements for the client/server network infrastructure and an assessment of how the existing network must be enhanced to meet it. This should include a proposed configuration of the physical network, with networking components such as hubs, bridges, routers, gateways, and communication line details.

This work demands a dedicated team of network experts. The team must have a complete understanding of the existing infrastructure and the technical depth to modify the network as required. This is an area where consultants must be employed if the skill is not available in-house. Chapter 6 provides a basic treatment of client/server network requirements, an assessment of the Boca Raton network, and the upgrade plan selected.

User Assessment

A complete count of users with associated organizational and job responsibilities is critical to scope the client/server migration and fuels the business case. This can be completed by the Finance or Client Rollout Teams. You should include all information technology users, including regular and nonregular employees (i.e., contractors and vendors). This information should be placed in a database and kept current as a base for measurements.

Supplier of Services Assessment

Your project leaders should gather information on each supplier of service to capture the company name, key contacts, type of work performed, breadth and depth of skills, fee structure, and availability. Key services are information systems support, application development, and information technology consulting (e.g., network analysis and design, application deployment).

The typical I/S (Information System) shop may be too mainframe-centric to provide the kind of unbiased and broadly experienced advice necessary to guide a successful client/server migration. Depending upon the situation, establishing a relationship with an experienced consulting firm may provide critical near-term guidance.

Boar [1993], in his book *Implementing Client/Server Computing,* leads the reader to the conclusion that an in-house, dedicated I/S shop is clearly preferred. If this is not feasible, then a long-haul partnership is recommended with a primary vendor. Outsourcing is an alternative for minor utility functions only.

In IBM Boca Raton, users have had a love-hate relationship with the internal I/S support team over the years. On occasion the users hated them, but they have been there when the users needed them. As the CIO contemplated making the leap into client/server, she was concerned that the existing ISSC team (Information Systems Solutions Company, the independent IBM subsidiary supplying information technology services internally and externally) lacked the necessary skills. Further, the CIO was frustrated in efforts to negotiate a clear, understandable service-level agreement with granular pricing indicated. However, the organizations finally came to terms, and using the existing team was without question the best decision made along this tortuous road. The key was that the

ISSC team members were, number 1, IBMers, and, number 2, Boca Raton people. They cared. They had nurtured the network from its earliest days. They had worried about power and cooling, when most users were just looking for the thermostat and plug. They were the bedrock of the site.

The lesson the reader should take away is that it is far better to work with an in-house information technology support organization and resolve any deficiencies in a team-spirited manner, than to abandon them and hire an outside vendor.

Standard Application Requirements and Selection

User requirements for client/server application programs need to be understood so that the right programs are selected for deployment. These selections are critical, as they drive PC, workstation, server, and network investment decisions. When selecting applications, it is important to define a standard suite for deployment to minimize cost and promote interoperability. Therefore, the Standard Tools team should complete a survey of users as to what applications they use in the current environment and how often (daily, weekly, monthly, yearly, infrequently) they use them. They should analyze the data to determine the sequence applications should be available in the client/server environment to meet the users' needs.

It is highly recommended that access to all legacy applications continue to be available to users for a defined period after they are migrated, if possible.

In IBM Boca Raton, this activity was performed by a Standard Tools Team composed of members from all site work areas. The results of their work are discussed in Chapter 3.

Business Plan Definition And Approval

The Finance team should create a client/server information technology business plan. The business plan should present a complete picture of intended expenditures over a defined period (typically five years) and contrast them against other alternatives. The goal is to be able to demonstrate a positive return on the investment and gain approval to proceed. The business plan is a critical piece of analysis and communication. Without its timely creation and delivery, the migration is impossible. Chapter 1 offers guidance.

Establish a User Council

A user council with participants representing every major business unit at your site is a forum for information sharing, user feedback, and critical decision making. With the right participants (committed, technically astute), it broadens the communications channel so necessary to win the hearts and minds of the user community. Regular meetings should be held—monthly is recommended. The meeting should be chaired by the site CIO. The agenda should include reviews of all current activities provided by team leaders, presentations of ongoing measurements by the provider of information technology services, and presentations of proposed additions or changes to the client/server computing environment.

Define Key Measurements

The business plan should be the source of many important measurement targets. These include the capital budget target, expense budget targets, number of rollout population versus total population, number of new PCs required, number of upgraded PCs required, and number of servers required.

A CIO database should be established to capture measurements on a regular basis (see Chapter 3 for a more complete discussion). Each migration phase includes the keeping and reporting of key measurements.

Test, Test, Test, Test, Test!

Testing new applications and processes *before* they are deployed to the general population should be standard practice throughout the entire migration process. Call them pilot tests, alpha tests, or beta tests, tests are needed prior to deploying applications, services, and infrastructure upgrades. The following IBM Boca Raton example should drive home this point.

The stability of each individual's desktop system was a major concern prior to the rollout. Informal pilot testing was performed with individual applications prior to deployment. During 1993, the interactions among the selected applications on OS/2 2.1 was rung out by over 700 users in the Personal Operating System (POS) organization. However, when the OS/2 2.11 Corrective Service Diskette was released in the spring of 1994, the Client Rollout Team delayed formal support until a full test of the application suite was completed.

The CIO negotiated with the OS/2 System Test department for them to formally test the site's Standard Applications as a test suite for the latest CSD (2.11) and any upcoming CSDs (Corrective Service Diskettes, IBM's name for a software maintenance release) and releases (the OS/2 System Test department is responsible for the final test of any new OS/2 release). After this comprehensive OS/2 System Test, a **beta-test** environment of the new operating system was made available to willing site users. In the future, when OS/2 code goes "golden" (i.e., ready for customer shipment), the Client Rollout Team will be able to upgrade all site PCs to the new level as soon as possible. This early testing process will improve stability for the office client users. This is a highly recommended practice for any client rollout project and for ongoing maintenance.

Phase 2—Build the Bedrock

This phase establishes the network infrastructure, the client preparation area, and the server farm. Education courses are prepared, user support is organized, and user communication goes into full swing. Now let's look at each of the main tasks in phase 2 (see Figure 2.4, page 42).

Upgrade the Network

The network team should execute the site network upgrade plan developed in Phase 1. This includes acquisition and installation of new wiring and network hardware (**bridges, routers, hubs, management consoles, gateways, cables**—these terms are defined in the Glossary and discussed in detail in Chapter 6).

The network team should ensure that the site is able to communicate with all other sites in the enterprise, making sure that this site complies with enterprise-wide standards for intersite connectivity. This includes the integration of existing **WAN** and **LAN** connectivity (WAN stands for

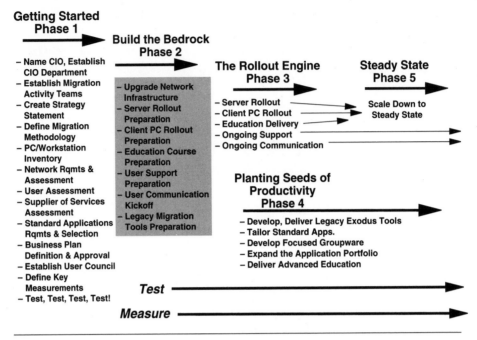

Figure 2.4 Client/Server Migration Methodology—Phase 2

wide area network or the connections among systems at distant geographic locations; LAN stands for local area network or the connections among local systems).

Network management must be in place to handle problems, performance, change, capacity planning, and configuration management. Chapter 6 provides definitions, organization, and additional details.

Server Rollout Preparation

The server team needs to complete pilot tests of critical applications in a controlled client/server environment. This provides a means to identify application problems prior to wide user deployment. A pilot test is the setting up of a fully configured application server with a small group of users (five to twenty) for a defined period. This should be done in conjunction with the client team. A typical pilot test should take from one to four weeks to complete.

Ordering hardware and software for application and gateway servers should occur in parallel with pilot tests. Orders should lead the client rollout so that adequate server capacity is available as clients are rolled out.

A well-designed site network will centralize access to all major LAN connectivity equipment. The **server farm** should be located at this central access point to allow flexibility in connectivity as the client/server environment evolves (a server farm is an area reserved for a large number of server computing systems). This allows for performance optimizations to occur easily, if required. Adequate server farm space should be reserved, allowing for reasonable growth. Ideally, the server farm area should have above-average cooling, line-conditioned power (incoming power is filtered for spikes and surges) with an uninterruptible power supply, and a raised floor to avoid wiring clutter. Office space for server administration and the network control center should be nearby. Spare parts should be located nearby as well.

Server storage space policies should be established in this phase. With adequate storage on each user's desktop, it is recommended that each user be responsible for archival of personal data. Policies should be set up regarding allocation of server storage by organization, personal e-mail data space allocation and policing, requests for additional space, and backup service requests. In IBM Boca Raton, the policy initially was to make each user responsible for personal data archiving. In the future, incremental, nightly backup of critical data for all PCs and workstations will be provided. The site could no longer afford terabytes (trillion bytes) of on-line disk storage on mainframe systems. (See Chapter 5 for details. It includes server requirements and how to set up and administer a server farm.).

Client PC Rollout Preparation

The client team needs to run pilot tests of new office applications in conjunction with the server team. At a minimum, these should include e-mail, a calendar, a directory for both office and mobile clients, and print services. (An office client is a PC with e-mail, calendar, phone directory, and, optionally, word processing, spreadsheet, and business graphics applications installed in an office. A mobile client is a PC that is not office-bound; it can be a truly mobile notebook PC or a home-bound desktop system). A plan and process for upgrading or replacing client systems should be created and tested. An office and mobile client configuration area should be established to set up new client systems with standard applications, operating systems, and services.

An office client rollout schedule should be created whereby departments or teams are rolled out in close time proximity. Sharing the migration pain will become a group effort in that way. Further, Phase 4 efforts to create and deploy targeted groupware will be enhanced. Other scheduling factors to consider are availability of hardware and business need. Hardware and software should be ordered according to the rollout schedule.

Based on the number of clients to be rolled out and the time objectives involved, a staff of trained installers should be hired to upgrade or replace client systems. Contractors should be considered for this role.

Chapter 4 provides additional information on client rollout and the IBM Boca Raton experience.

Communication and Education Preparation

The communications and education team should develop a communication plan to address user buy-in and ongoing awareness. Another key element is developing tools to capture end user satisfaction with the new environment and thereby improve the transition process.

The team should develop course material on the primary office applications. This should include hands-on education with handout materials. Class schedules should be synchronized with the client rollout team. Courses should be customized to user requirements in terms of course content and class duration. The ratio of customers who completed the education versus the total target rollout population should be tracked.

Chapter 7 provides additional details on communication and education. The IBM Boca Raton experience in these areas is summarized.

User Support Preparation

Implement a phone-based **help desk** facility that end users can access whether they are in their regular office, at home, or traveling. A help desk should have a staff of application and infrastructure experts who are available to resolve user problems in real-time. The staff must be trained to treat each and every user with patience and respect. Investment in on-site assistance to end users should be a priority. This can be handled by information technology team members identified to the help desk staff as on-site support personnel. Measurements of help desk responsiveness should be defined and tracked.

Office PC access to a problem report and network status database should be developed during this phase. This will reduce the load on the help desk and increase user satisfaction. Chapter 7 provides additional details on user support, and again, the IBM Boca Raton approach to user support is referenced.

Phase 3—The Rollout Engine

This phase is the critical path of the entire project. A critical path is that part of a plan in which, if problems arise, the plan will not achieve its target end date. Server rollout (setup and installation of servers in the server farm) should lead client rollout (PC installation in user offices). As organizations receive their new or upgraded clients, users should attend introductory education sessions. The project leadership should be ever present, communicating early and late with users to gauge satisfaction and react to problems (see Figure 2.5, page 46).

Server Rollout

Server rollout is the installation of servers in the server farm to coincide with the requirements of the client rollout. E-mail servers and any supporting gateways (e.g., OfficeVision/VM to Lotus Notes) are likely the most critical here—they are very sensitive to the number of users assigned. You should develop a solid understanding of number of users per server for this and other key applications. Chapter 5 offers more details on server rollout, including the IBM Boca Raton experience.

Client PC Rollout

Client PC rollout is the scheduled, managed process of installing PCs in user offices. Scheduling PC installations with busy users under considerable time pressure requires solid preparation, a smooth process, acute communication skills, and technical competence. Chapter 4 should be

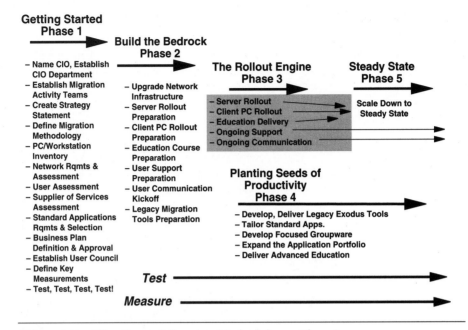

Figure 2.5 Client/Server Migration Methodology—Phase 3

reviewed in detail for the lessons learned in the highly challenging IBM Boca Raton 1994 rollout.

Education Delivery

Users unfamiliar with the basics of the new client/server interface need basic education just prior to client PC upgrade. Assuming that users still have access to legacy applications (in order to be able to continue to perform their jobs!), education on new applications should occur within two weeks after migration. Chapter 7 provides details on education alternatives.

Ongoing User Support

The Help Desk, covered in the Phase 2 discussion, must be armed and ready when the bell sounds for the rollout. Chapter 7 expands on the ongoing user support requirements and key issues.

Phase 4—Planting the Seeds of Productivity

This phase is motivated by the need to accommodate local user requirements—to tailor the new tools with functional or human factor improvements where needed. It is motivated by the need to bring some beloved features from the past (the legacy) into the present while encouraging users to leave the past behind where appropriate. Most important, it is motivated by the need to exploit the power of the client/server tools in targeted ways to improve productivity. It is also a phase that never ends! Phase 4 is where the application development team earns its stripes. Chapter 3 expands on each of the Phase 4 activities and IBM Boca Raton experiences. (See Figure 2.6).

Develop/Deliver Legacy Exodus Tools

Experienced mainframe application users sometimes require coaxing to take the leap into client/server computing. Specialized tools to migrate key data files from the mainframe to useful versions on the client/server

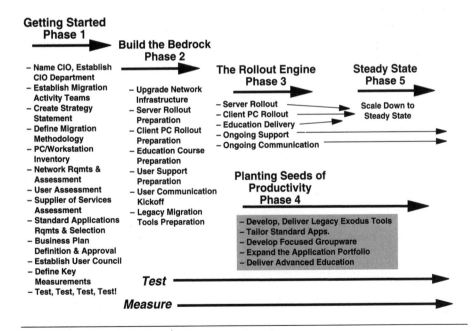

Figure 2.6 Client/Server Migration Methodology—Phase 4

platform are very helpful. User-friendly tools to reduce space used on the mainframe, archive files for safekeeping, or download them to the PC give that extra boost as well.

Tailor Standard Applications

Most PC applications offer some form of customization: default values, parameter settings, switches, smart icons (user or application supplied icons that are optional) and APIs (application program interfaces). By understanding user requirements and legacy application experiences, application customization can play a key role in user acceptance of and satisfaction with new client/server applications.

Develop Focused Groupware

In a large organization, there are many teams with unique work processes, as well as processes that affect the entire user community. With a powerful groupware development platform, such as Lotus Notes, focused groupware applications can be quickly developed. Like seeds planted in a garden, these applications sprout and blossom to create compelling examples of productivity for all to see.

The migration leadership should identify a set of key business application areas that are candidates for initial groupware development. Internal or external groupware experts should then set up short, focused group meetings with each business area to understand requirements and suggest a groupware application solution. If the reaction is positive, a prototype application should be created for evaluation. If this is accepted, the final application should be quickly deployed. In many cases, the prototype *is* the final application!

Expand the Application Portfolio

New applications and enhanced versions of current applications are part of a never-ending stream of evaluation, acceptance or rejection, testing, and deployment. Establishing a user-driven application review board aided by a workflow application (as was done at the IBM Boca Raton site) greatly smoothes this process.

Deliver Advanced Education

As users digest the new applications, become comfortable with them, and develop expertise, advanced courses should be available to enrich their use of the applications and, if able, develop new groupware applications. A key objective for IBM Boca Raton users was to educate a substantial percentage in Lotus Notes application development. See Chapter 7 for additional details. Also, the basic education should be expanded to include support for any new or enhanced applications.

Phase 5—Steady State

After a major migration, the rollout teams should be reduced in staff to reflect a steady state process. Support, communications activities, delivery of legacy migration tools, development of groupware, and expansion of the application portfolio should continue as in Phase 4.

Overall Planning and Project Management Processes

A well-thought-out planning and project management process must accompany the migration's execution. Regular, formal meetings are required to guarantee that the requirements, the plan, the financial model, buy-in, processes, and the organization remain on track throughout the migration. Note that meeting frequency and duration must be balanced against the need to get real work done (see the task management meeting approach discussed later in this section).

The planning process should result in concrete, documented, high-level plans. High-level plans establish major goals for the migration and document both tactical and strategic decisions. Ideally these plans should be placed in a centrally shared database. In IBM Boca Raton, high-level plans were placed in a Lotus Notes document database. A common title page format, containing summary information, was followed by a free-form in-depth section. This approach served two purposes: It established the central repository, and it acclimated the participants to data sharing via groupware.

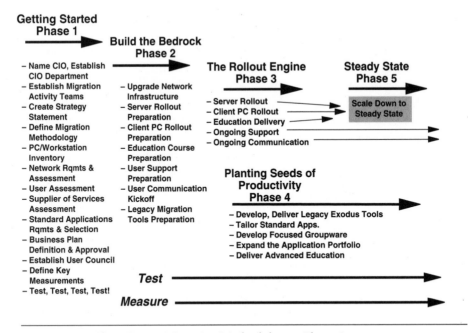

Figure 2.7   Client/Server Migration Methodology—Phase 5

The high-level plan documents should be living documents and form the basis for regular review meetings. In IBM Boca Raton, quarterly high-level plan reviews were initiated from the project's inception. The planners presented their work to representatives of each team. Key external consultants were invited to provide guidance and fresh opinions.

As high-level plans are formulated, detailed implementation task plans should be defined. The framework surrounding this effort should be a comprehensive project planning application leading to **PERT** analysis for the project. PERT stands for Program Evaluation and Review Techniques and is a method of deriving plans of action from a set of individual tasks. PERT analysis is key to understanding critical paths and intertask dependencies. In IBM Boca Raton, detailed tasks were placed in a Lotus Notes database. This was done for the convenience of the planners and implementers—all were Notes users. The Notes database contents were then automatically converted into input for the CA-Superproject application, which created the PERT diagrams.

The Notes database was used in a weekly task review meeting. It was run by a single project leader who was also responsible for coordinating input from every participant. There was a set agenda by major activity area (e.g., Client Rollout, Server rollout, etc.). Individuals only had to attend the portion of the meeting that reviewed their tasks. This approach minimized the impact to their work schedules. Duration of the meeting was a maximum of two hours. Tasks could not be of longer than one week in duration. If an activity took longer than one week, it had to be broken up into weekly tasks for checkpointing purposes. The project leader stepped down through each weekly task to determine if it had been closed. Minimal side conversations were allowed during task status reviews.

The task management meeting was an extremely successful forum for communications and decision making. The elements of its success were simplicity, regularity, and constancy of its leadership. The project leader did not miss a single meeting throughout the entire project.

It is important to note that, in addition to all of the technical concerns and activities, personnel management issues and group dynamics play a major part in the success of a project of this nature. Only seasoned leaders need apply.

From Migration Management to Information Technology Management

As you move from migration management to steady state, you must consider ongoing management of your overall information technology investment. Following is a set of objectives that should be considered:

Users in Control.   It is very important to have the users in control of the information technology infrastructure. This means that user representatives should be contributing to the information technology investment, deployment, and support processes on an ongoing basis.

Team-Oriented Management Structure.   The information technology management organization must be empowered and flexible to make short- and long-range decisions, and to deal with problems as they arise.

Processes in place.   Well-defined processes for investment, deployment of facilities, security of assets, disaster recovery, and ongoing support of the information technology infrastructure should be in place.

Measurements. A comprehensive measurement system for the information technology infrastructure, including operational status, financial status, security, and customer satisfaction, is key. Measurements should be reported regularly in summary form for decision-making purposes. See Chapter 8 for more details and examples.

Skilled support partners. A dedicated, highly skilled support organization should be in place for long-term information technology infrastructure support.

Management tools. Tools, including workflow and measurement databases, must be available to control information technology processes.

These goals are strongly recommended for effective information technology management. They achieve the overriding objective of a user-controlled information technology environment. The fallout from a well-executed migration will lead to accomplishing the rest of the goals as well.

3

Selecting Application Programs

Because they enable hundreds of workers to share information simultaneously, groupware networks can give lowly office workers intelligence previously available only to their bosses.

[Wilke, 1993]

Application programs are of paramount importance in any type of computing environment because they "are the computer system" as far as the users are concerned. For this reason, the selection of reliable, effective, and easy-to-use application programs is vital to any computing solution (client/server or not). This chapter will help you evaluate your particular application program needs and select the appropriate application programs to meet those needs. It will show how the Standard Tools Team used this application program selection process in the IBM Boca Raton migration and discuss the importance of proper application program management. The chapter winds up with some critical success factors.

Basic Application Program Requirements

You should define a set of basic requirements that all client/server application programs should meet. For the most part, these requirements will be obvious characteristics that all users would recognize and agree upon. Nevertheless, they should be explicitly defined up front so that they are addressed early on in the application selection process. Following are the ones the Standard Tools Team used in the IBM Boca Raton client/server migration.

Consistent, User-Friendly Interfaces.   A graphic user interface, or GUI, is a highly recommended standard. Consistent, friendly interfaces are easy for users to learn and remember.

Solid Performance.   Within a major application area, applications should exhibit acceptable performance on the site standard operating system and hardware platform (e.g., OS/2 on PC or AIX on RS/6000; see Chapter 4). Trivial user interactions, such as menu selections, should be instantaneous. File loading or saving time should be proportional to file size. For example, a small file (a page of text) should load instantaneously. Other interactions will vary by application, but a good rule of thumb is that the delay should not impede the user from completing his or her task.

Reliability.   Applications should have a track record of reliability in the user community at large prior to wide deployment. For standard application categories, such as word processors or spreadsheets, many solid candidates meet this criterion. For more specialized or new applications, an internal testing program may be required to assure reliability.

Interoperability.   Your applications should exhibit interoperability. Data files created in one application should be able to be used by a second application. Interoperability with **legacy** applications (i.e., existing mainframe applications) and systems is often mandatory. Applications where this is usually important include electronic mail, calendaring, and file transfer.

Low Cost.   Depending upon the size of your user community, there are alternatives to minimize application cost. These include purchase of an enterprise license covering all users or purchase of network licenses, where license fees are paid based on the number of simultaneous network users (not individual copies). For IBM Boca, IBM-developed applications were clearly preferred for this requirement because no license or support fees were required. However, where a vendor application was clearly superior or offered unique features, it was selected and a network license approach was used.

Application Program Categories

Figure 3.1 shows a conceptual view of an enterprise and its application programs. Most application programs can be placed in one of the three categories depicted in the figure. The outer ring corresponds to individual user applications, or personal applications, which aid the users in their daily office activities. The middle ring corresponds to team applications—applications that support teams of users. In a client/server computing environment, these applications are sometimes called workflow or groupware applications that run on servers. Team applications facilitate the flow of work among a group or team of users communicating on a network. There is an inner core of applications that support the enterprise. These are a subset of the general team applications category, some-

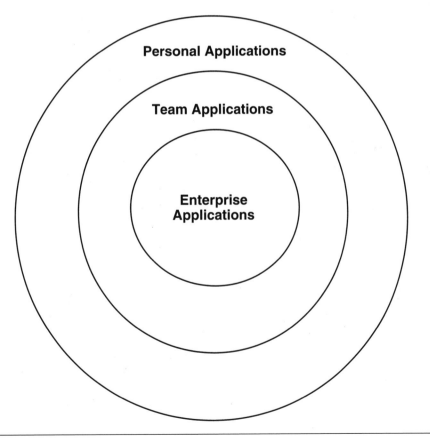

Figure 3.1 Enterprise Application Model

times called **decision support** applications, or applications that provide users with access to a database containing enterprise-level business information. Enterprise-level decision makers use these applications to make major decisions affecting the company (the really big team!).

Personal Applications Defined

Personal applications include electronic mail (e-mail), calendar, directory, word processing, spreadsheet calculations, business graphics applications, and database. This list represents, at a high level, the vast majority of individual application requirements in an enterprise. They are also "building blocks" for team applications, as we shall see.

Team Applications Defined

Team applications are defined at a high level as applications that are used by two or more individuals to share information. To understand them better, team applications can be categorized as e-mail, meetings, **forms processing** (e.g., surveys, requests for service, and applications), **document processing** (e.g., creation and review of articles, and other publications), decision support, and **groupware** (as a general-purpose, catch-all category).

E-mail shows up in both the personal and team categories—it is special. It is used by individuals for simple correspondence, so it fits within the personal category. It is also an important "building block" application for other team applications.

Clearly, personal and team applications are highly interrelated. Personal applications are the building blocks upon which team applications are built. Figure 3.2 shows these relationships. From the individual user perspective (row 1), e-mail is important to communicate with other team members, to inform others of meetings, to transmit a form or document, and to transmit information for decision support or group sharing.

Correspondingly, from the team perspective (column 1), e-mail draws on most or all of the office applications for information generation and addressing (directory). Aside from keeping an individual's schedule, the calendar application supports the scheduling of team meetings (row 2).

Team Applications

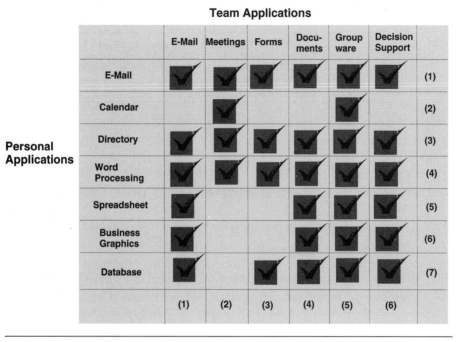

Personal Applications	E-Mail	Meetings	Forms	Docu-ments	Group ware	Decision Support	
E-Mail	✔	✔	✔	✔	✔	✔	(1)
Calendar		✔			✔		(2)
Directory	✔	✔	✔	✔	✔	✔	(3)
Word Processing	✔	✔	✔	✔	✔	✔	(4)
Spreadsheet	✔			✔	✔	✔	(5)
Business Graphics	✔			✔	✔	✔	(6)
Database	✔		✔	✔	✔	✔	(7)
	(1)	(2)	(3)	(4)	(5)	(6)	

Figure 3.2 Application Interrelationships

From the team perspective (column 2), the calendar application drives meeting scheduling through the use of the directory, supplemented by e-mail for notices and agendas created by the word processor. The directory application, aside from providing phone numbers to the individual, is a resource to workflow applications for e-mail addressing (row 3). The word processor (row 4) is useful to all workflow applications. The spreadsheet and business graphics applications (rows 5 and 6) create information useful for e-mail, documents, decision support, and group sharing. Forms processing (column 3) uses the word processor for creation, the directory for addressing, and e-mail for transmission. Document processing and groupware applications draw on most of the office applications for creation and distribution of information (columns 4 and 5). The database application stores information for the individual user (row 7) and serves as the repository for all forms of team applications. A general conclusion is that personal applications and team applications are inseparable, because their requirements are inseparable.

Applications: The "Make or Buy" Decision

For all but a very few businesses, off-the-shelf office applications make the most sense. There is a broad selection of maturing client/server application alternatives that satisfy the majority of user requirements. You will see that in the area of team applications, you will need to invest in application building.

Application Program Requirements and Selection

Once you have settled on your general application requirements, it is time to "peel the onion" and determine your specific application program requirements. Before any application programs are considered, it is imperative to clearly explore and define the actual and detailed needs of the users. The results of this exploration should be a set of documented application program requirements. We will look at the two major application categories, personal and team, in turn.

Personal Applications

Understanding the personal application requirements for a business is a major first step in most organizations. Generally speaking, IBM Boca Raton's personal applications requirements were not fundamentally different from those of any large business. To refine the personal application requirements at IBM Boca, the Standard Tools Team interviewed representatives from major site organizations and compiled a list of applications. To no one's surprise, almost all users employed OfficeVision/VM, IBM's flagship mainframe office application suite, and other VM tools for e-mail, calendar, directory, forms, and groupware. A potpourri of PC applications were in use for word processing, spreadsheets, business graphics, and database. This made the migration especially challenging. IBM Boca Raton's requirements included:

> **Electronic Mail.** Because of the daily use of **OfficeVision** (OV) by most of the site's users, e-mail requirements were well understood. OfficeVision was a mature, text-based system that was deeply

ingrained in the culture and workflow. The users were spoiled by outstanding OV response time, features, and reliability. The major requirements were rapid worldwide transmission, near-instantaneous response time to create and send a message, the ability to categorize and store incoming and outgoing messages, consistent worldwide addressing for individuals and groups, and easy printing. In addition, there were many "feature" requirements from users who were very familiar with all the "goodies" that OV offered. Some key features were mail reply (pressing a key initiated a new message with the incoming message's sender address filled in) and mail forward (pressing a key initiated a new message with the incoming message attached). Another example was a special kind of mail message, called a meeting notice. When read, OV recognized it as a meeting notice and supported a **function key** selection to add it to the reader's calendar.

Calendar.   The same story was true for calendar as for e-mail: clear requirements based on OV use. The major requirements were the ability to specify daily and recurrent meetings and appointments, the ability to view other site users' calendars, and the ability to conveniently print calendar information. Additional feature requirements included putting "notes" or memos on the calendar, allowing calendar entries to be large enough to include meeting agendas, and the previously mentioned interface with meeting notice messages.

Phone and Mail Directory.   A great strength of the IBM internal mainframe network was the global corporate phone and VM mail address directory used by the IBM CallUp program. The directory included name, phone numbers, OfficeVision mail and address (VM node and VM id), manager name, and other important data. The IBM CallUp program offered strict and fuzzy search from location-based directories and the ability to generate an e-mail message after a completed query. The requirements were to have this same facility in the new environment.

Application/Tools Access.   Selection of desired applications or tools had to be easily available from the office client user interface. Access had to be automatic after selection or, if installation was required, it had to be simple, fast and foolproof.

Word Processing.   A WYSIWYG word processor with a graphic user interface (**GUI**) was the requirement. **WYSIWYG** stands for What You See Is What You Get. It means that the on-screen view of the document created by the word processor looks like the printed output. The word processor had to support import and export of **ASCII** text files (ASCII text files, also called flat files, are the most common type of PC file). This enabled interoperability with OfficeVision files and files from simple text editors. The word processor's native file output format had to be interoperable with the standard e-mail application. Print output options had to include **PostScript** and PPDS data streams. Postscript is the de facto industry standard print file format for most laser printers. PPDS is the data stream supported by most IBM dot matrix printers.

Spreadsheet. Three-dimensional spreadsheet capability with a GUI interface was the requirement (a three-dimensional spreadsheet is one that supports multiple two-dimensional sheets in a single file). Because of the wide use of Lotus 1-2-3 for DOS on the site, the spreadsheet had to import and export the 1-2-3 file formats (wk1 and wk3).

Business Graphics. The ability to create visuals for presentations including text and graphics and the ability to create charts and graphs from numeric data was the requirement. The application had to have a GUI interface. The native file output format had to be accepted by the standard e-mail application selected. Print output options had to include PostScript and PPDS data streams.

Secretaries represent a special group with additional, important requirements for the office. They need the same office tools as the regular user population, but they may also need convenient access to their principal's e-mail and calendar to be able to provide appropriate support. They also may need the flexibility to back each other up on breaks or absences. Therefore, the ability to delegate access and control of a user's mail and calendar is an important requirement. Secretaries' roles and numbers have changed significantly over the past decade at the IBM Boca Raton site. As users became more skilled in e-mail and PC word processing, secretarial need was reduced for these tasks. The maturation of phone-mail services and its use in IBM Boca Raton reduced the need for live phone coverage. The number of secretaries was reduced as a result, and their workscope shifted to concentrate more on calendar management for the managers (principals) they supported.

Selecting the Personal Applications

Once the requirements are clear, the application selection process can begin. The Standard Tools Team (see "Migration Management, Phase 1" in Chapter 2) should gather information about available personal applications that meet the requirements. A good initial technique to employ is a paper comparison based upon vendor supplied features. Requirements should be rated numerically (a scale from 1 to 10 is fine), with mandatory requirements receiving the highest value. Each application under evaluation should then be numerically rated for each applicable requirement (a scale of 1 to 10 works here, too), with top features receiving the highest rating. Multiplying each requirement rating by the corresponding application rating and then summing all values for an application provides an objective measurement. Figure 3.3 provides a simple example of this method. This measurement can be used to narrow down a field of several competitors to two or three. At this point, installation and application testing (benchmarking) should be used to make the final selection.

The July 1993 establishment of the IBM Boca Raton CIO department led to the formation of the Standard Tools Team. It was formed to define a standard set of office applications for the client/server environment. In addition, it surveyed host-based tools requirements to create a convergence path. Drawing on representatives from across the site, the team focused on a single suite of applications that would provide comprehensive office function and maintain a dual environment (mainframe and client/server) during the transition period. This meant that users needed to be enabled for the new client/server environment and required continued access to current tools to avoid any loss in productivity. The Standard Tools Team approved

Requirement	Reqmt Rank	Application 1		Application 2		Application 3	
		Rating	Rank x Rating	Rating	Rank x Rating	Rating	Rank x Rating
Function 1	9	6	54	8	72	5	45
Function 2	5	5	25	6	30	8	40
Function 3	2	7	14	4	8	9	18
Function 4	8	8	64	3	24	10	80
Total			157		134		183

Figure 3.3 Application Comparison

the selection of Lotus Notes (a product of Lotus Development Corp.), IBM Time and Place/2, IBM Network Door/2, and IBM CallUp C/S as the standard applications in January 1994.

For E-mail, It's Lotus Notes

Lotus Notes is a client/server application that allowed users to communicate securely over a LAN or a WAN, with data (document data bases) residing on a server system. Notes was viewed primarily as group collaboration software consisting of two main parts:

A fully integrated e-mail system

An environment for the development and deployment of team applications (Notes as a team application development platform is discussed later in this chapter under "Team Applications").

Notes' adequacy as a replacement for OfficeVision/VM (OV) e-mail was a major concern during the transition, as OV/VM was deeply engrained in the work habits of the site's population. The creation of a standard mail template (e-mail form) for Notes with OV-like features met the users' requirements and enabled a successful transition.

One of the great strengths of Lotus Notes is that everything is a database and that every database is customizable. The beauty of the Notes design is that databases are customizable within a standard user interface framework. The Notes user interface presents the main body of the screen as a notebook with tabs (see Figure 3.4). Each section of the notebook graphically contains one or more icons, where each icon represents a Notes database. A Notes database is really a combination application and database. The menu items across the top of the screen are standard for the whole application, but (and this is important) the menu items offer different choices depending upon which Notes database is currently selected by the user. If the selected database is the Mail database, then by selecting Compose, the user will be composing a mail memo. If the selected database is some other application, Compose will be perhaps some other fill-in form. This approach is consistently applied throughout the application in a most elegant fashion.

The mail database has a set of forms that are user customizable. The IBM Boca Raton CIO hired Lotus Consulting to modify the supplied mail form and create a standard mail template (see Figure 3.5). They added buttons on the mail form for "reply"; "categorize"; "add to TaP/2 calendar" (if

Screen shot © 1994 Lotus Development Corporation. Used with permission of Lotus Development Corporation.

Figure 3.4 Notes User Interface

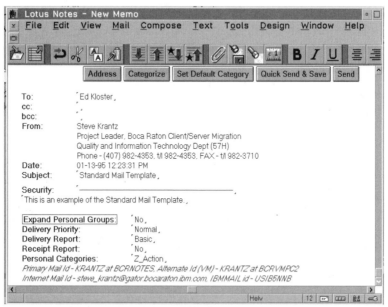

Screen shot © 1994 Lotus Development Corporation. Used with permission of Lotus Development Corporation.

Figure 3.5 Standard Mail Template

the received note was a meeting notice); and "quick send & save." They extended the form to include a prologue, epilogue, and security classification. These were OV standard features that the users insisted upon.

Two other customizations were done also. Lotus Consulting developed a mail delegate capability, similar to that on OV, whereby a user could indicate a period of absence and Lotus Notes would automatically notify senders that the user was away, and, optionally, forward all mail to another party.

The other customization was creation of an attachment viewer icon using the SmartIcons feature of Lotus Notes (SmartIcons are application-specific icons, which are smart because they simplify or automate tasks within an application. SmartIcons can be created by users, depending upon the application, to create a more customized environment). Files that are addressed to a Notes mail user arrive as attachments to a mail memo. In general, they must be detached (copied to the user's disk storage on his PC) to be examined. The attachment viewer icon was used when reading a mail memo with an attachment. Based on the attachment's file extension, an appropriate viewing application, such as the OS/2 system editor, was invoked by the viewer to allow the user to examine the attachment, and, optionally, print it.

For Calendaring, It's IBM Time and Place/2

The IBM Time and Place/2 (TaP/2) application program met the requirements as a client/server calendar application. It was a powerful, OS/2-based scheduling and calendar program for a networked environment. It provided the capability to schedule activities and meetings for a user or group of users. TaP/2 functions included a to-do list, memo pad, and event alarms. See Figure 3.6.

TaP Connectivity/2, a companion product to TaP/2, enabled IBM Boca Raton client/server and mainframe users to view and update calendars on either platform. It provided for free time search of calendars on both client/server and mainframe platforms. It generated meeting notices to Notes, OV and Internet addressees, if so requested. Chapter 5 describes the TaP/2 server configuration and installation.

In July 1994, the Boca Raton CIO team discovered that TaP/2 (Version 2.0) was missing a critical capability for the secretaries: TaP/2 did not offer full delegate capability. Some, but not all, TaP/2 capabilities

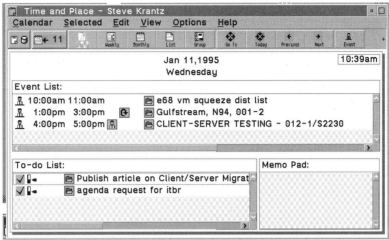

Courtesy International Business Machines Corporation

Figure 3.6 IBM Time and Place/2 User Interface

could be delegated, which was a serious handicap. This meant that a secretary could not truly act as the principal's proxy in calendar management. The TaP/2 developers came to the rescue by allowing a programmer on the team to create a local version that did support full delegate for the site's secretaries.

To jumpstart users in using TaP/2, a utility program, called CALMIG, was used to migrate the contents of an OV calendar to the user's TaP/2 calendar database. It was a one-time-only tool and it eased migration from the OV calendar to TaP/2.

For Conference Room Scheduling, It's CRS/2

Meeting or conference room scheduling was a separate VM application called CRS. Because conference rooms were shared and not all users were going client/server, any client/server application had to be synchronized with the mainframe CRS database. An internal client/server application, called CRS/2, ran on OS/2, offered the same features as the VM CRS, and communicated with the CRS database on VM. As a result, CRS/2 was installed and made part of the Standard Applications in the middle of 1994.

For the Phone Book, It's IBM CallUp C/S

CallUp C/S was an internally generated OS/2 application that borrowed considerable function from CallUp on VM. It provided the user the ability to look up other user's information about phone, fax, pager number, manager's name, reporting structure, and other such information. Directory search capabilities for CallUp C/S provided many of the functions provided with CallUp/VM, including fuzzy, partial name, and multiple field search. The IBM Address Book Synchronization/2 program was used to synchronize the CallUp/VM and CallUp C/S directories.

For Application Access, It's IBM Network Door/2 (NetDoor)

Built on OS/2 LAN Server 3.0, NetDoor provided convenient access to tools, applications, and documentation on OS/2 file servers on the site network, meeting the requirements for application access. After a simplified application installation via NetDoor, a user could access the application as if it were installed on his own workstation. The user accessed the network from a common network disk drive, with only the minimum number of local files installed on his or her PC. In this way, NetDoor saved a significant amount of hard-disk space for each user. NetDoor included a program called Vendor that kept track of usage of network licensed vendor applications. This means substantial cost savings for IBM Boca Raton (or any using enterprise), in addition to the advantages of central installation and support. By using Vendor on the network, the Boca Raton CIO only needed to purchase enough licensed copies to satisfy the maximum number of simultaneous users.

Lotus SmartSuite

For word processing, spreadsheets, and business graphics, Ami Pro for OS/2, Lotus 1-2-3 for OS/2, and Freelance for OS/2 were selected; i.e. Lotus SmartSuite for OS/2. Ami Pro is a full-function, WYSIWYG word processor, with features competitive with other leading word processors. Lotus 1-2-3 met the requirements for a three-dimensional, GUI-interface spreadsheet program, and it was a natural upgrade for the many 1-2-3/DOS users on site. Freelance for OS/2 met the requirements for business graphics. Most users required an easy-to-use package to create high-quality visuals for presentations. Freelance offered this, and many users had already upgraded to it on-site.

The most compelling reason for selecting the Lotus application suite was its easy integration with Lotus Notes, the centerpiece of the office client. SmartIcons for Ami Pro, 1-2-3, and Freelance were available for use on the Notes tool bar interface. This feature supported easy launching of the applications while in a Notes session. Notes supported both import and export of Ami Pro files, 1-2-3 files and Freelance files as well.

Behind the Scenes Utilities

Accompanying the Standard Applications were a set of service programs or **utilities** that provided the "behind the scenes" glue that allowed the office client to "talk" to the network (an office client is a PC with e-mail, calendar, phone directory, network connectivity, and, optionally, word processing, spreadsheet, and business graphics applications installed in an office). These service programs are sometimes called network connectivity software or protocols. Figure 3.7 lists them.

Communications Manager/2 was selected to communicate with IBM mainframe systems. Over the coming year, the reduced need for everyday

Application

OS/2	**Callup C/S**
Communication Manager/2	**NetDoor**
LAN Requester	**LPRMON**
LAPS	**TCP/IP**
DOS Dual Boot	**PCPRINT**
LAN Station Manager	**IBM AntiVirus/2**
Lotus Notes	**ACPM/ALMCOPY**
TaP/2	

Figure 3.7 Standard Applications

mainframe access and the general availability of TCP/IP will reduce the need for Communications Manager/2 on the site.

IBM LAN Requester was required for communication with the PS/2 servers running OS/2 LAN Server 3.0. DOS Dual Boot is a feature chosen to allow alternative access to a native DOS environment. This was included purely for transition purposes.

IBM LAN Station Manager (LSM) was an application selected to help automate asset management data collection over the network (it was also used to monitor network bandwidth utilization; see Chapter 6). When used in conjunction with the IBM LAN Network Manager application running on a server, LSM passed PC and user information to a database for subsequent analysis. This database is one of the "federation" of databases to become part of the CIO database currently under development (see Decision Support section later in this chapter).

The remaining utilities served a variety of other purposes:

IBM **TCP/IP** 2.0 was selected to support a growing set of data transport requirements across the network. TCP/IP is an industry-standard protocol, developed by the Department of Defense, that supports internetworking telecommunications. This IBM product included not only transport level protocol support for applications, such as LPRMON, but other tools to access the Internet (see Chapter 6 for a description), to access support databases (see Chapter 7 for a description of HelpPlus), and as a future mainframe access protocol.

LPRMON, a TCP/IP print monitor utility, was included to provide a bridge between the current host-based printing capability and the new client/server environment. The site had invested over the years in over two hundred IBM page printers (3816, 3820s, etc.), all mainframe-attached and aging. This means that most printing, other than that performed in offices with PC-attached printers, was done from a VM mainframe to one of these printers. The mainframe-attached printers needed to be replaced with LAN-attached printers, but the capital plan would not allow it. LAN-attached means that the printer will receive print jobs from a server on the network rather than a mainframe.

So, ISSC stepped in to invent a seamless means of using the host-attached laser printers from the standard OS/2 desktop with LPRMON. For users without a personal printer in their office, the default printer driver pointed to the LPRMON printer monitor. It transparently routed print requests back to the mainframe via TCP/IP, invoked the required mainframe print program, and sent the print data stream to the assigned site printer. This supported Notes Mail printing and other critical print requirements. As the site's current printers are replaced with new PostScript printers, each client's printer drivers will be replaced to address LAN-attached printer servers.

PCPRINT, an internal application, met the requirement of users to route OfficeVision/VM print files to their office printers. This was included as a transitional application only.

IBM AntiVirus/2, an internal application, was included to guard the user's PC against software viruses.

ACPM/ALMCOPY was a PC to mainframe upload/download (data copy from system to system over a network) internal application that was included as a transitional application only.

Team Applications

A team application is a general term for an application that facilitates information sharing among users on a network. The types of team applications include meetings (face-to-face, telecon, and videocon), mail, document processing, and groupware. Both technological advances and financial pressures have combined to alter team applications significantly over the past decade.

Meetings: Face-to-Face, Telecons, Videocons

Business meetings have evolved over the past decade to incorporate advanced telephony and video tools to save dollars and shrink schedules. This was partially due to the impact of lower profit margins, which shrank travel budgets, and greater worldwide competition. At the IBM Boca Raton site, this caused the continuous reduction of site-to-site travel, which has led to the increasing use of teleconferences and, to a lesser extent, videoconferences with off-site participants.

Because of easy availability of telephones with improved conferencing features, more often than not, telecons have become a standard for remote attendees. Coupled with fax or softcopy transmission of visuals for display, telecons have been as effective as face-to-face interactions on many occasions.

At the present time, videoconferencing remains impractical for general use due to extreme demands on local and wide area networks. At the IBM Boca Raton site, although the number of videoconferences, or videocons, has increased, they have been relatively little used. Primary limitations to use have been availability of resources (limited to major IBM sites) and limitations on motion video transmissions. The original video conferencing facility offered only static image transmission. See "Future Applications" later in this chapter, which discusses the near-term potential for this technology.

Mail

Mail has already been discussed as a personal application in the previous section. However, it is also the foundation of most team applications. The evolution of mail technology has accelerated in recent years. The availability of inexpensive and easy-to-use fax systems over the past decade has revolutionized the transmission of paper images worldwide. This has been accompanied by an explosion of use by businesses large and small through both public and private electronic mail (e-mail) services.

In IBM, OfficeVision/VM (OV) was the primary e-mail tool during the 1985–1992 period. OV was limited to character text with single monospaced characters. The transition to Lotus Notes in 1993–1994 ushered in an era of WYSIWYG e-mail. Proportionately spaced fonts of multiple point sizes, both monochrome and color, improved text readability and communication impact. The use of tables (of which the author is particularly fond!) was supported nicely within Notes to improve information organization. Finally, the ability to import graphics of different sources further improved information content. Paper mail has showed a steady decline over the past ten years with the broad deployment of OfficeVision/VM throughout IBM.

Document Processing

As a team application, document processing is the creation, review, and edit cycle employed to produce finished documents, such as a newsletter, magazine article, or book. At the heart of this process is the WYSIWYG word processor. What-You-See-Is-What-You-Get (WYSIWYG) word processors with PCs are gradually replacing more primitive mainframe tools and typewriters. A WYSIWYG word processor, such as Lotus Ami Pro, uses the graphics processing capability of the PC to display proportionately spaced characters of multiple sizes and fonts exactly as they will appear on the printed page. Through features such as revision marking built into word processors, teams can electronically share, review, revise, and ultimately publish a finished product.

Another approach, long used within IBM Boca Raton, uses a simple text editor to enter text along with tags that describe how the text is to appear when printed (e.g., the tag ":h1" before a line indicates the fact that the line is a title). This is called **Generalized Markup Language**, or **GML**. A program called a document compiler processes the marked up text to produce the printed output. On the mainframe, IBM's VM-based product **BookMaster** application was typically used by a team of writers, or information developers, to create their publications in this manner.

The IBM Boca Raton community of information developers (publications writers) required BookMaster because of its extensive features. Unfortunately, a large percentage (over 30%) of the mainframe expenses for their respective organizations was used in the document compilation process. An alternative explored was using an IBM OEM Personal/370 Adapter/A (P/370). The P/370 was a standalone IBM System/370 processor (yes, a mainframe processor!) that ran in a PS/2 computer running Operating System/2 (OS/2). This created a personal workstation that could run System/370 applications concurrently with OS/2 applications. A PS/2 server was acquired and equipped with a Pentium processor and a fast SCSI adapter for high performance. Then the VM operating system was installed along with the BookMaster application. The pilot test results for a 150-page document were excellent. This led the CIO leadership to invest in a GUI interface from the OS/2 desktop to the P/370 to create a simpler, production quality interface for the information developers. During the fall of 1994, a production test was in progress. It is expected that eight P/370 servers will be added to the Server Farm to process documents for the ID organizations on site in early 1995.

As WYSIWYG document creation tools with the necessary processing power have matured, a slow transition has occurred away from GML/Script for internal documents to WYSIWYG.

Because external publications sometimes require intersite contributions and review, this trend will proceed more slowly in the publications area. In the future, the use of **Standardized General Markup Language,** or **SGML,** may actually run counter to the WYSIWYG trend industry-wide. SGML is required by the U.S. Government for certain documents.

Decision Support

For many years, IBM has earned a reputation for leadership in database technology. The hierarchical database system, IMS, has been used for decades on IBM mainframe platforms. Built on solid theoretical and practical results, the relational database model, created by IBM's E. F. Codd, is an established industry standard. Most large corporations have built large databases using the DB/2 and SQL/DS relational database products sold by IBM for MVS and VM mainframes, respectively. Moreover, the IBM defined interface, Structured Query Language or SQL, is a widely supported standard for database access on platforms from PCs, to workstations and to minicomputers from many vendors.

The IBM Boca Raton site is no different in its dependence upon an assortment of IBM mainframe databases These databases include finance and accounting information, personnel information, product planning, inventory, and supply. Through 1993, database access has been accomplished primarily through batch queries submitted interactively from a mainframe-interactive terminal (typically a PC using terminal emulation software).

Vaskevitch [1993] draws the distinction between analytic databases and operational databases. Operational databases tend to contain real-time information for immediate decision making. Analytic databases require summaries of information to provide comparisons over periods of time. Operational databases should feed analytic databases at regular time intervals. With a solid design, the analytic database can provide consistent and correct views at any level of the business. Both should be available locally to satisfy operational or analytic requirements, but they should be linked such that upper levels in the business hierarchy can perform operational or analytic decisions. Vaskevitch has created the term **federation of databases,** which is a set of internally consistent databases that are tied together by another database that is "designed to meet the needs of senior management," to define this linkage.

An example of a federation of databases is the CIO database project in IBM Boca Raton. It was an analytic database built with Lotus Notes. Its purpose was to provide a set of weekly measurements of the client/server environment. It was fed weekly from two operational databases: initially, the Network Status and Help Desk databases. The Network Status database periodically gathered network performance statistics and client workstation asset data. The Help Desk database contained a record of each user problem encountered by the Help Desk staff. Figure 3.8 illustrates this approach.

Another significant decision support project was the construction of a product planning database by the IBM PC Company. Its goals were:

- Create a central database containing all PC Company product plans.

- Enable distributed input across the PC Company planning community.

- Share plan information in a user-friendly, yet secure, manner for timely decision making.

A DB/2 relational database design was created to describe the PC Company products—desktop systems, mobile systems, servers, displays, monitors, and peripherals. Using the IBM Personal Application System/2 (PAS/2) tool, a GUI interface was created to enter product plan data into the database from an OS/2 desktop. A set of batch queries was completed

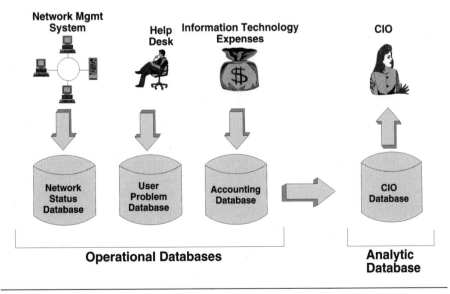

Figure 3.8 Federation of Databases Example: A CIO Database

to generate summary reports to be distributed to PC company-approved recipients in a secure manner. Significantly, a Lotus Notes database was created to extract periodic information from the DB/2 repository, called PSPLAN. It gave convenient access to the data to authorized users for analytic purposes. Ultimately, PSPLAN data tables will become part of a PC Company **information warehouse** (an information warehouse is a large centralized repository for multiple databases which can be accessed with a common query tool) linking the critical processes of the business to a central repository. In this way, the federation of databases idea will become a reality for critical PC Company decision support information.

During 1994, the migration to PC-based, GUI query of legacy (mainframe) and client/server databases occurred for these and a few other key applications. These represented process-driven, local extractions from central databases. This is consistent with industry expert recommendations to bridge to legacy databases using client/server tools when appropriate [Boar, 1993]. Centralized databases continued to be used in most cases in 1994, however.

In the future, the business rules, programmed in mainframe applications in the past, will be programmed in server-based, workflow (or team) applications. Business processes will define the workflow for these next-generation applications [Vaskevitch, 1993].

For Groupware, It's Lotus Notes

Groupware, workgroup computing, and workflow automation are three of the hottest buzzwords in client/server jargon. The objective of groupware is, in general, to improve the sharing of information among members of a group or team.

A simple example is a database on a server containing articles to be published as a newsletter by a team of writers. Each writer can add his or her own article and create comments about the articles of others. These comments are stored in the database associated with the article, and, again, all writers can "share" the comments. By adding an approval form to be used by the editor to approve an article, which also resides in the database, everyone can be made aware of the progress of the newsletter.

Spectacular benefits can be achieved if business processes are reengineered and groupware applications are developed to support them. Organizations can gain a competitive advantage by improving their responsiveness to the marketplace. They can enjoy improved coordination of effort and collaboration between members of local or widely dispersed teams.

Many groupware products on the market today use client/server computing elements to create groupware applications. They incorporate a shared, distributed, document database which resides on a server, an easy-to-use GUI on the client, a wide-area e-mail function, and built-in security to allow access control for critical information. A notable feature, discussed later in this chapter is **rapid application development**, which means that a groupware application can be changed as rapidly as required to meet business needs. Finally, many groupware products support documents that contain **rich text**. Rich text describes a document that can contain text, graphics, scanned images, audio, and full-motion video data. Sometimes such documents are called **compound documents**. This feature alone can improve the communication quality of shared information.

According to the trade press, Lotus Notes has a two-year lead on all competition in this key application area. The primary reason for its selection as a centerpiece of the client/server desktop was precisely this ability to improve business productivity through groupware.

By contrast, a form of groupware on VM emerged and achieved widespread use within IBM during the past decade. Some very creative programmers developed a VM program called **TOOLSRUN**. At its heart was the notion of a **TOOLS disk**, managed by the TOOLSRUN program, which could be active on a **VM Service Machine**. The TOOLS disk was a collection of user-created files managed by the TOOLSRUN program. A VM Service Machine operated like a **daemon,** or a program that was waiting to be triggered into action by an incoming request. In this case, the events were user requests for files and user transmissions of files to a TOOLS disk. A **control file** defined user access (by VM node and ID). Users could deposit, retrieve, and subscribe to TOOLS disk files if their VM ID appeared in the CONTROL file. Within a disk, files could be grouped into named **PACKAGES** for easy retrieval. The TOOLSRUN program ran as an independent entity on a VM service machine, allowing users on local or remote VM nodes to access the repository. Through automatically generated replicas, called **shadows**, local copies could be maintained for faster access. VM notes, triggered by TOOLS disk events, maintained communication among authorized users. The concepts embodied in TOOLS disks are identical in many ways to other client/server groupware application builders, such as Lotus Notes. Unfortunately, difficulties in establishing and maintaining TOOLS disks greatly limited their general use (even a knowledgable VM user required considerable support in setup and maintenance). Further, the files on a disk, although not restricted in terms of format, were primarily documents with no inherent database or interactive features (e.g., they didn't support viewing alternatives as does Notes). This ruled out workflow automation.

Another feature of TOOLS disks was support for **Forums**. A Forum was a sequential collection of e-mail notes that represented a discussion among a community of interested users, typically highly technical users. Over the past decade, Forums have proliferated across IBM, established by the technical community to exchange information and engage in question/answer discussions. Unfortunately, Forums were limited to penetration of the technical communities due to complexity of user access and user interface.

Figure 3.9 compares Lotus Notes with TOOLS disks and Forums to identify the ingredients in Notes that have fueled its marketplace success. Highlighted in bold in the figure, the advantages of Notes make the transition from the mainframe capabilities compelling. Based on the IBM Boca Raton experience, groupware applications could be developed as much as 90 percent faster with Notes than with traditional development tools. Using Notes, teams can share, distribute, and build upon existing work, whether they are on site or traveling. Users can post documents where other users can immediately see them, regardless of the document type: text, graphics, CAD drawings, images, spreadsheets, tables, and so on.

	TOOLS Disks & Forums	Lotus Notes
Function	File sharing and discussion databases on multi-user system and across IBM corporate WAN	File sharing, discussion databases, **workflow applications** over Boca network **and across IBM corporate** WAN
User Interface	Line mode and page-mode character menus	**GUI, Presentation Manager/Windows interface.**
Developer Interface	Limited set of line mode commands, supplemented by REXX	**Object-oriented, macro function language.**
Platform	VM on S/390	**OS/2, Windows on PCs**

Figure 3.9 TOOLS Disks and Forums vs. Lotus Notes

Everything in Notes is a database. The database is a single file (xxxxxxxx.NSF) with one or more documents (records) contained in it. A document can be a single data item, a simple text file, a form with one or more data fields, a graphics file, and so on. The document format and views of a document in a database are easily specified (programmed) through the Notes GUI interface. Multiple forms can be defined for a database. A critical feature is the ability to route e-mail to and from a Notes database (the mail message can be one of the forms). This provides the basis for workflow applications. Through simple commands, access to the database can be granted to one or more users.

A key Notes database feature is replication. According to Vaskevitch [1993], replication provides "automatic tiered storage" for Notes users. This keeps geographically dispersed Notes databases in line automatically through the routine transmission of changes. This is different from the traditional, central database where only a single copy is maintained and all users must log in to the central repository for update and or access. The advantages are that geographically dispersed users can each have a copy of a Notes database on their PC for convenient independent access and consistent performance. The disadvantage is that the data may be backlevel and that periodically the users must connect to the network for replication of changes to occur. This is a two-way process in which users' changes propagate to the server and vice versa. Eventually, all users are at the latest level. Vaskevitch calls this, appropriately, "sophisticated self-adaptive storage migration." Note that updates to a document by two independent users must be manually resolved (they are noted as conflicts in the database however). Clearly, this approach is not appropriate for on-line transaction-oriented databases and their applications. But, for today's team-oriented, data-sharing environment, replication is perfect.

It is much more efficient to post files (e.g., accounting ledgers) in a Notes' database than distributing that information through mail. The advantages of groupware databases over mail include:

- Less traffic on the network if it is a multiple server network like IBM Boca's.

- Notes (groupware) databases enable sharing of information in one repository.

- Notes databases enable different types of applications to be built on top of the basic data store, including workflow, discussion, and broadcast applications.

Notes easily allows development of data-sharing applications coupled with e-mail that improve business processes. In IBM Boca Raton, this development was actively encouraged across the site through education classes (see Chapter 7) and focus groups as the migration proceeded. A focus group was the term for a short meeting (up to two hours) with a department or work team and a Notes consultant.

Out of necessity, the first groupware tools were built to aid the Client Rollout Team in successfully managing the client rollout itself (see Chapter 4). With the aid of Lotus Consulting and IBM LAN Business Solutions consultants, several focus groups were run to identify other candidates for groupware solutions. A few examples follow:

- The migration of a competitive analysis spreadsheet database to an easily distributed Lotus Notes database. This database required strict security, which the Notes 3.0 application supported.

- A database for the site library offerings, including periodicals, new books and new CDs.

- A Usability Issues Tracking database. This was a standard database on everyone's Notes desktop. Every site user could compose a document (i.e., fill in a form) describing a usability issue or suggestion. The lead client/server administrators monitored this weekly. The administrators could assign a specific individual to follow up with a simple name lookup and button press, put the issue on hold, or respond to the issue author via an e-mail message directly from the database.

- A mail-logging database for the site's secretaries. This allowed them to conveniently record receipt of paper mail, fax, and other deliverables for the people they supported.

These tailored application drove home the value of Notes and client/server computing to the users. It is highly recommended that you adopt this same practice in your rollout. Chapter 2, "Migration Management," highlights this in the Planting Seeds of Productivity Phase of the migration (Phase 4).

Team Applications: The Make or Buy Decision

Team applications, unlike personal applications, have many business-unique requirements, in particular in the data and process areas. You need to have an understanding of how to build them when the need arises and have the resources on hand to do so. This means software developers, development tools, development schedules, and testing.

Boar [1993] observes that software development has evolved through three stages:

1. The craft stage, in which artisans and brute force predominated.

2. The commercial stage, in which business needs added procedures and training as additional elements.

3. The engineering discipline stage, in which science, standards, and professionalism are introduced.

The craft stage of software development was the 1950s and 1960s. There were no well-defined programming development practices until the very end of this period. The 1970s and 1980s roughly correspond to the commercial stage. During these decades **structured programming** (a strict method of writing code without goto statements), **code inspection** (a team review process of software prior to test), and other methods were combined to become the discipline called **software engineering**. Software development management insisted on these practices and trained their programmers in them.

The trends toward use of **object-oriented design** and **open system standards,** introduced in the late 1980s, appear to have brought software development into the engineering discipline stage. Object-oriented design is a method of software development in which code and related data are developed and treated like self-contained objects. In many cases, these objects only need minor modifications to adapt them to the new requirements. This approach promotes software reusability and simplifies development. Open system standards are well-defined software interfaces and protocols (data exchange formats, for example) that promote interoperability among software and hardware systems.

Database management systems (DBMSs) provide a framework (a relational database is an example) and platform (software services to interface to the database) to standardize and simplify software development. Application development platforms that combine DBMS and object-oriented tools foster very **rapid application development**. Lotus Notes and IBM's Personal AS/2 are recent examples. The previous sections on groupware and decision support describe examples of their use in activities at the IBM Boca site.

What is interesting to note here is the rapid application development approach used to create and deploy useful Notes and PAS/2 applications.

Traditional application development followed a **waterfall model** (see Figure 3.10), in which one development phase cascaded into the next. A typical sequence was, from start to finish, requirements definition, functional specification, detailed specification, design, coding, testing, installation, and maintenance. Cycles tended to be long because all software was built from the ground up. With the new tools, multiple, shorter development cycles occur in the same time period that a single traditional waterfall cycle would occur. The approach is to quickly create a prototype, test it, deploy it, and then go into a new cycle with refinements to the previous prototype. With Lotus Notes in particular, this approach is producing useful applications very quickly with great user satisfaction.

Another interesting trend is the movement to more end-user software development versus central I/S development. The Notes database platform generality and ease of programming is making this happen to great success in IBM Boca Raton.

Legacy Application Programs

Depending on the extent of software investment in a prior mainframe environment, the number of legacy applications may be quite extensive.

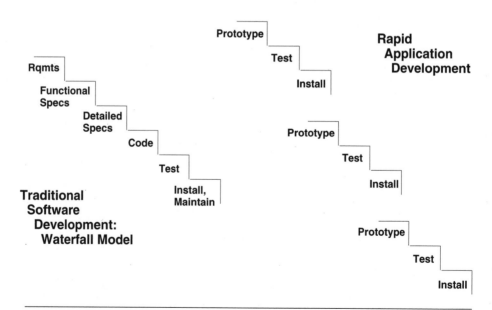

Figure 3.10   Traditional vs. Rapid Application Development

Server Requirement	High Storage	Medium Storage	Low Storage
High CPU	Mainframe Server	RISC Server	RISC Server
Medium CPU	Mainframe Server	PC Server	PC Server
Low CPU	Mainframe Server	PC Server	PC Server

Figure 3.11   Server CPU vs. Storage

Inevitably, some legacy applications may have to be used during and after a client/server migration for an assortment of reasons. Some applications should be replaced.

The Legacy Replacement Decision

When considering application replacement, it is important to recognize that client/server applications require a division of labor decision between server and client systems. The division of labor will imply best fit of technology for the server system. Figure 3.11 provides a simplistic guideline to decide the best fit of server technology for an application. The best fit for the client system should be based on the prospective users. In general, the preferred approach is to develop the client portion of the application to run on all standard client platforms.

Once a legacy application has been mapped to a client/server solution, its replacement schedule (if any) can then be decided based on:

Development Cost versus Ongoing Mainframe Expense.   In some cases, the cost of application development and purchase of required PC servers is well below ongoing mainframe expenses (see preceding P/370 example).

Importance to the Business.   If two applications have equally good business cases, the application with the greatest user impact should be developed first.

Integration Requirements with Other Applications.   This means, for example, that if the application must work with the calendar program it should integrate well with the office desktop applications.

At the IBM Boca Raton site, there was no escaping the need to use many mainframe-based applications, both during and after the major migration period. Most came under the category of corporate applications, applications that interacted with corporate databases or were part of corporate processes. The CIO could not afford to replace these applications or create client/server front-ends for them. Being out in the lead compared to sister sites in IBM, the Standard Tools Team knew it had to wait for most to catch up for these applications to be replaced or upgraded. Examples were the on-line time and attendance recording application, the on-line forms handling applications, and personnel records handling applications.

Legacy Exodus

Winning user hearts and minds with words and slogans so that they will migrate is one thing (see Chapter 7), making it easier for them to migrate is another. Sometimes it is necessary to invest in migration tools, programs that bring some familiar parts of the old environment into the new and save part of the old environment for safekeeping.

The IBM Boca Raton CIO leadership was concerned that many users just wouldn't make the leap from tried-and-true OfficeVision/VM. The CIO leadership decided to invest in a set of migration aids that would make it easier for users to embrace the new office tools and a communication program to inform users of the value of the new environment (Chapter 7 discusses the communication program in detail). In addition, the CIO was under pressure to "make the numbers," that is bring down information technology costs. Migrating users off VM, which would reduce CPU cycles and storage, was a path to success.

The CIO leadership first looked at critical personal OfficeVision files that users were dependent on. Four types were identified:

- Distribution lists, flat text files containing VM mail addresses, were almost universally used to simplify mail distribution on VM. Notes provided a similar capability with Groups, which could be defined in both personal and public Name and Address book files.

- Nicknames Files were specially named files containing a list of nicknames with associated mail addresses to simplify e-mail. The Notes Personal Name and Address Book provided a similar capability.

- Notelogs are flat text files containing saved mail memos. An OfficeVision user would typically have several notelogs, each being named with a personal category. The Notes Mail database provided a similar capability.

- Documents were special OfficeVision files that were stored in a central database where they could be shared by many users. They were typically used to communicate information from management to a large group of employees. The Notes database provided a similar capability.

It turned out that IBM Somers had invested in the creation of three conversion programs that a user could employ to migrate all four types of files to his PC. There were picked up and enhanced for generalized use. Figure 3.12 summarizes these programs.

Next, the CIO leadership concentrated on VM WIHAT (pronounced *why-hat*) files. You might ask, "What is a WIHAT file?" WIHAT is an acronym that stands for "What In Hell Are These?" Most VM users had many storage cylinders devoted to WIHAT files. Simple tools were needed that would enable a user to easily archive or download these files to his PC to relieve WIHAT anxiety. **ADSTAR Distributed Storage Manager (ADSM)** was selected for personal VM storage archive (see Chapter 5 for details about ADSM) where a large number of WIHAT files were involved. For a relatively small number of files, a program, which compressed a set of WIHAT files and downloaded them to a user's PC, was readied.

These set of utilities were placed on public disks (either VM or site network as appropriate) for easy user access. Chapter 7 discusses the aggressive communication and education plan used to migrate the site's users.

OfficeVision File	Conversion Program	Notes File
Distribution Lists	DLIST Conversion Program	Notes Groups
Nicknames File (Private Mail Address Lists)	DLIST Conversion Program	Notes Personal Name & Address Book
Notelogs	OV2LNOTE	Notes Mail Databases
Documents	DOCS2LN	Notes Mail Databases

Figure 3.12 OV to Notes Conversion Programs

Other Applications

As defined, personal and team applications comprise most of the applications required to run a business. Other, more specialized and important, application categories include **computer-aided design (CAD)**, **computer-aided software engineering (CASE)** and **computer-integrated manufacturing (CIM)** which are used by design, development, and manufacturing companies. If applicable to your business, these and other applications should be evaluated as part of your overall requirements gathering and selection process. An important success factor to consider is the integration of these applications along with standard office applications on the user's desktop. A successful integration improves usability, saves dollars, and saves office (desktop) space for the user in question.

For over twenty years, electrical and mechanical engineers have used CAD tools to design new products. In the past decade, software engineers have increasingly used CASE tools to design software. A number of aggressive startup companies developed workstation-based applications to wrest control of this industry from the companies providing minicomputer-based and mainframe-based products in the 1980s. Engineers and programmers increasingly selected workstation-based tools because of higher productivity. A personal, high-performance workstation with high-resolution graphics for key engineers significantly reduced schedules and raised quality.

The IBM Boca Raton experience is consistent with this broad industry-wide experience. Both CAD and CASE applications use are discussed along with the client workstation in Chapter 4.

Ongoing Application Management

Interoperability, user productivity, and low costs are very important to information technology management. A highly effective way to foster all three is to control software application use. You can accomplish this by buying, installing, and supporting only standard applications on the enterprise network. With only standard applications available for use (e.g., one word processor, one spreadsheet), interoperability is assured. All users learn one, and only one, tool, resulting in increased knowledge sharing and expertise. Volume purchase discounts for licenses are possible, resulting in lower costs.

A major success story for IBM Boca Raton was the early establishment of an Application Review Board during the client/server rollout. Its job was to promote standardization of application usage across the site as the users changed from mostly host-centric applications and roll-your-own PC applications to a common, networked environment. First, it was staffed with representatives from each major organization. Next, a wise and skillful leader was installed to both administer and adjudicate disagreements. Then a Lotus Notes database was created to accept nominations for new applications and made it available to all site users. The database was a classic Notes workflow application that combined nomination forms and response forms so that the entire process of nomination, evaluation, and decision making was tracked and public. This approach has kept the site on track toward a low-cost, interoperable set of standard applications and productive users.

Future Applications

With the right analysis, you should be able to select applications for a client/server migration that will provide a solid base for a three- to five-year period, and perhaps beyond. At the IBM Boca Raton site, this base has been established.

Looking beyond the short term, future applications based on leading technology and development advances should be anticipated. The broadest category of future applications on the tip of everyone's tongue is **multimedia** (an application that combines at least two of the following: text, graphics, image, sound, and video). The technology behind multimedia includes denser storage media and faster processors. The approach is to digitize multimedia information rapidly, store it efficiently, and reproduce it rapidly. To digitize multimedia information means to convert it to a sequence of 0's and 1's, the fundamental way all information is encoded in a computer system. With sound, images and especially video (a rapid sequence of images), a very long sequence of 0's and 1's results! If we consider an 8½" by 11" page with regular text, about 3,000 bytes of storage are needed to store the information (3,000 bytes equals 24,000 bits of 0's and 1's). If we scan this same page and convert the result to a compressed, digitized image, the information load increases to about 60,000 bytes. This is an increase of twenty times! This affects not only the storage meant to hold the image, but the capacity of communications links over which the image is to be transmitted. [IBM Image, 1990]

A hot subcategory of multimedia applications is person-to-person videoconferencing. Person-to-person videoconferencing is exciting because it is the next logical step in improving person-to-person communication in a large organization or among organizations. What is involved is providing the user the software application, a video camera (to capture the user's image), supporting software services, and, optionally, a video processing card to compress, decompress, and transmit video data over the network. Another related subcategory is called video-on-demand, where users can select video information from a central server to play on their PC. This is exciting because it can provide a new, improved means of delivering user education directly to a person's office, among other applications. Both of these application subcategories are highly dependent on the network infrastructure and may be infeasible today for wide deployment in a large organization. It was estimated recently by a noted industry expert that with today's leading edge technology, person-to-person videoconferencing among 500 people could be supported on a single network, however 5,000 people was infeasible [Semilof, 1993]. If the application deployment can be carefully monitored and controlled, you can introduce these new applications to many of your users.

Another very interesting multimedia application category is **visualization**. Applications that replace numerical tables and low-resolution graphics with images of high information content are called visualization applications. These applications enable users to see complex information and data relationships quickly and easily. Today, this technology is usually associated with scientific supercomputing or high-end graphic workstations. However, it is expected that as the cost of computing continues to fall, visualization applications will start to appear on future PCs with enhanced graphics displays. In the future, a large visualization application may result in "movies" that range in length from seconds to minutes, again with very high demands on the network data transmission capacity.

Critical Success Factors

Application selection is a lynch-pin activity in your client/server migration. Select well and many of the critical challenges to follow—in particular, winning the hearts and minds of your users—will be easier. Following are a few critical success factors to focus on:

- You should invest in standard applications to promote interoperability, reduce training costs, and reduce support costs. The IBM Boca Raton site was extremely fortunate to have achieved a consensus in this highly charged decision.

- You should consider establishing an Application Review Board to control acquisition and deployment of new applications. This is a very cost-effective decision in the long run. Supporting the process with an easily accessed team application will solidify its use.

- You should provide committed, accessible application support for *all* vendor and internal applications. Deployment of a number of important internal applications were held up at the IBM Boca Raton site due to lack of a formal support organization.

- Lotus Notes is an outstanding platform for development of team applications. It combines ease of use and ease of programming to drastically shorten development of new applications.

4

Client Rollout

Host computing dictated a master-slave relationship with respect to attached devices such as user terminals. Network computing, however, leads to a client/server approach. The workstation becomes a client platform that requests information and processing services from "servers" connected to local and wide area networks.

[TAPSCOTT, 1993]

After all of the planning, there comes a point when you actually give the users some computers and say go! This is the **client rollout**. This rollout is a major component of any client/server migration project. Careful planning must be performed prior to and during a client rollout to guarantee user satisfaction. This chapter details the IBM Boca Raton experience during a large-scale client rollout in 1993–1994, with a look back at the relatively small-scale client migrations in the 1991–1992 timeframe. It will focus on each of these client migrations in turn, detailing requirements, the transition to client/server computing, future considerations, and some critical success factors. Although this chapter focuses on the IBM Boca Raton experience, most of the activities can be generalized and applied to your client rollout.

Client Categories

Typically, you can organize most client systems into three broad categories: **office clients, mobile clients,** or **workstation clients.** The office client probably represents the bulk of the users and should receive the greatest attention throughout your client/server migration project. In IBM Boca Raton, over 2,700 computer systems fit this category. An office client is a PC with e-mail, calendar, phone directory, network connectivity software, and, optionally, word processing, spreadsheet, and business graphics applications installed in an office.

A mobile client is a PC that is not office-bound; it might be a truly mobile notebook PC or a home-bound desktop PC. The mobile client is undergoing the most substantial transition during the IBM Boca migration period. Several hundred mobile clients are currently enabled.

A workstation client is defined to be an engineering workstation, such as an IBM RISC System/6000 system, or a very powerful PC used to do design or development activities. Software programmers and hardware designers require special tools to perform their jobs—that is, create designs. Programmers require **text editors** to create their **source programs,** which are then converted by a **compiler** into executable programs. They typically use a very-high-performance industry-standard PC as a workstation. Hardware designers require **computer-aided-design (CAD)** applications to create logical and physical hardware designs. They typically use a RISC-based computer system with high-performance graphics as a workstation (a RISC-based or Reduced Instruction Set Computer system has a simplified instruction set capable of operating faster than other computer systems). In IBM Boca Raton, many of the workstation clients, representing over 400 systems, were defined and rolled out prior to 1993.

Office Clients

Within the client/server paradigm, the industry-standard PC is a generally accepted platform for the office client. As the office client will be used by most, if not all, office workers, professionals and managers in a business, understanding its requirements is very important. Basic requirements for an office client are illustrated in Figure 4.1. Let's examine each element in the figure:

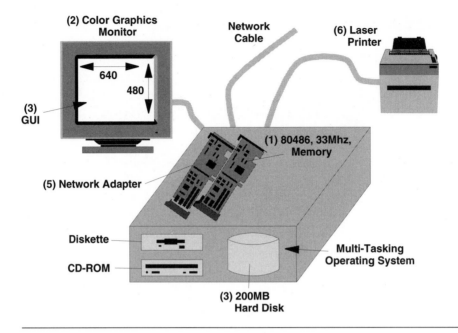

Figure 4.1 Typical Office Client

1. Industry-standard PC system. The system must contain adequate memory and disk storage to support the selected operating system and applications. An Intel 80486 processor operating at 33 Mhz or higher, 8 to 16 megabytes (MB) of memory and a 200 MB hard disk should be considered a typical configuration for a full-function office client.

2. A color graphics monitor capable of supporting from 640 by 480 (VGA) to 1024 by 768 (XGA, SVGA) graphics resolution. This is a widely supported industry standard, adequate for most user applications. Fifteen-inch diagonal screen size and **noninterlaced** image support are optional requirements. A noninterlaced image is one in which all display lines are drawn every time the graphics display is refreshed, resulting in a more stable image.

3. A robust, **multitasking operating system,** able to support a broad range of office and nonoffice applications with good performance. A multitasking operating system is one that allows more than one application (task) to run at the same time.

4. A Graphic User Interface (GUI), with consistent human factors and good performance. A GUI interface provides users an easy-to-learn and proven application environment with point-and-shoot, mouse-driven commands.

5. Network connectivity able to provide adequate bandwidth for all office applications. This should be a 16 Mbps token-ring or 10 Mbps Ethernet LAN adapter for starters.

6. Peripherals support may be a requirement for a subset of users. Typical peripherals requiring support include CD-ROM (internal) or a personal laser printer. Some users requiring multimedia support may require a sound card with stereo speakers or a video card to display video clips.

The Office Client Past

It is useful to take an historical perspective to appreciate the rate of progress and identify trends in many cases. In few other industries has the rate of progress been as dramatic in terms of technology advances, cost reductions, and user impact. Figure 4.2 identifies the past, present, and future office clients in Boca Raton. We can see that PC use in IBM Boca Raton was not unlike the experience at many major companies. As the birthplace of the IBM PC and the home for its development over the past decade, it is no surprise that IBM Boca was a heavy user of IBM PCs as office clients. During the 1985–1992 period, a typical office PC (not yet a client) had an Intel 80386 processor, 2 MB of memory, an 80 MB hard disk, and a 3270 emulator adapter card (enabling the PC to act as a mainframe terminal).

User Interface

A user interface is a general term for the way the user interacts with a computer system to get it to perform useful work. There was not a standard office desktop user interface in the 1985–1992 period. Most users utilized the **page-mode** (full-screen, menu-driven) OfficeVision interface on VM via **terminal emulation** (a PC operating as a terminal with the help of software called a terminal emulator and a communication card)

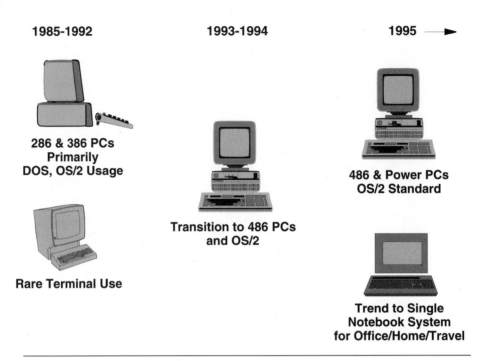

Figure 4.2 IBM Boca Raton Office Client: Past/Present/Future

for most office activities. They also used one or more DOS-based PC applications. The PC applications offered little consistency. Some were command driven, a few had their own graphical interfaces. A growing number of users installed OS/2 or Windows to gain a consistent graphic user interface.

Consistency and user-friendliness were the key user interface requirements during the transition period. A common, graphic user interface was the obvious choice as provided by OS/2 Presentation Manager. It offered a flexible windows application environment with consistent controls and rich customization capabilities.

Operating System

It is important to select a single operating system for the office client that meets your requirements. The operating system is a layer of software that allows applications to run on the client system. If it is designed well, it will support multiple applications efficiently, allowing them to share the client system hardware resources (i.e., processor, memory, and input/output devices) without error or conflict. It should support the broadest set of industry-standard applications to give you the broadest latitude in application selection. It is also a complicated piece of software that requires occasional service—bug fixes, upgrades for new features or releases, or customization for new applications or system hardware. When a single operating system is selected, fewer support staff are required to assist users (see Chapter 7). Standardized maintenance procedures can be created, thereby minimizing cost (see discussion of Configuration, Installation, and Distribution in Office Client of the Future section later in this chapter).

From all angles, OS/2 was the best choice as IBM Boca Raton's standard client operating system. It is a robust, 32-bit (data can be processed 32 bits at a time), true multitasking (more than one application or process can be active at one time) software system that supports most of the PC-based applications available, including DOS, Windows, and OS/2 applications. Over two thirds of the users were OS/2 literate and had early versions installed (OS/2 1.3, 2.0) already. Not the least significant in the selection was that IBM Boca Raton is the home of OS/2 development. This led to key advantages in support, quality, and (most important) acceptance.

OS/2 provides an industrial-strength base for client/server migration. It is a fully architected operating system with the most advanced **object-oriented** user interface available today. Object-oriented means that most items visible in the user interface (the icons) can be treated as objects by the user and moved about to accomplish things. This includes files, icons, and devices such as printers. For example, the icon for a file can be moved by the mouse to a printer icon, which will cause the file to be printed.

OS/2 has superior crash protection and the needed application protection. This means that if an individual application fails, other applications are not affected. It is designed to support true multitasking and has more memory available for individual applications than its competition. OS/2 becomes a superior performer as the number of applications increases. In addition, OS/2 performance will improve even more as applications convert to 32-bit implementations. Freelance Graphics and Lotus 1-2-3 already have 32-bit versions. Most applications were implemented to run on Intel 80286 systems which only supported 16-bit data access and so must be converted to take advantage of the Intel 80386, 80486 processors, which support 32-bit data access.

Hardware

Selecting industry-standard hardware simplifies upgrades and maintenance. The broadest array of hardware upgrade and peripheral products are available. Since Boca Raton is the home of the IBM PC Company, almost all of the PCs were to be either IBM PS/2 or PS/ValuePoint systems (see Figures 4.3 and 4.4).

One mistake that was made was allowing individual departments too much leeway in ordering specific PC systems. The diversity of systems, even within a single department, added difficulty to the PC manufacturing process (see "Office Client PCs off the Assembly Line" later in this chapter).

The Intel 80486DX, operating at 33 Mhz (million cycles per second),

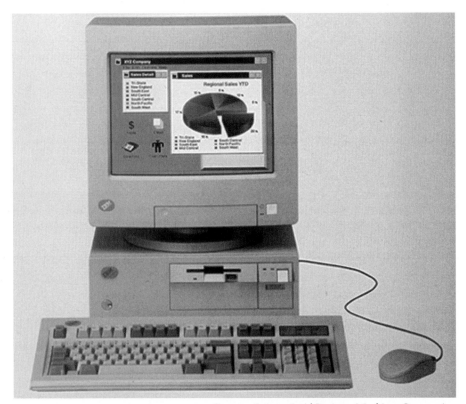

Courtesy International Business Machines Corporation

Figure 4.3 IBM PS/2 Model 77

Courtesy International Business Machines Corporation

Figure 4.4 IBM PS/ValuePoint

and 16 MB (million bytes) of random access memory (RAM) were selected as the minimally capable processor complex based upon informal benchmark testing performed in 1993. The bottom line was that application performance was too slow without this processor-memory combination. The minimum disk storage capacity of 240 MB was selected based on two factors. First, the Standard Applications plus utilities took up approximately 160 MB of disk storage, so a reasonable additional amount needed to be available for data and other applications. Second, several models in PC Company inventory offered a 240 MB hard file.

Hard disks were logically partitioned in a standard manner (a physical disk is said to be logically partitioned when the operating system treats it as more than one disk, each with its own drive letter). The disk partitioning was based upon practical experience with PC operating systems. A 100 MB space was allocated to the C drive to contain operating system-related code. This included OS/2, IBM Communications Manager/2, LAN Requester, DOS Dual Boot, and LAN Station Manager. Isolating the operating system and its utilities into its own logical drive enabled update or replacement of this code with minimal impact to any user applications.

A **VGA** CRT display, with 640 by 480 resolution and up to 256 simultaneous colors, was deemed adequate graphics display resolution for the office client, although many systems were equipped with either **XGA** or **SVGA** resolution. VGA stands for Video Graphics Array, the graphics standard IBM introduced with the PS/2 systems in 1987. XGA stands for eXtended Graphics Array, another IBM graphics standard, which supports up to 1024 by 768 resolution. SVGA stands for Super VGA, a de facto industry standard, which also supports up to 1024 by 768 resolution.

The Standard Applications utilized the NetBIOS protocol for local LAN communication. Some of the utilities used TCP/IP for both LAN and WAN communication. SNA, IBM's standard mainframe network architecture, was used for **terminal emulation** communication from PC to mainframe. Terminal emulation is software that runs on a PC, allowing it to log on to a mainframe to run mainframe applications. The site network supported these multiple protocols transparently, as all the LAN internetworks were connected using bridges, which do not see the differences in the higher level protocols (i.e., NetBIOS, TCP/IP, and SNA). Chapter 6 describes this in more detail.

The standard hardware interface to the site network was a **token-ring** adapter card (token-ring is a standard physical LAN communication protocol, introduced by IBM), operating at 16 Mbps (up to 16 million bits can be transmitted per second). All existing site PCs and workstations were already equipped with these adapter cards, and the site network was already operating at the 16 Mbps speed (see Chapter 6 for details).

The most common peripheral in user offices was a personal printer, either a dot matrix or a laser printer. Host-attached laser printers supplemented this capability. A migration to LAN-attached printing is expected, however. Chapter 5 describes how the old host-attached printers were used and how the LAN-attached printers will replace them over time.

Some less common peripherals were CD-ROM drives and multimedia adapter cards (sound, video), which appear to be increasing in number during the transition period.

Office Clients Rolling off the Assembly Line

Once you have selected your standard office client's software and hardware, you face the daunting task of upgrading each user with the minimum system so that all can participate in the new environment. Chapter 2 discussed the organization and methodology necessary to make this happen. It requires a well-run team of trained specialists working closely with users and other support teams. For a large rollout, assembly line processes are called for to achieve success.

In January 1994 in IBM Boca Raton, over 2,700 office client PCs were to be either upgraded or replaced by the end of the third quarter of 1994 by the Client Rollout Team. Approximately, 700 systems were completed in 1993, so just over 2,000 remained in 1994. This meant that the target of installations in 1994 had to average 50 systems per week (or roughly 10 per working day) for the rollout to be successful. Based upon the inventory of installed PCs, the Client Rollout Team made the assumption that 70 percent of the systems were to be replacements (brand new systems) and 30 percent were to be upgrades.

The team started with the following general objectives, which are applicable to any client rollout:

1. Minimum disruption to user's current work.

2. All standard software preinstalled.

3. Final software customization would occur in the user's office by trained installer.

4. Installation would take no more than 4 hours.

5. All user data from current system would be migrated by the installer at time of installation.

6. Up to three applications from the former system would be migrated to the new system.

7. Users must return old PCs that had been replaced. The returned systems were to be reused or scrapped.

Your approach to client installation or upgrade should be comprehensive. It should be based on the Golden Rule (Do unto others as you would have others do unto you), because each office client upgrade has a significant psychological, intellectual, and physical impact on a new user. This was the approach used in IBM Boca Raton.

The IBM Boca Raton process was comprehensive and included the following steps:

1. Department focal points were identified to handle early information gathering and keep department members informed.

2. Area meeting presentations were performed to set expectations and communicate the plan.

3. Completion of a comprehensive user questionnaire, to establish user PC requirements, was required of every user.

4. Hard disks of new PCs were personalized with software through replication over the network from a "custom" master disk for the department.

5. Personalized PC replacements or upgrades were carefully scheduled. This included installation of the standard desktop and maintenance of all prior capabilities (VM access, print, and up to three PC applications).

To support this ambitious effort, the Client Rollout Team set up a private local area network. It was used to efficiently transfer disk images of the Standard Applications software suite to fully configured PC systems (see Chapter 3, Figure 3.7).

The assignment of user focal points is highly recommended for your rollout. The focal point should be a person in each area or department to serve as your local agent to communicate directly with each person to receive a new or upgraded PC. The goal should be to have a focal point in each department (10 to 20 clients). At the IBM Boca Raton site, this proved to be unrealistic. A few organizations of 100 to 200 clients only assigned a single individual to serve. In addition, this was a part-time responsibility for the majority of the focal points. The focal point key duties should be:

1. Ensure completion of client questionnaires. The questionnaire should be taken on-line by most clients. It gathers comprehensive

information of client requirements. Appendix D includes a sample copy.

2. Order network identifiers and key software licenses. At IBM Boca Raton, the Client Rollout Team ordered TCP/IP identifiers and Lotus Notes licenses for clients.

3. Track new PC orders and gather complete data on PCs to be upgraded.

4. Communicate with the Client Rollout Team and the clients throughout the rollout period. A weekly meeting run by the team should review all progress and problems. This proved to be a vital activity in IBM Boca Raton.

A well-defined group-by-group rollout process should be initiated once a focal point is identified. In IBM Boca Raton, the Client Rollout Team defined an 8-week rollout process for each group. It was viewed as a week-by-week countdown, where week 8 was the kickoff leading to week 1's eventual in-office installation (depicted in Figure 4.5). Week 8 began with a presentation to the users (Customer Communication #1).

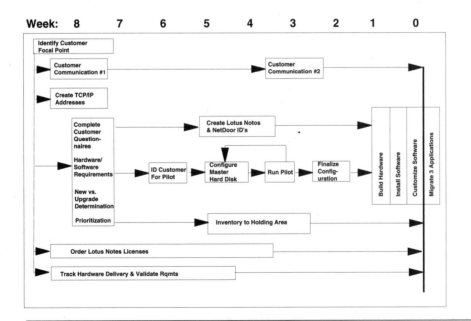

Figure 4.5 IBM Boca Raton Office Client Rollout Process Flow

This was an overview of the Client/Server Migration with specific emphasis on the client rollout. Other activities initiated during week 8 were creation of TCP/IP addresses, ordering Lotus Notes licenses for each user, tracking of hardware deliveries, and validating their accuracy versus requirements.

During week 7, emphasis was placed on completing user questionnaires. As these were accumulated, user requirements were solidified, in particular the breakdown of replacement PCs versus PCs to be upgraded. This assessment was important in that it impacted installation resources. Through experience the Client Rollout Team learned that complete PC replacements took from 2 to 4 hours in the user's office whereas upgrades took from 5 to 12 hours. The accumulated user requirements were prioritized along with available inventory, as well. This resulted in transference of inventory meeting those requirements to a holding area awaiting final customization.

By week 6, the user group's requirements were sufficiently solid to enable initiation of a pilot master build—the creation of a master hard disk to undergo testing during weeks 5 through 2.

In week 5, the Server Administration team (see Chapter 5) created Lotus Notes and NetDoor identifiers for each user. These identifiers allowed users to access the applications.

In week 3, each customer was contacted individually to set up a replacement or upgrade appointment. After the appointment was made, careful follow-up with the user was the rule to minimize no-shows.

At week 2, the master hard disk configurations for an area were finalized. They included the Standard Applications plus any unique area requirements. Unique area requirements were specific applications that an area needed to do its job. For example, all OS/2 developers required an application which linked them to their software code library and problem tracking database.

During week 1, the PC manufacturing process began. Figure 4.6 details the manufacturing process for new builds and identifies the staffing employed. Figure 4.7 shows a set of client systems ready to be delivered. The last step completed the manufacturing process with the in-office installation. Typical in-office installation time for new systems was 2 to 4 hours.

Figure 4.8 details the original manufacturing process for upgrades, which was completed entirely in the user's office. However, due to the variability of results with this method (from 5 to 12 hours), it was

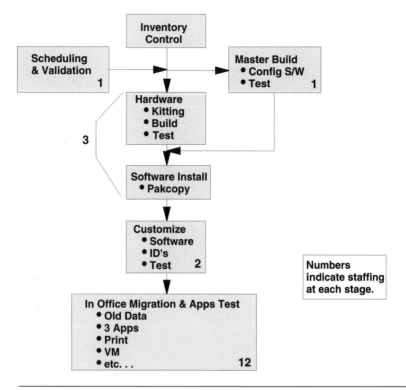

Figure 4.6 Manufacturing Process—New Builds

enhanced in June 1994 to combine in-office and manufacturing line sections (see Figure 4.9).

Deliveries of new PCs or upgrades to existing ones received the personalized attention of a trained and skilled installer. The installers were contractors, specially trained to perform the installation or upgrade function. Every effort was made to provide same-day functionality for all user PC requirements. A complete information package was provided with the installation to answer most, if not all questions (see Chapter 7 for a description of the Client/Server Office Solution Guide). Up to three personal applications were migrated to new PCs by the installer, provided proof of license was presented and original diskettes were available. All old PC data were migrated to new PCs during the installation as well. This was accomplished by copying the entire existing hard disk files to a backup server on the network at the beginning of the installation/upgrade

Courtesy International Business Machines Corporation

Figure 4.7   Office Clients Ready to Go

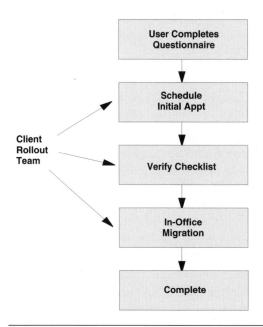

Figure 4.8   Manufacturing Process—Upgrades (Original Process)

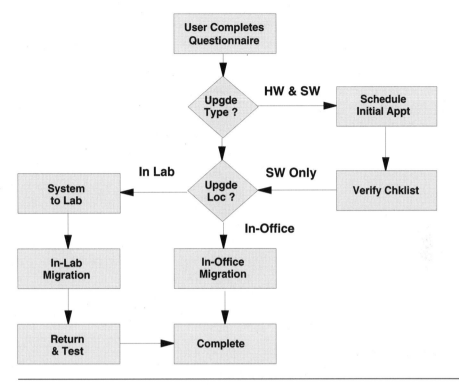

Figure 4.9   Manufacturing Process—Upgrades (Revised Process)

process. After installation/upgrade, the reverse copy was performed to an OLDDATA directory on the new or upgraded PC. If a PC was replaced, the old system remained in the user's office for about two weeks, just in case it was needed if the new PC failed. At the end of two weeks, the PC Returns department, a site services group, reclaimed the old system for either sale to another IBM site or refurbishment and redeployment as a Mobile Client (see next section).

The Lotus Notes application played a critical behind-the-scenes roll for the Client Manufacturing process. Eleven Notes databases were employed, serving as information repositories, workflow automation and tracking applications. The Client Implementation Library Notes database contained procedure, process, and forms documents specific to the client rollout. The ISSC Document Library, another Notes database, contained general application installation procedure documents. The User Questionnaires were **imported** and maintained in a consolidated Notes database (imported means that the data required conversion to the Notes format. This was required because most users employed VM to complete the questionnaire). The Master Configuration database contained descriptions of the hard file masters to be used by the Client Manufacturing process. Three Notes databases were used for client tracking and scheduling by the Installation Team. Three Notes databases were set up to inform users of their migration schedule, provide a migration checklist and, most importantly, track purchase orders for new equipment.

The IBM Boca Raton 8-week client rollout process was highly successful. It can easily be generalized to apply to your client rollout.

Managing the Challenges of a Client Rollout (Keeping Murphy at Bay)

A client rollout is extremely challenging, requiring a highly synchronized "manufacturing" process, worthy of a case study in industrial engineering! Many things can go wrong, and will (according to Murphy's Law), unless careful planning is performed. Several elements require synchronization, including:

- **Gathering and Logging Customer Data Profiles and Requirements.** The comprehensive user questionnaires (see Appendix D), when consolidated in a readily available database (e.g., Lotus Notes), meet this requirement.

- **Inventory Delivery, Staging, and Control.** Hardware delivery schedules can be unpredictable. They can be minimized through flexibility in schedule management, establishment of a 3- to 4-week inventory of readily accessible hardware, and supported by a (Lotus Notes) tracking database.

  •**Work-in-Process Management.** Well-laid-out processes (see Figures 4.5 through 4.8) make the difference.

  •**Technical Requirements Changes.** This is inevitable, as software levels change or last minute user requests filter in. The rollout team must be flexible and responsive to properly handle these changes.

  •**Workload Balancing.** The client installation team must be well-trained and proficient in their tasks to accommodate this. Installers should be PC-familiar at least, with application and some operating system modification experience.

•**Network-Based Software Installation Delivery.** This is a critical technology for a large-scale client migration. See discussion of Configuration, Installation, and Distribution in the Office Client of the Future section, next section.

•**Setting Customer Expectations.** Customer expectation of each phase of the process should be appropriately set. A mass client migration takes a good deal of the "personal" out of a user's personal computer. This is increasingly inevitable as client/server technology matures.

•**Scheduling with the User.** This is a delicate matter. If your installer is late, the installation opportunity may be missed, and the user is angry. If the user doesn't show, again, the installation opportunity is missed, jeopardizing the overall schedule. This problem can be minimized through use of the airlines' method of overbooking (a key insight) and up-to-the-minute scheduling communication with the user.

•**Additional User Visits.** Installation problems requiring additional user visits by installers add schedule pressure. These are inevitable given a large and complex rollout. They can be minimized through the use of carefully documented procedures and upfront testing by the installation team. The use of (Lotus Notes) tracking databases for sharing of information can help here.

By the end of the third quarter of 1994, the IBM Boca Raton Client Rollout Team rolled out over 2,000 new or upgraded PCs. They met the goal of over 2,700 enabled PCs delivered to the users.

The Office Client of the Future

If the past 13 years of industry progress are any indicator, office applications will offer continuously improving human factors and PCs will offer increased speed and capacity in the future. Consistency in look and feel will be emphasized to the application providers as critical requirements in IBM Boca Raton. In addition, the CIO leadership are adding customized features to the Standard Applications in response to customer input (see Chapter 3).

Application developers will continue to exploit new PC functionality to provide additional productivity for end users. It is good practice to plan to upgrade office client PCs on a 3-year cycle to maintain competitiveness. This will maintain user productivity balanced with affordability. Plan on equipping PCs with faster processors and more internal memory to keep pace with the demands of new, more powerful applications.

A counterbalancing trend to this suggested 3-year replacement cycle is the trend to provide a single notebook system PC for office, home, and travel. In IBM Boca Raton, this is under consideration as a cost-saving approach in the future. Today, almost one third of the site's population has a second PC for home or travel use.

It is unclear whether additional office client disk storage will be required in the future. Two factors may combine to control this. First, by making applications available over the network via applications such as NetDoor, less personal storage is required for each user. Second, the ease of creating shared data repositories on servers, with applications such as Lotus Notes, should reduce personal storage requirements in the future.

A major leverage point for a LAN or a site network is its ability to deliver information from a central place (e.g., a server) to one or more PCs or workstations. Using the network to deliver new software and software upgrades with convenient central administration or user selection is highly desirable. It saves time for users and support personnel, and it simplifies and improves user support because software versions will tend to be consistent across the user community. Basically, it is significantly cheaper than diskette distribution and installation for a large user population.

IBM has defined some features that, if supported by an application, allow it to be installed over a network. The application is then called CID-enabled. CID stands for Configuration, Installation, and Distribution. To be CID-enabled, an application must be installable from any disk/diskette drive, accept all user installation input from a file (as opposed to a keyboard), and be able to be started from the command line. Starting with a CID-enabled application, a simple program can be written to prompt users for necessary information to initiate installation of the application to the user's PC from a server on the network. This is called a **pull** installation process; that is, the user initiates the installation and pulls the code to his or her PC or workstation. Pull network installation procedures tend to be customized.

A second approach to network installation is the **push** approach. A program on a server on the network initiates the installation of one or more programs to one or more user PCs or workstations. Typically, this is administered by the I/S support organization on a regular, automated basis. It is used most often for operating system and services software where a standard operating environment is important. The IBM NetView Distribution Manager/2 is an OS/2-based application that supports push software installation over a network.

During 1985–1992, IBM Boca site I/S supported configuration, installation, and distribution for mainframe applications. Individual users took care of their own PC applications. Toward the end of that period, OS/2 CID facilities (the ability to install OS/2 and other CID-enabled programs over the network) were exploited by I/S support for users requiring OS/2, Communications Manager/2, TCP/IP, and other operating system services. At the same time, **AIX** (the IBM version of UNIX) users were the happy recipients of automated push upgrades over the site network for AIX and related applications via IBM SoftDist/6000.

During the 1993–1994 transition period, NetDoor provided convenient user application selection and automatic upgrade (i.e., push and pull support) for PC applications. In addition, NetView Distribution Manager/2 was set up on a network server to push operating system and services upgrades to a set of three CID servers that supported user-initiated CID pull upgrades.

The use of automated and user-initiated software installation and upgrade over the site network is planned to continue into the future in IBM Boca Raton. It improved user satisfaction and quality by improving support—Help Desk personnel could focus on a standard set of operating system, service, and application software. See Chapter 5 for NetView Distribution Manager/2 and CID server configuration.

Nightly, incremental backup of user-selected office client files (by file extension, e.g., .wk3, .txt) is an important application to consider for the future. A user's worst nightmare is that moment when he or she realizes that the hard disk has crashed. In the simple world of DOS, recovering was relatively simple. In the complex world of OS/2, client/server applications, and network connectivity, recovering is far more difficult. However, by taking advantage of the client/server network, the difficulties of recovery can be minimized. First, support for installation of all operating system, network services, and standard applications can be available over the network with a convenient and easy-to-use **CID** installation process (i.e., menu-driven process). What remains to recover are the user's personalized configuration files (e.g., CONFIG.SYS) and data files (e.g., .wk3, .txt, .prs). With nightly, incremental backup of just these files, a user can recover from a hard disk crash with relatively little difficulty. At the present time, a 500-user pilot test of this process is being run using the ADSM backup application on the Boca site. If successful, it will be expanded to ALL site users in 1995.

Increasing use of larger size, higher resolution, higher color content graphics displays is expected. As manufacturing yields improve for large, color **LCD flat panel displays** (the display used in color notebook systems), they will start to be used more frequently in offices, displacing **CRTs** (Cathode Ray Tube displays).

Chapter 6 describes the plans to standardize on TCP/IP as the primary communication protocol and to increase the **bandwidth** (transmission speed) of the network. Initially, office PCs will not be affected. But toward the end of the millennium, network adapter cards will probably be replaced with higher-speed versions, capable of supporting 25 to 100 Mbps. Higher bandwidth from the network will facilitate an expanding array of **multimedia** applications to enrich the current office application suite (multimedia is a term to describe the combination of text, graphics, images, sound, and video in an application). This includes the following:

- Full multimedia presentation support

- Intelligent multimedia mail with transparent outgoing mail media (e-mail, fax, paper)

- Information Access inside and outside the company with no visible boundaries

- Groupware for collaboration

- Print data stream (e.g., PostScript) viewing capabilities

- Multimedia computer conferencing

With the expected increase in multimedia applications, a percentage of office clients will be upgraded with CD-ROM drives and multimedia devices, such as stereo sound cards.

Increased use of LAN-based and personal use of laser printers is expected in the future. A reduction in use of dot matrix printers will follow this trend.

Mobile Clients

The term **mobile client** is defined to be a client system with access to the enterprise network, but not present in the same building or campus as the network. This includes truly mobile notebook systems as well as desktop systems permanently stationed at a user's home.

The key requirements for a mobile client platform are very similar to those of the office client. General industry requirements for a mobile client are illustrated in Figure 4.10. Let's examine each element in the figure:

1. Notebook-sized (8 1/2" by 11" by 2") computer for travelers, a desktop system for home users. Figure 4.11 is a photograph of the popular IBM ThinkPad, which is a leading notebook system.

2. An industry-standard, Intel-based PC system unit. All systems must contain adequate memory and disk storage to support the selected operating system and applications, but reduced functionality from office clients should be acceptable. For the mobile client, a single active application was acceptable, whereas the office client had to support multiple active applications, for example. An Intel 80386 processor operating at 25 Mhz, with 8 MB of memory and a 120 MB hard disk is considered a minimum configuration.

3. Some notebook system users require a docking station in the office to allow convenient connection to the site network and peripheral devices when not traveling.

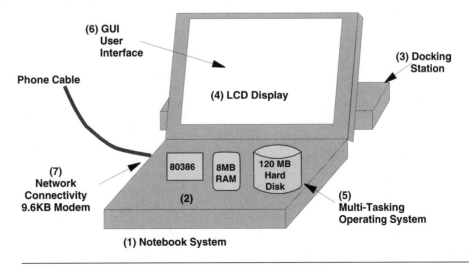

Figure 4.10 Typical Mobile Client

Courtesy International Business Machines Corporation

Figure 4.11   The IBM ThinkPad 750C

4. Monochrome or color graphics LCD (a flat-panel, liquid crystal diode) display capable of supporting 640 by 480 (VGA) resolution.

5. A robust, multitasking operating system, able to support a broad range of office and nonoffice applications with good performance is a must. Consistency with the office client is key. OS/2 Warp is a perfect choice.

6. A Graphic User Interface (GUI), with consistent human factors and good performance. Consistency with the office client again is key. Presentation Manager, the OS/2 Warp GUI, satisfies this requirement.

7. Network connectivity to the site server farm with adequate bandwidth for critical office applications is mandatory. Reduced performance vs. on-campus use is acceptable. A high-speed modem providing 9.6 Kbps or 14.4 Kbps is assumed to meet this requirement. For travel to other company sites with a notebook system, a

network adapter (token-ring or Ethernet) is required. Wireless communication is a future requirement.

8. There are no critical requirements for mobile client peripherals support other than occasional connectivity to a low-resolution personal printer.

The mobile client should support the same applications as the office client where practical. Because of the difference in bandwidth between off-site and on-site communications (9.6 Kbps vs. 16 Mbps), application software must be completely installed on a mobile client, whereas it can be network accessed from an office client. This means that an application like NetDoor is impractical on a mobile client, unfortunately (for more details on NetDoor see Chapter 3).

User access and data transmission security is a more serious requirement for mobile clients than office clients, as they are connected to the site network via the public telephone network. Additional authentication measures are required to handle this. Chapter 6 discusses how to address mobile client authentication.

Traveling users without notebook systems may require the ability to access their e-mail while at remote company sites. An office client "terminal" room for employee visitors is a possible solution.

Two approaches are becoming increasingly popular in the industry to support the remote connectivity requirement:

1. **Remote Client.** A WAN/LAN server allows mobile clients to share its resident data and applications. The remote client approach supports small single-server networks, but does not scale well to support large or distributed environments.

2. **Remote Node.** The mobile user accesses a communications router whose only function is to convert incoming data from WAN to LAN and vice versa for LAN to WAN communications. Growth in the number of remote users can be easily accommodated by adding communications routers without duplicating and maintaining data files across numerous WAN/LAN servers (the remote client approach).

Figure 4.12 shows the differences between the office client "software stack" (the software programs used to communicate to the network) and the mobile client "software stack." They are identical until the transmitted or received data is prepared for the physical network. In the office

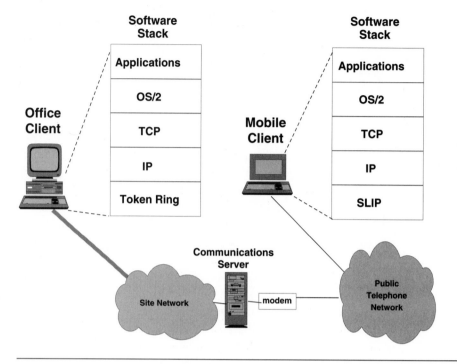

Figure 4.12 Office Client vs. Mobile Client Connectivity

client case, a token-ring physical protocol is used. In the mobile client case, **SLIP** (Serial Line Interface Protocol, an industry-standard point-to-point protocol) is used for transmission over the public telephone network (the public WAN). The data is received by the communications router, where it is converted to the token-ring protocol for communication with the site network servers.

Due to the size of the network, the remote node approach was implemented in IBM Boca Raton, discussed in detail in Chapter 6, Network Infrastructure (see Figure 6.14). Figure 4.13 illustrates past off-site alternatives, the current transition period, and future plans.

The Lovable Luggable Era

Through most of the 1985–1992 period, travelers reluctantly schlepped IBM P70 portable systems when on the move. Hand-me-down systems

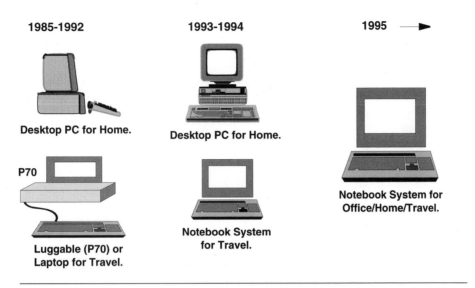

Figure 4.13 IBM Boca Raton Mobile Client: Past/Present/Future

were used at home. These were 286- to 386-based IBM PCs of various stripes. The typical software was IBM PC DOS and an assortment of PC applications. A simple DOS-based program, called the Home Terminal Program, provided terminal emulation capability to VM or MVS mainframes from remote locations. In this way, the IBM Corporate mainframe network was extended to operate over the public telephone network. Over 1,000 site residents were authorized users of this facility during this period. For text e-mail with OfficeVision and occasional file downloads, the Home Terminal Program, a 286- or 386-based PC, and a 2,400 bps modem was adequate. Only toward the end of the 1985 to 1992 period did practical mobility arrive in Boca, through the use of IBM laptop systems such as the L40SX. A few key users were able to secure IBM ThinkPads, but this was rare.

As the site entered the transition period of 1993–1994, notebook system use became more widespread for IBM Boca travelers. The use of 386- and 486-based systems at home and on the road increased. VGA graphics became the standard, and both memory and disk storage increased. As modem prices fell for the next generation of 9,600 bps units, the IBM mainframe network was extended to support these increased speeds.

Moving to Mobile Client

Your client user survey should identify the users requiring mobile client support and their specific needs. There are more variables than meet the eye initially when attempting to satisfy a large and diverse community. Following are some major issues to be considered for your mobile client rollout:

- Users may need to use a mobile client at home, while traveling, and in the office. Software installation and setup on the mobile client must consider all three environments to be complete. This also implies that the system unit may need both a modem for home and travel access, and a LAN adapter card for office connectivity.

- Mobile client delivery is not as straightforward as office client delivery. Replacement systems could be handled in a manner similar to the office client process—installers could deliver the system to the user's office for final customization. However, a LAN adapter would be required (at least temporarily) for this process. Similarly, for upgrades, the user could bring his or her system on-site, a LAN adapter installed, and network-based upgrade accomplished. Where on-site delivery is infeasible (user travel cost is prohibitive or network attachment is unavailable), diskette installation should be a second choice, but carefully scripted for the non-techie user. Software installation occurring at 9.6 Kbps over the telephone network (the typical telecommunications speed), a possible third choice, is impractical due to the megabytes of operating system and application code required to be transmitted. Another alternative that can be employed for completely compatible systems is to copy a complete disk image from one to the other. A personally owned system may present other unforeseen obstacles, such as incompatibility with the site network.

- Telephone services needed to tie in to the site network can vary in terms of performance, availability, cost, and billing alternatives. Today's performance standard is 9.6 Kbps over the generally available analog public telephone network, but faster alternatives, such as the digital ISDN, are coming rapidly (see "The Mobile Client Future" later in this chapter). The most common telephone service billing approach is to have charges directed to the caller's bill, with employees providing receipts for compensation. A superior alternative is to contract 800 service, which bills the employee's individual office phone extension.

As the client/server rollout came into full swing in the first half of 1994 in IBM Boca Raton, the LAN-enabled Mobile Client solution was in beta-test across several IBM southeastern sites. Over 300 IBM Boca users participated. Home and travel users required a PC or notebook system, respectively, equipped with, at a minimum, a 386 processor, 8 MB of RAM, a 120 MB hard file, and a 9.6 Kbps modem (travelers to a few IBM sites, such as Somers, New York, could also use a token-ring PCM-CIA card for network connectivity instead of a modem).

The two critical standard applications for the office client, Lotus Notes and TaP/2, running on OS/2, were fully supported. This allowed the traveling or occasional home user to continue to use the same office applications as when on the site.

OS/2 2.1 and a DOS/Windows version were tested initially, but only the OS/2 version was supported in the end. The Windows version was developed due to its ability to perform well in systems with lower memory. This met the needs of a number of home and notebook systems which could not be expanded to the required 8–16 MB of memory. However, OS/2 Warp resolved this problem in the fourth quarter of 1994 with its ability to run effectively on systems with only 4 MB. This meant that only OS/2 would be supported for office applications across the site, greatly simplifying support and maintenance.

TCP/IP was the protocol used to communicate over the public telephone network to the site network (see Chapter 6 for the connectivity and communication details). TCP/IP was selected because it is an open system solution that scaled well to the IBM Boca Raton environment. It minimized traffic from the site to the remote user which provided good performance. Furthermore, IBM's TCP/IP products had excellent SLIP support for OS/2 and AIX.

User password authentication was performed by a **Kerberos** server. Kerberos is the name of a security application developed at MIT (again, see Chapter 6).

Upgrading underpowered home or mobile PCs was handled through replacement with refurbished office PCs that had been reclaimed (see "Office Client" in this chapter). Initially, software installation for mobile clients was performed by the user over the network using a **CID** pull installation process. The CID architecture supported a simple, user-initiated installation process over the site network for OS/2 itself as well as services and application programs. Using the **REXX** programming language, the Client Rollout Team created a menu-driven, user-friendly interface for this process. As the Client Rollout Team soon recognized the great variability in user home or mobile PCs, they improved the process by offering a dropoff/pickup service for mobile client software installation, performed by the existing Office Client Rollout Team. This greatly eased the user installation burden and improved quality. Target turnaround was 48 hours for a completely installed and tested mobile client.

The requirement for travelers without notebook systems to access their Notes e-mail was troubling. Being at the forefront of the client/server migration in IBM meant that most sites were still OfficeVision only. The solution was to support mail-forwarding capability from Notes to VM in addition to Notes to Notes. This allowed the user at a remote IBM location to log onto VM and, using the VM/CMS Mailbox program, read his or her mail.

The Mobile Client Future

The use of a single notebook system for office, home, and travel is becoming common industry practice. Hand-me-down upgrade processes slowly trickle faster desktop systems with more memory and disk storage out to users with a home system requirement.

Future performance requirements vary based upon the user category. As user applications expand to enable WYSIWYG graphics and multimedia data streams, external network (WAN) speeds become increasingly important. The replacement of SLIP with the faster PPP (Point-to-Point Protocol) is planned for 1995. Faster modems, with 28.8 Kbps capability, will become increasingly affordable, so their support is planned for 1995 as well. Digital **WAN** (Wide Area Network) connectivity for services such as **ISDN** (Integrated Services Digital Network, a relatively new, high-speed digital data service) must be anticipated in 1995, with **ATM** technology (Asynchronous Transfer Mode, a basic data transport technique for high-speed WAN and LAN applications) a possibility in 1996.

Wireless connectivity is an emerging requirement with an assortment of competing protocols, products, and vendors vying for critical mass. Called nomadic communications, it is envisioned as a means to have personalized telecommunications follow one around from place to place [Personick, 1993].

X-Windows support in the UNIX world is the logical equivalent of terminal emulation (a program that runs on a PC which allows it to communicate with a mainframe as if it is a dumb terminal), but for a client/server environment. The entire application operates on the server while the client sends mouse clicks/keystrokes and receives screens in return. The server is called an **application server** in this case. The Citrix company of Coral Springs, Florida is a leader in this technology for DOS, Windows, and OS/2 environments. Figure 4.14 characterizes the three alternatives in terms of impact to the network, user system, the server farm, and application installation on the user's PC. The application server approach requires the least network bandwidth and least-capable PC, but server resources must be beefed up to provide computing power. Two advantages of this approach are the ability to continue to use older PCs (a money-saver) and minimizing the installation impact of new or updated applications. Both advantages are very important for a large mobile client community. The NetDoor approach is to install only an application stub on the user's system and transmit the complete application image over the network when the user selects it. Behind the scenes, the user's PC is given access to a network disk as if it were on his own system by using the facilities of IBM's OS/2 LAN Server program. This facility is called **redirection**. This saves hard disk storage at the user's system, minimizes installation impact as in the application server alternative, but requires higher network bandwidth. Hence, it is inappropriate for a mobile client communicating over relatively thin pipes (i.e., the public telephone network at 14.4 Kbps). The alternative that IBM Boca has selected for 1995 is to use the traditional "install it all"

Impact Category	Application Serving Impact	Redirection Impact (NetDoor Approach)	Install It All Impact
Network Bandwidth	Low to medium bandwidth required	High bandwidth required.	Low bandwidth required.
Client System	Low speed processor, small memory, and small disk storage required.	High speed processor, large memory, small disk storage required.	High speed processor, large memory, and large disk storage required.
Server Farm	Additional servers with high speed processors	Additional file servers for applications.	No impact. File servers only required.
Application Installation on Client System	Low	Low	High

Figure 4.14 Mobile Client Application Delivery Alternatives

approach. This requires a full-function system, and users are impacted if software upgrades are required. The CIO project leaders will be looking seriously at application serving in the future for the mobile client.

Workstation Clients

The workstation client addresses the needs of engineers, programmers, architects, and other highly skilled professionals requiring the highest level of performance and capacity in a client system.

UNIX-based workstation technology exploded in the 1980s and became increasingly compelling for these specialized workers. It became clear that a dedicated, high-performance computing system with high-resolution graphics, a workstation, dramatically improved productivity for individuals. The organization of workstations into networks with high-performance servers was much cheaper to acquire and support than competing minicomputer and mainframe alternatives, as well.

Figure 4.15 is a photograph of an IBM RISC System/6000 POWERstation and POWERserver 590, which form a typical workstation installation. Let's examine Figure 4.16, which illustrates a typical workstation. The system unit will typically contain a RISC-based processor (1), operating at 66 Mhz or higher speed, 16 to 32 MB of memory, and a 1 GB hard disk (2) containing a multitasking operating system such as UNIX (3). A diskette and CD-ROM drive (4), and a network adapter (5) will be in the system unit as well. Connected to the system unit will be a 19-inch, high-resolution, color graphics display (6), typically capable of rendering 1280 by 1024 picture elements, and presenting a GUI interface to the user (7). Some workstations will occasionally have peripheral devices, such as a laser printer (8), attached.

UNIX-based workstation technology became compelling for IBM Boca's engineers and programmers by the end of the 1980s. Accompanying this was an increase in excellent tools on a UNIX base to aid in data and problem management. These realizations and the on-site investments made by the engineering and software developers presaged the broad-based client/server migration of 1993 and 1994.

The competitive pressures of the PC hardware and software industry, led to the following goals:

1. **Productivity.** Time to market for new products was critically affected by development schedules. Engineers and programmers

Courtesy International Business Machines Corporation

Figure 4.15 RISC System/6000 POWERstation and POWERserver 590

were the site's creative developers. Tool investments leading to increased productivity and reduced development time were a priority (see Chapter 1 for a discussion of the process changes undertaken to achieve this goal as well).

2. **Quality.** Tools that provided complete design evaluation prior to manufacture, testing, and tracking were a priority. Chapter 1 discusses the external forces which drove the quality goals.

3. **Lower Development Cost.** This was particularly acute for the engineers, because competition with PC clone manufacturers was driving prices and profit margins ever lower.

These goals led to specific requirements:

1. **High Performance.** The fastest available processors (CPUs), large memory (greater than 16 MB), and fast and plentiful storage (above 250 MB) were crucial.

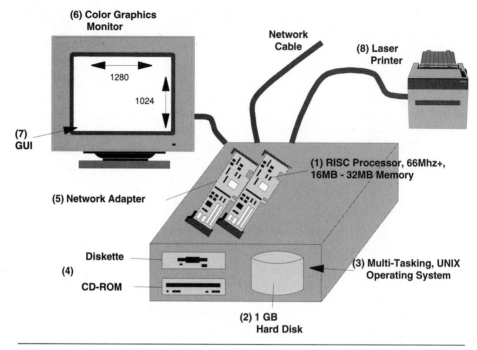

Figure 4.16 Typical Workstation Client

2. **High-Resolution Graphics.** For engineers this meant 1280 by 1024 display resolution driven by special-purpose graphic hardware capable of drawing graphic primitives (e.g., circles and polygons) at high rates of speed.

3. **Information Sharing.** Large development projects are team efforts where data and information must be shared. Designs and software must be located in a common place for common availability over a high-speed network.

4. **One System.** Development applications and standard office applications had to be installed on a single system.

The Birth of the PS/2 Family

In 1987, the designs for the first IBM PS/2s brought IBM mainframe chip technology to the personal computer world. This effort began in 1985, as the independent PC business unit took its first major steps as an integrated IBM division called the Entry Systems Division (ESD).

Electronic CAD

During the 1970s and 1980s, IBM technology enabled rapid design and manufacture of chips mostly for the large, mainframe computers called the System/370s. The IBM internal **CAD** tools were a combination of batch and interactive graphic mainframe applications. A subset of these tools were selected to design three critical PS/2 chips, which, in combination with the Intel 80286 or 80386, did most of the function on the PS/2 system board (the PS/2 system boards were designed using a mainframe, MVS-based, internal program).

The mainframe applications were developed by the IBM CAD tool development organization. They required central I/S organization support for installation and maintenance. Local CAD specialists were required to support these tools. This included tasks such as library maintenance, batch job submission, setup, and local testing. Local CAD specialists were required to perform design services as well, due to the complexity of the tools.

However, the decade of the 1980s saw the emergence of powerful CAD workstation technology from companies such as Mentor Graphics, Sun Microsystems, and CADNETIX. Because these CAD workstations were basically turnkey systems, they did not require central I/S installation or maintenance support. However, local CAD specialists were still required for library maintenance and local testing. The most significant benefit of CAD workstations was to put the design tools directly in the hands of the designers. This eliminated the need for design services and, in fact, improved quality and turnaround by simplifying the entire process.

This trend was observed by a few savvy design managers in the IBM Boca lab in 1986. Independently, they purchased vendor workstations for their engineers. There were some technical problems with an independent workstation approach. For example, there was difficulty in transmitting design files to manufacturing because of nonstandard file formats. However, the advantages in design turnaround and quality became clear over time.

During this same time period, the IBM Austin Laboratory was developing the RISC System/6000 series of workstations. They were announced in 1990 to great success in the marketplace. The operating system was AIX, the IBM version of UNIX, which was (and is) the standard for IBM's CAD workstations.

In 1991, the IBM Boca Lab electronic designers invested in RS/6000 workstations and application software. The migration of most electronic CAD design work from the MVS applications to the RS/6000 resulted in dramatic savings (over 75 percent) in 1993 for the over 200 electronic designers on the site.

Mechanical CAD

The standard within IBM for mechanical design and drafting was MVS, mainframe-based applications until the 1987–1988 timeframe. The original PS/2 frames and covers, for example, were created using a 2½D (dimension) design application on MVS. This was superseded by another MVS, mainframe-based program, which offered true three-dimensional, solid modeling facilities. This meant that mechanical parts could be realistically portrayed in three dimensions, thus improving the designer's productivity.

In the early 1990s, PC-based and RS/6000-based versions of these applications were developed. The IBM Boca Raton facilities engineering department was therefore able to migrate from mainframe-based to the PC-based version in 1992. In 1994, a three-dimensional, solid-modeling application for the RS/6000 was in pilot test in IBM Boca Raton for use by the site's mechanical designers in 1995.

CAD Support

The support costs for the CAD environment included vendor license fees, I/S site network support charges, corporate tools development charges, and local support personnel costs. The vendor software license fees were optimized by purchasing a number of network licenses, which floated among the user community. This was more than offset by the large drop in corporate tools charges due to the migration to vendor tools. The rolloff of local support charges was substantial as well, due to the steady reduction in support personnel required over the 1986 to 1993 period.

Software Design

Software design and development for IBM DOS and OS/2 was performed on IBM PCs during the period 1985–1992. Most code was developed with an assortment of C compilers and Intel assemblers as required for performance. Some IBM AIX development was performed on RS/6000 workstations in the latter part of this period.

During the 1993–1994 transition period, an assortment of C compilers, including the world-class IBM C Set/2 and IBM C ++ for AIX compilers, were used for OS/2 and AIX development. OS/2 development used IBM PCs. RS/6000s were employed for the AIX developers.

A **software library** is a database where one or more versions of all software code is stored. Most large software development shops use such a tool for the safekeeping of their code. It is useful to link the library to problem management so that changes to any code can be tied to specific problems accurately.

Between August 1991 and July 1992, a major transition occurred in the replacement of an internal, mainframe system for software library maintenance and problem management with the RS/6000-based **CMVC** program in the DOS and OS/2 development area. CMVC stands for the IBM Configuration Management Version Control 6000 Program Product. A similar transition from the internal application to CMVC was undertaken by the PC Company engineers for BIOS development and problem tracking in the 1992–1994 time period.

Both transitions were motivated by the technical advantages of CMVC versus the internal mainframe tool and the anticipated cost savings in support and expenses of the workstation environment versus the mainframe. The mainframe tool required six support personnel with no enhancement support. CMVC is supported by only four personnel, with two additional people providing local enhancements to improve productivity. Further, there is a five to one reduction in ongoing expenses with CMVC.

Office Applications for Workstation Users

The unification of development and office tools on a single platform is highly desirable for cost and space economies (only one desktop system is required for a developer), as well as user productivity for workstation users.

From 1991 through most of 1994, the workstation users had electronic mail using **IP**-based **SMTP** (IP is the Internet Protocol, which is part of TCP/IP. SMTP is the Simple Mail Transport Protocol, an e-mail protocol over TCP/IP networks). This interoperated with the IBM Office-

Vision-based e-mail system and, in 1993–1994, with Lotus Notes mail via gateway server systems. In the latter part of this period, access to the corporate directory via the CallUp application was provided. By the end of 1994 or early 1995, Lotus Notes and TaP/2 clients and servers are expected to provide a "unified" and interoperable office suite on most AIX workstation systems.

The Workstation Client Future

Standard office applications, such as Lotus Notes, will be available for the UNIX-based workstation client/server environment in the future. They will improve human factors and reduce cost and space requirements for workstation users. It will also improve interoperability between office client users and workstation users, enabling them to use common applications.

Workstation applications, such as three-dimensional solid modeling, require large files to describe complete designs. Sharing and distributing these files over a network requires high network transmission rates. Networking technology improvements, such as ATM (see Chapter 6), will improve network throughput, and therefore performance for future workstation users.

Critical Success Factors

The client rollout is the heart of any client/server migration. It touches all users squarely on their desktops, in their offices, while they are on the road, and at home. Following are some key recommendations that will lead you to success in this critical phase:

- *You should carefully identify the minimum hardware requirements for client PCs.* This should be based upon performance evaluations of selected applications on a real system. Ensure that processor, memory, and disk storage can be upgraded if required. Secondarily, allow installation of peripherals as upgrades.

- *There is no substitute for a complete inventory database of all user clients.* This is required initially to scope the investment necessary to migrate to a client/server environment. It is required on an ongoing basis to track asset ownership and identify upgrade candidates. Investing in automatic client inventory maintenance (see Chapter 6 regarding LAN Station Manager) is very worthwhile.

- *You should create a completely defined process for a large-scale client PC rollout, including user communication (gaining buy-in, setting expectations), installation logistics, and tools.* Flexibility in scheduling is critical. Through careful schedule management and overbooking client PC installations, your rollout team can achieve success.

- *Invest in groupware, groupware, groupware.* The use of Lotus Notes databases enabled the incremental improvements made by the IBM Boca Raton client rollout team in their process.

- *You should define both office and mobile client solutions at the same time.* The Client Rollout Team was fortunate that the users were very patient in waiting several months for mobile clients to "catch up." It turned out that the analysis required to select the right solution for the site was more complex than the office client analysis.

- *If you have a large number of users (more than 1,000), a LAN-enabled, remote node solution for mobile clients should be your goal.* It was scalable to a site as large as IBM Boca Raton's, where over 1,000 site users required off-site capability. The industry-standard TCP/IP using SLIP or PPP, as implemented in IBM TCP/IP for OS/2 2.0, provides an excellent remote communication solution. In addition, you should invest in a simple installation process for mobile client users. The number of steps, choices, and customization required (e.g., CONFIG.SYS and INI files) can be too daunting for the average user.

- *Don't ignore your CAD or CASE environments.* The evolution in CAD tools at IBM Boca Raton from a relatively expensive mainframe-centric environment to a relatively cheaper workstation-based environment provided a measure of validation for the anticipated gains in office and mobile client/server computing. Planning for a unified workstation tools suite, including CAD or software development tools with office applications, is highly desirable as well.

5

The Server Farm

In the days of mainframe hosts and terminals, information systems were driven from the center, with one of the key questions being how many terminals the host could support. Tomorrow's information systems will put the user at the center, with the main question changing to "how many servers can a support a workstation?"

[FLINT, 1992]

The organized collection of servers necessary to support a large number of clients requires careful planning, staged acquisition, and staged installation. This chapter will discuss the overall requirements for server systems, how this evolved on the IBM Boca site, future considerations, and some critical success factors.

A large-scale client/server migration requires a well-managed, centralized server or assembly of server systems to support client/server applications, user data storage, and networking services. Chapter 3 analyzed client/server applications and focused on those chosen for the 1993–1994 IBM Boca Raton rollout. How these applications drove server organization, user data storage, and administration is the primary subject of this chapter.

Server Systems Requirements

Most applications are targeted for a specific client and server combination. However, user requirements are driving application developers to provide multiplatform client support, if not multiplatform server support. For example, the Lotus Notes application supports OS/2 and Windows clients and OS/2 servers. It currently supports OS/2 servers and plans to support UNIX-based servers in the near future. For applications that offer multiplatform server support, best fit of technology should dictate server selection.

Three primary hardware technology variables affect this selection. They are the **central processing unit (CPU)** speed, storage capacity, and network throughput. CPU speed very roughly corresponds to number of instructions processed per second. At the top end of this spectrum are large mainframes, followed by **RISC**-based systems (e.g., RS/6000 systems) and then PCs, which are CISC-based (RISC stands for Reduced Instruction Set Computers, which tend to be faster than Complex Instruction Set Computers). Storage capacity refers to hard disk storage. Again, mainframes offer the greatest capacity and expandability, followed by RISC-based and PC systems. Figure 5.1, introduced in Chapter 3, is repeated here for clarity. Network throughput refers to the capacity of a server to transmit data over the network. Most PC, RISC, and mainframe servers offer expansion in network throughput in line with their relative CPU and storage capabilities by addition of network adapters or channels. So this additional variable, although important, can be ignored in the initial decision-making process.

Once the type of server is determined from general application requirements, specific server features should be carefully reviewed. Following is a good checklist:

- Reliability and Fault Tolerance. The server's design should be inherently reliable. Further, it should have the ability to compen-

Server Function	High Storage	Medium Storage	Low Storage
High CPU	Mainframe Server	RISC Server	RISC Server
Medium CPU	Mainframe Server	PC Server	PC Server
Low CPU	Mainframe Server	PC Server	PC Server

Figure 5.1 Server CPU vs. Storage

sate for internal and environmental failures and continue to operate. This includes recoverability for failure of some or all hardware subsystems, loss of external power, and extremes of external environment (e.g., temperature). The investment in fault tolerance depends upon the criticality of the server's application to the business. The ideal server should offer choices in this area.

- Systems Performance.   This refers to the ability of a server to offer adequate processing performance under anticipated load, which depends upon the server's processor complex and memory. The ability of the server to support multiple processor complexes to increase performance should be an option.

- Network Performance and Capacity.   This is the ability of a server to offer adequate data throughput over the network, which depends upon the design of the network interface hardware or adapter. Server design should support the addition of multiple network adapters to increase network bandwidth as required by the application and the number of users.

- Storage Performance and Capacity.   The speed of access to stored information and the total available hard disk storage of the server should be adequate for the selected application. Disk storage expansion is required as well.

- Peripherals.   Peripherals such as modems, tape drives, optical drives, and printers must be attachable.

- System Management.   Local and remote (lights-out) systems management is required. Remote management should support on-site and off-site connectivity. This means that server administrators will be notified of any server failure and have the ability to correct it from local or remote control systems.

- Operating Systems.   The server must support one or more industry standard operating systems. Examples are OS/2 and Novell's NetWare.

- Architecture.   The server architecture should support expandability via industry-standard interfaces. This is a general statement of expandability applying to all aspects of the server design—processors, storage, peripherals, and so on.

- Communications Flexibility. The server should support all the necessary LAN and WAN connections and protocols.

- Service and Support. A single point of contact from an experienced vendor with a well-defined response level is important.

- Installation. The system should be easily installed by internal staff.

- Technical Documentation. All technical documentation should be complete, accurate and easy to read by internal staff.

- Common Parts. To as large an extent as possible, major components should be interchangeable from server to server. This includes disk storage devices, network interface cards, power supplies and processor complexes. This is particularly important for a large site such as IBM Boca Raton. A secondary requirement is for parts, such as hard disks, to be "hot-pluggable" replacements if a failure occurs.

- Backup and Recovery. Easily administered, nightly, incremental backup and recovery, as required of all server data, is critical. Vital records must be stored at a remote location in the event of a site disaster. Mission critical information must be maintained in a "hot-backup" environment to assure minimal downtime in the event of server failure.

- Price Performance. Given that other requirements are satisfied, the lowest price is always preferred.

Figure 5.2 depicts a typical server configuration. Let's walk through the figure, step by step:

1. Software will include an application, such as Lotus Notes, the operating system, such as OS/2, and the network operating system or NOS, such as OS/2 LAN Server. The network operating system will contain service programs which handle the transmission of data over the network.

2. The system unit will have a processor, memory, and hard disk storage. Many servers will have multiple hard disks to contain large amounts of information.

3. Most servers will have one or more network adapter cards. The network adapters are connected via cables to the site network.

4. Sometimes servers are connected to modems through a serial port to communicate over a WAN.

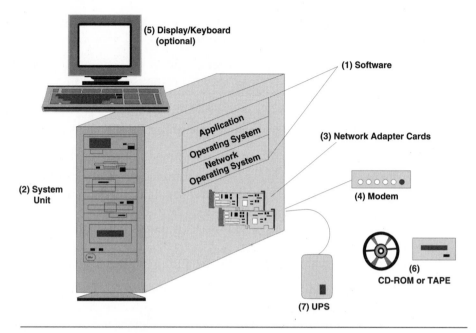

Figure 5.2 Typical Server

5. Displays and keyboards are optional on server systems, as they may be controlled (managed) by a remote PC console.

6. Servers may also contain other peripherals such as tape drives for backup or CD-ROM drives containing software or other data.

7. Mission critical servers will typically have an uninterruptible power supply (UPS) in series with the connection to the main power source.

Server Farm Considerations

The centralized Server Farm has its own requirements that you should consider along with the specifications of individual servers. The Server Farm should be accessible to major network points of presence (connectivity ports). As discussed in Chapter 6, a well-designed client/server network will centralize access to major connectivity ports, such as network backbones. By locating the Server Farm in close proximity to the major network points of presence, server administrators have the flexibility to shift server connections to balance network traffic or improve network performance.

The Server Farm should be in its own access-controlled room. It should be on a raised floor, which avoids wire clutter and prevents unintentional disconnects. If planned in advance, a Farm-wide uninterruptible power source can be installed, which is superior in both cost and capability to individual UPS devices. Enhanced air conditioning is another serious consideration based on available space for the Farm, especially if hands-on support is required.

Server management is the function of monitoring server activities and capacities, taking appropriate action(s) in the event of problems, initiating changes to optimize performance and capacity, guaranteeing security, and generating appropriate bills to users. Both local and remote access to the Server Farm should be supported for problem identification and remote management, at a minimum. Don't ignore provisions for convenient administrator access to servers requiring hands-on management and administration. Chapter 6, Network Infrastructure, expands on server management in the context of overall network management.

The IBM Boca Raton Server Farm Experience

The IBM Boca experience with servers over the past decade started with isolated deployment (1985–1992), followed by centralization driven by PS/2 server acquisition (1993–1994), leading to a best-fit-of-technology heterogeneous server environment (1995 and beyond). Given current industry trends, it appears that 1995 will be a watershed year for applications to support multiple client and server platforms. This will enable businesses seeking to migrate to client/server to be able to plan a highly efficient (and cost-effective) best-fit-of-technology Server Farm at the beginning of a migration.

Random Server Growth in IBM Boca Raton—1985–1992

In the period 1985–1992, server deployment in IBM Boca Raton was fairly random, despite the strong PC and LAN heritage. Isolated PC LANs were employed in departmental labs for testing and development purposes. PC LANs were occasionally installed for departmental print server use.

At the end of 1991 and early 1992, RS/6000 servers were deployed to support electronic CAD (ECAD), library maintenance and problem tracking for DOS and OS/2 development (CMVC), problem tracking for PC engineering (CMVC), and AIX operating system and application code distribution (IBM Softdist/6000). RS/6000 servers were selected for their world-class price performance and because they were IBM products. These steps marked the earliest, organized client/server thrusts on the site. The CAD application and CMVC application migrations replaced mainframe-based tools and were undertaken as the result of careful business case analyses (Chapter 4 provides additional detail regarding the CAD and CMVC migrations). They were managed and supported by their owning organizations in separate server facilities, while being fully interconnected with the site network infrastructure (see Chapter 6). The ISSC support team provided centralized support for AIX software distribution via the IBM SoftDist/6000 application.

System/390 systems were not used or viewed as servers in this time frame. They were employed as multiuser, multitasking hosts, running either MVS or VM, and supported a diversity of mainframe applications.

IBM Boca Raton's experiences were no different from those of other large corporations making ad hoc investments in new LAN technology during this period. Compelling improvements in LAN-based applications, however, soon drove the site to more organized, planned deployment.

Plowing Ground on the IBM Boca Raton Server Farm

The OS/2 development organization requested Lotus Notes support at the end of 1992. A single PS/2 Model 95 server was brought into the administrator's office to serve 20 Notes users. Shortly thereafter, this server was communicating with PS/2 servers in Somers, New York, and Austin, Texas, two other Personal Systems sites. Administrative meetings continued weekly among Somers, Austin, Atlanta, and Charlotte ISSC administrative personnel until May 1994. By this time, the sites' skills had matured so that they were relatively independent. The Server Farm grew little by little—the team continued to accumulate privately owned and managed servers, and install them by connecting them directly to the site network. During the early part of 1993, TaP/2 servers were added.

To organize the growing Farm, simple (half-wide) tables were used for displays and keyboards with the PS/2 95 system units underneath. Racks with shoulder-height stands for displays and keyboards, adopted from other labs, soon replaced the tables. Displays and keyboards were needed for each server because of the complexity of administration.

By the end of 1993, many more seeds were sown in the Server Farm—60 PS/2 Model 95s grew in Building 013, first floor for the roughly 700 users. In March 1994, the Server team moved the entire Farm to the second floor of Building 002 to take advantage of the mainframe-vacated raised floor, uninterrupted power supplies, enhanced cooling and additional space available there. At that moment, it happened: the PC replaced the mainframe in IBM Boca Raton, the birthplace of the PC.

The Server Farm continued to grow significantly in 1994 to accommodate the remainder of the OS/2 development employees and the PC Company employees, a total of over 2,700 users. One hundred and ninety-one are currently installed (see Figure 5.3). These provide support for the site's key applications, including Lotus Notes, mail gateways, application access, calendar, directory, software distribution, problem

Courtesy International Business Machines Corporation

Figure 5.3   IBM Boca Raton's Server Farm

Server Application	Server System	January 1, 1994	May 1, 1994	October 1, 1994
Lotus Notes Mail, Data, Hubs, Code Share	PS/2 95, 195	16	42	63
IBM Mail LAN Gateway/2	PS/2 95	2	5	10
Time and Place/2	PS/2 195	3	4	23
Callup C/S	PS/2 195	1	2	2
NetDoor	PS/2 95	15	18	37
Domain Controllers	PS/2 95	2	2	3
File Servers	PS/2 95	2	2	3
System Monitors	PS/2 95	2	2	6
Netview Dist. Mgr/2	PS/2 95			1
CID	PS/2 95			3
FAX	PS/2 95	0	0	1
Spares	PS/2 95	0	1	12
PS/2 Server Total		**43**	**78**	**164**
CMVC (SW Library & Problem Tracking)	RS/6000	7	7	7
SoftDist/6000 (AIX SW dist)	RS/6000	2	2	2
Callup/6000 (directory)	RS/6000	1	1	1
gator (Internet gateway)	RS/6000	0	1	2
AFS (file sharing)	RS/6000	5	5	6
X-Station Support	RS/6000	1	1	1
Kerberos (Remote access authentication)	RS/6000	1	1	1
ADSM/6000	RS/6000	0	1	2
Print (PSF/6000)	RS/6000	0	1	5
RS/6000 Server Total		**17**	**20**	**27**
Grand Totals		**60**	**98**	**191**

Figure 5.4   IBM Boca Raton Server Rollout Status—1994

tracking, print, fax, backup, and sundry gateway server applications necessary to allow the site's users to communicate around the world. Figure 5.4 summarizes this growth.

The Server Team learned as it went, making investments and technical decisions to incrementally establish a strategically located and expandable Server Farm. With the right planning, your Server Farm can be built step by step as well.

Selecting Server Systems

When you are selecting servers for your Server Farm, a good initial technique to employ is a paper comparison based upon vendor-supplied features, an exercise similar to that recommended for application selection (see Chapter 3). Requirements should be rated numerically (a scale from 1 to 10 is fine), with mandatory requirements receiving the highest value. Each server feature under evaluation should then be numerically rated for each applicable requirement (a scale of 1 to 10 works here too), with top features receiving the highest rating. Multiplying each requirement rating by corresponding server rating and then summing all values for a server provides an objective measurement. Figure 3.3 provides a relevant example. This measurement can be used to narrow down a field of several competitors to two or three. At this point, installation and application testing (benchmarking) should be used to make the final selection.

PS/2s as Servers

PS/2 Models 195 and 95 met IBM Boca's requirements for server systems. Both products are highly competitive in the industry and well-regarded by customers as noted in the June 1994 issue of *Network Computing* [Harrison, 1994].

The IBM PS/2 Server 195 (Figure 5.5) was selected primarily for its fault tolerance and remote manageability for use in critical applications, such as Notes hub servers. Dual processor upgrade potential (to the Server 295), support for **SCSI** devices, **RAID**, a dual power supply, and MASS/2 remote management software were the critical features.

The IBM PS/2 Server 95 (Figure 5.6) was selected primarily for its high performance as a file server. SCSI device support, RAID storage, and the **IBM Serverguard** card with **NetFinity** management software were the critical features (the Serverguard card with NetFinity enables remote server management). The Server 95 was used for Notes mail, Notes data,

Courtesy International Business Machines Corporation

Figure 5.5   IBM PS/2 Server 195

and other applications where the fault tolerance of the Server 195 was not required.

Of significant value to server administration was the ready ability of the 95s to swap parts as needed. This was due to excellent **guardbanding** used by the 95 engineers in its design. Swappable parts included hard files, processor complexes, adapter cards, and power supplies.

The value of SCSI device support and RAID in a server system cannot be underestimated. SCSI, which stands for Small Computer System Interface, typically refers to a controller (adapter) card in the server which supports the SCSI interface standard (see Figure 5.7). Devices that support this standard can be connected to the SCSI controller for communication with the server system. One advantage of SCSI in a server is that the SCSI controller can interleave access to the devices that are connected to it, thereby increasing server system overall throughput. Another advantage is SCSI expandability and diversity—up to seven devices can

Courtesy International Business Machines Corporation

Figure 5.6 IBM PS/2 Server 95

be attached to a SCSI controller and they can be of varying types (e.g., hard files, CD-ROMs, and tapes). Figure 5.8 contrasts SCSI to IDE, the most common PC controller type. A SCSI controller is used in every PS/2 in the Boca Raton Server Farm.

RAID, which stands for Redundant Array of Inexpensive Disks, is a storage system design in which a group of smaller disk drives can be made to appear as a single disk drive to the operating system or application program. Also called a **PDA** (Parallel Disk Array), a RAID storage system retrieves information from many disks in parallel and, depending on the organization of information on the disks, can be much faster than a single large drive [Vaskevitch, 1993]. The RAID architecture defines "levels" of RAID implementation that offer different facilities to the server administrator. The simplest level, level 0, defines disk mirroring, in which two disks store the same information in parallel for backup and recovery purposes. RAID level 3 defines a data organization in which

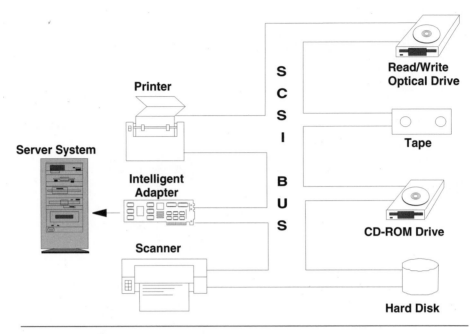

Figure 5.7 The SCSI Story

data is interleaved in large blocks across all of the disks, called a stripe set (see Figure 5.9). Data is read and written in full stripe units, thereby simultaneously accessing all disks in the stripe. An extra drive is used to contain redundancy information for data recovery should a drive in the array fail [Katz, 1992]. Both RAID levels are used within the Boca Raton Server Farm where backup/recovery and high performance are required.

	SCSI	IDE
Device Flexibility	One adapter can support up to 7 devices: disks, CD-ROM, tape, etc.	One or 2 hard disks
Connectivity	Internal or external	Internal only
Performance	Fast/Wide at 20 MBps	Up to 6.67 MBps
Cost	High	Low
Multimedia Capable	Best	Limited
System Environment	Servers: Multimedia desktops	Desktops

(Bryan, 1994)

Figure 5.8 SCSI vs. IDE

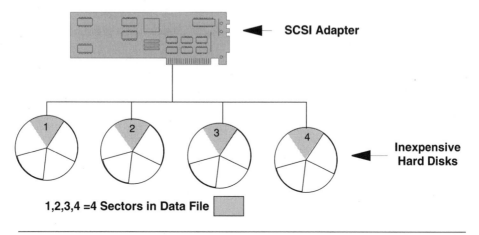

SCSI Adapter

Inexpensive Hard Disks

1,2,3,4 =4 Sectors in Data File

Figure 5.9 RAID Example: Data Striping

RS/6000 Servers

Since their introduction in late 1990, the RS/6000 servers running IBM's AIX operating system have been price/performance competitive with other UNIX-based server products. Because of highly efficient and powerful processor complex and storage subsystem designs, they make outstanding server solutions for AIX applications. They are used by the site's developers for CAD, software library and problem tracking storage (CMVC), support for distributed file sharing (**AFS cell**), software distribution, and other special purpose uses (Internet access, Kerberos security support, X-station support, and mail/phone directory).

With regard to office applications, RS/6000 servers were selected in situations where server application software was available that could support OS/2 clients. The ADSM application for backup and recovery and the PSF application for print serving, met this criterion. Both are implemented as true 32-bit applications for the RS/6000. With the relatively high performance of this system versus a PS/2, a much higher ratio of PCs to servers, in the case of ADSM, or printers to servers, in the case of PSF, is possible.

Mainframes as Servers

Many major corporations worldwide have a significant investment in mainframe applications. These span the spectrum from mission critical financial applications, large-scale reservations systems, corporate databases, computer-aided design applications, e-mail, and forms processing.

The client/server paradigm, when coupled with a "best-fit-of-technology" strategy, leads many businesses to rightsize their information technology infrastructure. In some cases, this means abandoning the mainframe entirely for a downsized environment. In other cases, it means shifting some applications to other platforms that are more cost-effective. Mainframes can be price/performance leaders for very complex problems (high CPU and high storage applications) and handling enterprise-wide data (high storage and high access) [Rothfeder, 1993].

A transition is taking place as to how mainframes can fit in with the client/server paradigm. Figure 5.10 contrasts the two approaches. Most mainframe applications and the data they processed operated entirely on the mainframe system itself. Users accessed the applications through dumb terminals (also called dependent display terminals). The mainframe rotated access to the application(s) through a multitasking operating system; users received a time slice of the mainframe for their own processing, which, in most cases, was adequate for their needs. The client/server paradigm splits the processing among client and server systems, with the server being the data storage repository. By creating distributed applications processing and treating the mainframe as a server with a less-encompassing role, it can be used where it best "fits."

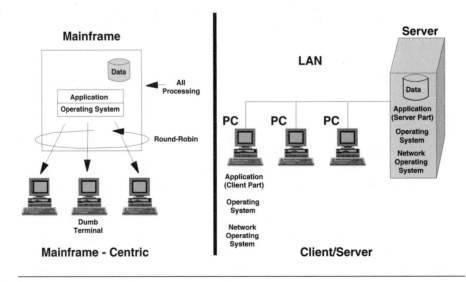

Figure 5.10 Mainframe-Centric vs. Client/Server Computing

System/390 systems, heavily used in the past for IBM corporate applications, office applications and decision support, are the focus of use reduction during the 1994 transition period (see "Legacy Exodus" in Chapter 3) in Boca Raton. During this transition period, they are not regarded as servers per se. However, by 1995, mainframes will be used effectively as enterprise-wide database servers as part of several key distributed applications.

Server Administration and Support

Central server administration and support is extremely cost-effective when compared with individual organizations maintaining their own servers in their own areas and worrying in isolation about backup, recovery, and security. In IBM Boca Raton, administrative and support skills, practices and policies evolved through the central leadership of the server administrator over the 1992–1994 time period.

Server Administration

Server administration includes a variety of important tasks, both general-purpose and application-specific. We will discuss server capacity and file organization, network user access, directory, application access (Net-Door), planning, installation, configuration, software distribution, backup/recovery, and security administration in this section.

Capacity and File Organization Administration

In general, these are application-dependent activities, which should be bounded by well-defined policies. For example, a mail application may specify a maximum number of users per server based upon the server's CPU. Hard disk storage availability may further dictate limits on a user's mail storage limits. These two factors can be the basis for a documented server capacity policy.

File organization can be simply administered through allocating a directory to a major organization with subdirectories for each subordinate department. Again, a documented policy should be created.

At the IBM Boca Raton site, server disk space administration was relatively informal, originally. At the start, there was no roadmap for Notes databases, file server space, and so on. Lotus recommended no more than 75 users per Notes mail server, with a limit of 10 MB of storage space per user. The practice was 100 users per PS/2 Server 95 mail server, which appeared to be providing adequate performance. Based on the strong dependence and experience the users had with OfficeVision mail, the Server Team doubled Lotus' mail file size recommendation to 20 MB of storage space per user. The goal is automation for mail file size threshold violations, but today it is a manual process.

As users are rolled out, their mail files are set up on a Notes mail server. Since the client rollout is by organization, this naturally segregates departments on a single server. However, as users transfer to different site organizations, their mail files will remain on their original mail server to minimize administrative overhead.

A major change for the users is the new practice of archiving personal mail files to personal PC storage, as opposed to a central archive. It is expected that this will result in overall cost savings for archival storage across the site, as users must optimize the use of their personal storage as opposed to exploiting seemingly limitless, but really very costly, on-line mainframe storage.

Notes database servers are allocated by major organization. This allows organizations to create database applications tailored to their environment with relative freedom. General-purpose file servers are allocated on a request basis only, with the server being supplied by the requesting organization. A general-purpose file server does not contain Notes databases, only assorted files for access by the owning organization.

Uncontrolled Notes database proliferation led to a painful reorganization of existing database servers in June 1994. A formal request process for future databases, administered through a Notes database (of course) was then instituted. The Lotus Notes Administration Request database is available to site users to place user-developed database applications on their area's servers. Databases designated as mission critical will, after approval by the site's Application Review Board (see Chapter 2), be mirrored to a backup server for near-real-time recovery should the database server go down.

A Lotus Notes Guidebook, created by Lotus Consulting in early 1994 as an on-line Lotus Notes database, serves as a central repository for server administration policies and procedures for Lotus Notes. ID administration, installation procedures, operations procedures, maintenance procedures, and disaster recovery planning among other topics are documented in the Guidebook. Being on-line, it is easily reviewed and main-

01 - Introduction
02 - Components of Notes
03 - Site Planning & Preparation
04 - ID Administration
05 - Installing Notes Servers
06 - Installing Notes Workstations
07 - Operations & Maintenance
08 - Mail
09 - Replication
10 - Remote Notes Access
11 - Development Process and Standards
12 - Production Applications
13 - Database Maintenance
14 - Disaster Recovery Planning
Appendix A - The Name and Address Book
Appendix B - Troubleshooting
Appendix C - Other Important Stuff
Appendix D - Notes Network Assessment/Analysis
DOCLINKS Listing
Glossary

Figure 5.11 Lotus Notes Guidebook—Table of Contents

tained. It is strongly recommended to create such an information base for any major client/server migration. The table of contents is in Figure 5.11.

The TaP/2 application data servers also require space administration. The TaP/2 developers recommended that approximately 200 to 250 users share a PS/2 data server with 2 GB of storage. This organization is being followed by the Server Farm administrators.

Network User ID Assignment

A network user ID is the string (usually 6 to 8 characters) that identifies a user to the network operating system (NOS). Coupled with a password, the network user ID allows the user access to network resources, such as file servers and network printing. The user typically logs on to the network with a logon command, is prompted for a password, and, if the correct password is given, may then access network resources. The administration of network user IDs is performed by the Server Farm administrators. Most often, it is a manual process of updating a central file. In IBM Boca Raton, network user ID maintenance is currently a manual process, synchronized with the client rollout. It will be incorporated into a Lotus Notes workflow application by the beginning of 1995 that will eliminate or minimize manual updates.

Directory Administration

This area is one of the major problems of any budding client/server environment. A directory is a database containing, for example, user names and their associated telephone numbers, e-mail addresses, TCP/IP identifiers, and so forth. A directory could also contain names of network resources (e.g., printer names) and their associated network addresses (e.g., TCP/IP addresses). It is common for a client/server application, such as an e-mail program, to define its own directory database, with little relationship to any other application's directory! In IBM Boca Raton, the Server Team is currently wrestling with five separate repositories containing directory information for site users. Figure 5.12, titled "Directory Cacophony," depicts this situation. (A cacophony is set of inharmonious sounds. Its use here is not precisely accurate, but irresistible!). Previously, the OfficeVision environment utilized a single, consolidated directory—the CallUp database on VM (1). The Server Team continues to support this for lingering OV users. This database is migrated to the client/server environment as a DB2 for OS/2 database to be used by CallUp C/S (2). An internally developed utility program is used to create a Lotus Notes database version of the CallUp C/S directory for use by Notes applications to identify site users (5). The TaP/2 application utilizes its own directory, stored as a DB2 for OS/2 repository, containing user and group identifiers (3). Finally, the Lotus application utilizes its own directory, called the Public Name and Address Book, containing information for Notes users on site (4). TaP/2, however, can also address Notes and VM users, through the **VIM** interface and a gateway, respectively (see Figure 5.18). Clearly, this situation cries out for a single, consolidated, industry-standard directory, such as **X.500**, to be used by all applications. X.500 defines a standard, general-purpose format for distributed directories and a standard application program interface (API) for applications to access information.

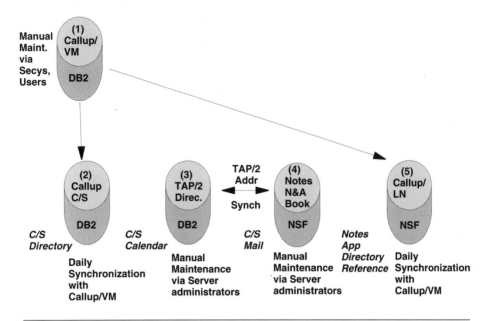

Figure 5.12 Directory Cacophony

The Lotus Notes Name and Address book contains the names and associated e-mail addresses of Notes users and groups with associated administrative data. Groups represent mail distribution lists for public use. A single Notes domain is defined for IBM Boca. A Notes domain is a grouping of Notes servers and users for security and administrative purposes. It is defined by the primary Name and Address Book file (directory) used by the servers. An early domain approach, where major corporate organizations irrespective of location defined a separate domain, was abandoned in late 1993 due to the complexity of administration. As a result, each IBM site using Notes will maintain a single Name and Address book.

NetDoor Administration

As discussed in Chapter 3, NetDoor is an IBM application that provides convenient network access to a catalog of applications and tools. For each application in the NetDoor catalog, a front-end must be written in **REXX** to allow installation on the user's PC (REXX is a language used to create applications that can access system-level commands and resources). This front-end performs application icon setup on the user's PC, transference of the minimal amount of application code, and modification to local system files. When complete, the application is invoked from the NetDoor server and saves user-created files on the user's PC. Server administration monitors the Vendor program statistics of simultaneous application use to make sure that vendor license agreements are not violated. Additional licenses are ordered if the number is exceeded. The site's Application Review Board, discussed in Chapter 3, directs the NetDoor administrators to add or remove applications to the catalog.

Planning, Installation, and Configuration

Planning includes projection for server system requirements, including configuration, connectivity, spare parts, space, backup, cooling, power, and racks. The planning process should reflect your users' application requirements. In IBM Boca Raton, a quarterly meeting is conducted to review server plans and application requirements, among other items, to guarantee that user requirements will be met.

Installation and configuration means server setup, application configuration, testing, and production installation within the Server Farm. Creating standard operating system, network operating system, and application configurations greatly simplifies these activities.

Software Distribution and Maintenance

Both Chapters 3 and 4 mentioned network-based distribution of software to install operating system and application code on client systems. It is up to the Server Farm administrators to establish the server environment for this capability. Offering a combination of both push and pull software installation over the network is the ideal approach to this problem. Push software installation is a process that updates client system software over the network automatically. Pull software installation is a process in which the user requests software installation over the network. Initially, in IBM Boca, NetView Distribution Manager/2, installed on a PS/2 server, pushed (distributed and maintained) the office client software (operating system, services, and applications) to three PS/2 servers. The three servers were set up as CID (Configuration, Installation, and Distribution) servers. Site users were able to "pull" office client application code sim-

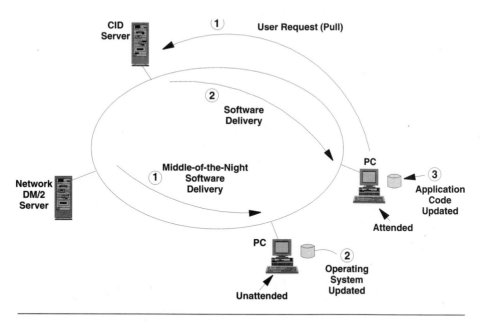

Figure 5.13   Configuration, Installation, and Distribution

ply and conveniently to their PCs with a simple, menu-driven process from any one of the three. The 1995 plan is to use the push features of NetView DM/2 more extensively to maintain operating system and services code versions on client PCs automatically (see Figure 5.13).

The AIX application Softdist/6000 is used in the RS/6000 workstation environment to distribute (push) AIX operating system code and AIX applications. It will be replaced by NetView Distribution Manager/6000 by 1995.

Backup and Recovery

Byte Magazine reports that in a survey of 450 information systems executives, computer downtime cost over $78,000 per hour, with outage and recovery costing an average of $330,000 [Wallace, 1994]. Clearly, centralized, automated control of backup and recovery of client/server network's distributed data is critical to ongoing operations.

The typical backup and recovery system operates on a set schedule based on administrator-defined criteria (time, types of files, full or incremental backup, etc.). Backup operations create sets of backed-up files retained in a mainframe's storage system or copied to a tape subsystem connected to a backup LAN server. The backup program retains a database noting each file saved so that network can recover them on user demand [Carr, 1992].

Backup and recovery of the Server Farm was a problem in early 1993, due to lack of funds for tape backup devices. As an alternative, two available IBM PS/2 Server 95 systems were set up as hot backup servers. This was done by swapping OS/2 critical configuration files as required (INI and CONFIG.SYS files). This approach is still employed for critical servers only, providing 10-minute recovery time if an outage occurs.

Later in 1993, the IBM WDSF (Workstation Data Save Facility) was used for Server Farm backup. In early 1994, the ADSTAR Distributed Storage Manager or ADSM replaced WDSF. ADSM runs on a VM mainframe and performs incremental nightly backup of all Notes, TaP/2, Net-Door, and CallUp C/S data servers to mainframe hard disk and tape storage. As all mainframes that service IBM Boca Raton are physically located in Research Triangle Park, North Carolina, vital records on the Server Farm are protected from any site disaster.

ADSM operation is set up and monitored by LAN administrators. Seven-day archiving is employed. The system has proven to be very reliable. In mid-1994, over 250,000 files with over 28 GB of information were being incrementally backed up nightly and were fully recoverable.

ADSM for VM will be replaced in early 1995 by ADSM/6000, which will run on an RS/6000 930 Server in the Server Farm. The 9333 SCSI drawer subsystem and the 3494 Tape Library Dataserver are planned to be used for backup storage. Vital records will be selectively backed up to another IBM site.

Security Requirements and Auditability

In a client/server computing environment, the servers are the storage repositories for most, if not all, critical business information. Controlling access to server data is mandatory for operating a secure computing environment. General-purpose file server access is typically controlled by the network operating system at user network logon time. In the case of OS/2 LAN Server, the user logs on to a server, called the domain controller, where he or she is given access to the servers assigned to the domain (a domain may contain one or more servers, as defined by server administration). Client/server applications, such as Lotus Notes, control access to application data on associated servers through authorized user logon and password, as well. Server administration should be responsible to guarantee that trivial passwords are not allowed (e.g., the user's name as a password) and that passwords are changed at regular intervals (every 6 months at a minimum). In addition, access logs (files containing server transactions, including logons) should be maintained (for at least 6 months) and periodically reviewed for unauthorized logon attempts. The logs will help determine the culprit if data theft is suspected.

IBM corporate operational guidelines and specifications dictate the security and auditability requirements. Primary concerns are the physical security of the servers and data security. Badge lock entry to the Server Farm resolves the physical security requirement. User authentication for application data access via ID and password verification is the first line of defense against unauthorized access or sabotage. Password expiration for Lotus Notes, TaP/2, and NetDoor applications, which occurs every 6 months, is administered by the Server Farm team. The Server Farm Team maintains server data access logs to meet corporate auditability requirements.

Server Support

If you have a large and diverse user population with multiple time zone requirements, you should plan on 24-hour-a-day, 7-day-a-week server availability. At a minimum, this means on-site server support during prime shift and one or more administrators on call for off-shift coverage. A proactive approach is (1) to invest in servers that support both local and remote management access and (2) to invest in server management applications that monitor server availability and capacity thresholds, and automatically notify server administrators if a problem occurs.

Server local management access is simply direct hands-on analysis and correction performed in the Server Farm. Server remote management access usually means a server adapter card with a built-in modem that allows a remote administrator to access the server for diagnosis and perform remote correction (e.g., restart) over the public telephone network. This allows on-call administrators to work from home and sometimes avoid an on-site visit, thereby controlling cost and improving availability for the users.

Server management applications that monitor the Server Farm should be part of an overall network management system that consolidates network management alert information to a central station or console from which pages can be generated to the appropriate support person. Chapter 6 discusses server management in context with other network management applications.

In IBM Boca Raton, most support activities for the Server Farm are manual. If a server goes down, the administrator is paged and must physically come in to restart the system. The MASS/2 application, which is in use on the IBM Server 195s with the remote maintenance processor (RMP), enables some remote administration (e.g., remote restart). The IBM NetFinity program is installed on the IBM PS/2 Server 95s. It uses the IBM Serverguard card to enable remote management by the server administrator on call. NetFinity supports remote reboot for simple server stoppages. However, a dirty drive on a PS/2 with OS/2 demands an operator's presence, unfortunately.

Pager alerts for server application outages are generated by the locally developed Server Availability Monitor/2 (SAM/2) program. An internally developed OS/2-based application, SAM/2 communicates with a paging program (EZPAGE), which generates the appropriate page to the server administrator on call. SAM/2 also sends an alert to the mainframe system monitored by the Help Desk. This alert also communicates server status to a database for display at user desktops on the HelpPlus application (see Chapter 7).

By contrast, lights-out operation is common practice on large mainframe systems: Remote management is mature. VM or MVS systems can reside hundreds of miles away from system administrators with no impact to the end user. This is an area where mainframe systems offer features that are superior to the budding client/server environment.

Server Farm Staffing

Server Farm administration staffing should be based on the number of applications and the number of servers supported. Specialists are required for individual application support. In addition to one or two team leaders (primary leader and backup), general-purpose hardware setup and maintenance skills are required as well.

In IBM Boca Raton, the Server Farm administration/support team is composed of 19 people to support the 191 servers—a ratio of 1 support person for every 10 server systems. This included a mixture of regular employees and skilled contractors. Figure 5.14 shows the breakdown by

Application	#Support Personnel
Notes, IMLG/2	8
TaP/2, Callup C/S	2
NetDoor	3
AIX Apps	2
Other	4
Total	19

Figure 5.14 Server Farm Staffing

application area. The "Other" category includes the primary and secondary team leaders and two setup and maintenance persons.

The server team members have considerable mainframe administration skills. These roots provide a good deal of discipline and experience in a general sense. In some ways, they try to emulate the prior VM environment with the new distributed environment. As they become expert in the new applications and support responsibilities, this experience has bred a strong desire to return to a more automated administrative environment, resulting in innovative applications, such as SAM/2 (see "Server Support" in this chapter).

Server Farm Application Support

Each application selected for your client/server computing environment will require specialized server setup, administration, and support. These tasks must be completely understood prior to application installation and user access. The IBM Boca Raton Server Farm organization reflects the specialized setup for each of the major applications selected for the rollout as well as critical supporting applications, such as the IBM Mail LAN Gateway/2. Following is a description of how each of these requirements were addressed.

Lotus Notes Server Organization

As the Farm grew and remote communication became more important, a Notes hub-and-spoke design (Figure 5.15) was implemented. Notes mail destined for remote sites was sent by individual mail servers to the local

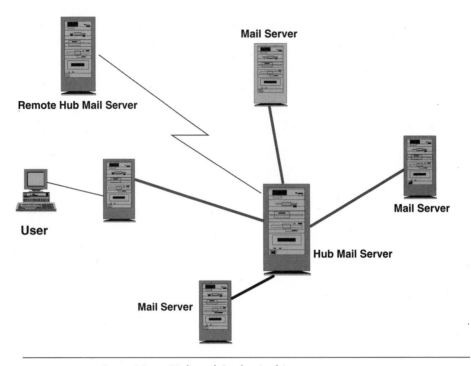

Figure 5.15   Lotus Notes Hub-and-Spoke Architecture

hub. The local hub then sent it to the correct remote hub. A backup Notes mail hub was installed. If the main hub fails, the backup hub automatically picks up the work. This was a basic capability handled by Notes.

The interconnection of the Notes mail, Notes hub, and IBM Mail/LAN Gateway/2 servers is described in Figure 5.16. Notes mail traffic between Boca and IBM Somers in New York is characterized. The first Notes hub server (8) is the primary Notes mail hub server. The second Notes hub server (10) transfers mail from the primary Boca hub (8) to the Somers hub (11). The third Notes hub server (not shown) is a hot backup to the primary hub (8).

IBM Mail LAN Gateway/2 Server Organization

The IBM Mail LAN Gateway/2 (IMLG/2) was an IBM program product that offered interoperability between OfficeVision (OV) electronic mail and Lotus Notes mail. It ran on a PS/2 server with OS/2, IBM Communi-

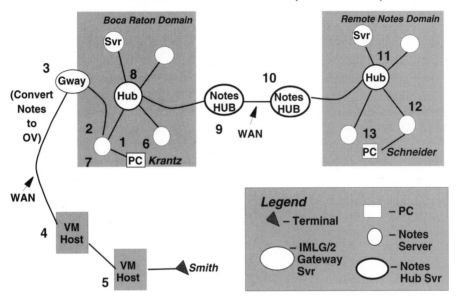

1 - 5: Lotus Note from Krantz to Smith (Notes to OfficeVision/VM)

6 - 13: Lotus Note from Krantz to Schneider (Notes to Notes)

Figure 5.16 Lotus Notes Mail Routing Examples

cations Manager/2, and the Lotus Notes server code. A single PC server gateway system supported a single Notes domain. Through most of 1993, a single gateway system was adequate to support the relatively few Notes users communicating with OV users.

In Figure 5.16, an IBM Mail/LAN Gateway/2 server (3) receives Notes mail from one or more Notes mail servers to be converted and sent to VM. It will receive OfficeVision mail from a VM host (3) to be converted and sent to a Notes mail server.

As more users were rolled out with Lotus Notes, the single gateway system became a serious bottleneck, threatening the success of the entire project. The capacity limits of the PS/2 running IMLG/2 were exceeded in early March 1994 (19,000 notes/week), requiring the Server Team to install a "Scalable Gateway" version.

Figure 5.17 depicts the relationship of a set of Notes mail servers and four gateway servers. The set of gateway servers is supported on VM by an application that treats the gateway server traffic as if it came from a single server. In order to support the large Notes-to-VM mail traffic for

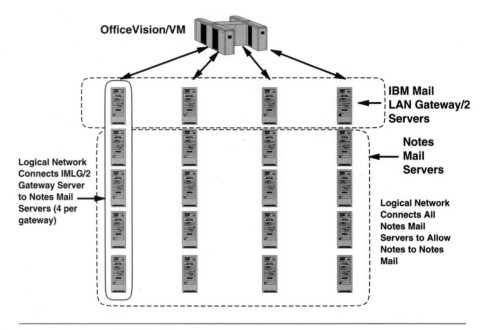

Figure 5.17 Scalable Mail Gateway in IBM Boca Raton

Boca in 1994, ten gateway servers are currently installed. Each supports four mail servers. Using a network routing strategy support by Notes server administration, mail is routed to alternate gateways should the primary gateway go down.

Over 60,000 notes per week were efficiently processed by this the scaleable gateway in June 1994. As the client/server migration progresses, it is projected that as many as 12 to 14 PS/2's may be required to handle the workload until the site goes "over the hump," when most mail traffic is expected to be Lotus Notes-to-Notes.

IBM Time and Place/2 Server Organization

The IBM TaP/2 application servers offer a diversity of calendar and meeting schedule features that imply a fairly complex server organization (see Chapter 3 for details about TaP/2). Figure 5.18 outlines this organization. The user PC (1) logs on to the TaP/2 master server (2) to gain access to the application. The user is given access to a TaP/2 data server (3) that

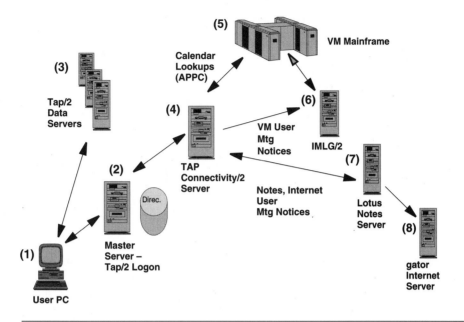

Figure 5.18 IBM Time and Place/2 Interfaces

stores his calendar in a DB2 for OS/2 database. Meeting scheduling among IBM Boca TaP/2 users is a basic function of the application. In addition, the TaP/2 event gateway server (4) can perform the following:

1. Interface with one or more VM mainframes (5) to determine free-time availability for OfficeVision calendar users.

2. Send meeting notices to IBM OfficeVision/VM-user attendees worldwide via IMLG/2 (6).

3. Send meeting notices to Lotus Notes user attendees (7).

4. Send meeting notices to Internet-user attendees (8).

OS/2 LAN Server 3.0 Server Organization

LAN Server 3.0 is installed on NetDoor servers (see the following section), shared-code servers, and general-purpose file servers. It supports sharing of resources and devices on the network. The user logs on to an assigned domain controller (server), which gives him transparent access to one or more network servers, associated with the controller.

Lotus Notes code is installed on eight shared-code servers, supported by LAN Server for user network access. This avoids private code installation and thereby simplifies application upgrade.

IBM Network Door/2 (NetDoor) Server Organization

NetDoor provides application access through a NetDoor catalog to client computers provided by servers on the site network. The NetDoor servers are organized into four groups (Figure 5.19 depicts the organization):

1. **Domain Controllers.** Three PS/2 Server 95s with 32 MB of RAM, 1 GB of storage, and 4 IBM LANstreamer adapters are employed. User logons are assigned to a primary domain controller as they are rolled out in the migration. If a domain con-

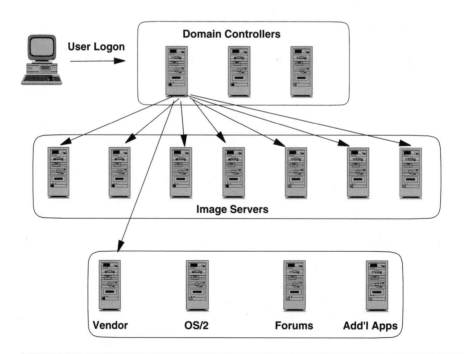

Figure 5.19 NetDoor Server Organization

troller is down, the user will automatically be logged on to the next controller. A **daemon** (a program waiting to be triggered by an external event) running on the domain controller performs automatic load balancing among the seven identically configured NetDoor Image servers for user access assignment. This provides some fault tolerance and allows for dynamic increase or decrease in network resources as the user population changes.

2. **Image Servers.** Seven PS/2 Server 95s with 32 MB of RAM, 1 GB of storage, and 2 IBM LANstreamer adapters are employed. They are each configured with the complete NetDoor catalog of applications and tools. The original developer recommendation was 200 users per server. However, the installation of two IBM LANstreamer cards in each Image server has enabled this to be increased to 250 to 300 users per server.

3. **Vendor Server.** One PS/2 Server 95 monitors vendor application usage to ensure that the number of active application requests is less than or equal to the number of network licenses.

4. **OS/2 Tools and Forums Servers.** Two Server 95s with 2 GB of storage provide access to OS/2 tools programs and Forums. OS/2 tools are internally developed programs for aid in OS/2 use and development. Forums are discussion databases that contain serial dialogs among developers and users across the IBM corporation on specific topics of technical interest.

AIX, RS/6000 Server Applications

A set of RS/6000 servers in the Server Farm are used to support an assortment of individual AIX-based applications. Some of these perform behind-the-scenes, infrastructure type work for all site users. Others support specialized user segments. These include:

- AFS Cell for Distributed File Access Services. AFS stands for Andrew File System. An AFS cell is a set of data servers that can be freely accessed by a set of users for file storage and file sharing over a network. Users can be local to a site or remotely linked.

- Internet Access. Internet refers to the large and growing public domain network developed by DARPA that uses TCP/IP as its communication protocol. It is shared by universities, corporations and private individuals. Site users logon to a special purpose server to access the Internet. Files are transferred from and to the external Internet only via this special server. After the user logs off the server, he may then request the file(s) to be sent from the server to his PC or workstation. This indirect, two-step process protects the internal network from potentially damaging transfers (see Chapter 6, IBM Boca's WANs for more details). E-mail to and from Internet users is also supported with Lotus Notes.

- Print Servers. The Print Services Facility/6000 (PSF/6000) application will be installed on RS/6000 server systems attached to network campus rings (see Chapter 6). They will be used to receive, queue, convert (if necessary), and route print files to the site's convenience laser printers.

- SMTP Gateway. This is for e-mail interoperability among AIX users, Internet users, Notes users, and OV/VM users. SMTP is the Simple Mail Transport Protocol which utilizes TCP/IP. It is a widely used e-mail protocol developed for the Internet and widely employed by UNIX users.

- Kerberos. This is for security authorization for mobile client access. The mobile client communications router (a XYPLEX router) accesses the Kerberos server for user password authentication. See Chapter 6 for details.

- IBM SoftDist/6000. This is used for AIX operating system and applications code distribution.

- CMVC. This is used for software library and problem tracking. CMVC is discussed in Chapter 4.

The Heterogeneous Server Farm of the Future

The future of client/server computing is very bright because of the rich set of information technology solutions that are expected in the area of server applications, tools, and systems. This is particularly evident after examining the server system alternatives available today and projecting forward to the maturation of this environment. Following are some focus items and emerging technologies that will probably play an important part in your ongoing Server Farm investments.

Centralized, Automated Administration and Management

Once you establish your initial Server Farm, consolidated and automated administration should be a primary goal. This will enable you to control support costs over time. Central administration includes user ID and password maintenance, database organization, data space administration, and access authorizations (e.g., network userids). In addition, you should seek to create a unified management environment for the network infrastructure and the Server Farm for additional leverage over increasing support costs. In IBM Boca Raton, network infrastructure and server management is expected to converge in 1995 (see Chapter 6).

X.400 and X.500

The international standard for electronic messaging, X.400, should become the basis for your future e-mail infrastructure. X.400 is implemented on a worldwide basis and has recently gained momentum as the solution to interconnect multiple LAN and mainframe-based proprietary e-mail systems. It will enable your Server Farm to support multiple e-mail clients (e.g., Lotus Notes, cc:Mail) with a single e-mail "backbone" server application, thereby minimizing support costs.

IBM Boca was able to achieve consensus regarding Lotus Notes as the standard e-mail application. IMLG/2 provides necessary interoperability with OfficeVision/VM. However, many users have requested cc:Mail for e-mail, a very popular application from Lotus Development. An X.400 gateway "backbone" server would support this new requirement behind the scenes, maintain the current Notes-OV/VM mail interoperability, and position the site to support additional e-mail clients with little impact. Essentially, client e-mail applications would maintain their user interfaces but would change the file format of each e-mail message produced to conform to the X.400 standard. Correspondingly, they would each accept the X.400 format for incoming e-mail messages. The X.400 server would then handle the messages from any number of unique e-mail applications transparently.

X.500 is gaining momentum in the marketplace as the industry standard for directory services, in particular with respect to X.400 directory synchronization issues. The X.500 requirement is easily understood considering the directory mess described earlier (see Figure 5.12). Recent developments with Novell, Microsoft, and Lotus indicate a strong push toward X.500-compliant directory services over the next few years. Again, implementing this industry standard minimizes support costs, as each application requiring directory information selects from a single, centrally managed database.

RISC Systems as Super Servers

Application vendors are increasingly developing their applications to run on multiple systems. For example, Lotus Notes, originally developed for Intel-based systems, will soon be available on UNIX-based systems. This implies that high-performance, RISC-based server systems will increasingly be used in Server Farms to consolidate application support.

In IBM Boca Raton, as other server applications are written for the RS/6000 (e.g., Lotus Notes), and additional fault tolerance features become available for this system, it is anticipated that the Server Farm will utilize relatively more RS/6000s. This will ultimately reduce the number of systems in the Farm and correspondingly reduce support costs.

Mainframes as Servers

Where PCs and RISC-based servers offer clear advantages, they will be employed in the future. However, for big jobs in big companies, "heavy metal will rule" [Meyer, 1994]. A critical place where the mainframe will continue to be used in IBM Boca Raton is as a server for very large databases, such as a large DB2 database. Mainframes will be used also to support "legacy" applications, such as those that support corporate data processing, until a client/server equivalent is developed.

Dual Processor Servers

In a shared memory system, such as the IBM PS/2 Server 195, the addition of a second processor brings a significant performance gain. According to Ga Cote [1994], "a performance advantage of as much as 3 to 1 has been demonstrated for dual-processor, Intel-based servers for an SQL-transaction client/server environment vs. a single processor system." For applications requiring medium to large relational databases, dual-processor servers are a solid choice—one processor would service data queries while the other would support general system processing.

Tertiary Storage

Katz [1992] has stated that a revolution has taken place in tertiary storage with "near-line" storage systems. Robotic pickers select optical or tape media aligned on shelves in these devices. When these are used in conjunction with secondary storage for data caching, near magnetic disk speeds are attainable with a much lower cost per megabyte of storage. These "juke-box"-like devices will be welcome additions to the Server Farm's backup system in the future.

Critical Success Factors

The Server Farm supports the client rollout in your client/server migration. It is the storage place for your critical data and runs the critical "back-room" applications that make your client/server environment work. Following are some key recommendations that will lead you to success in building a Server Farm.

- You should take advantage of the superior scalability of small PC-based servers in deployment within your client/server environment. This scalability comes at a price—system administration and management is more difficult and more costly.

- You should take advantage of the granularity of PC and workstation-based server systems to select different levels of fault tolerance and recovery options based on need. This flexibility is an advantage of the client/server environment.

- The potential to create a heterogeneous Server Farm, as in IBM Boca Raton, is perhaps the best balance of scalability and manageability. As Boar [1993] writes in his *Implementing Client/Server*

Computing: A Strategic Perspective, specialized servers offer "the ability . . . to perform specific functions in a superior price/performance manner." He further observes that "monolithic systems could not take advantage of discrete specialization. Client/server computing enables entrepreneurs to develop advantageous and specialized solutions with the ability to plug them into the network due to modularity and interoperability." Nineteen ninety-five appears to be a watershed year, in which you will be able to take advantage of many important applications that support multiple server platforms, simplifying the establishment of a heterogeneous server environment.

- Despite living with a Directory Cacophony (see Figure 5.12), the IBM Boca Raton site is quite fortunate that it is living with only two e-mail systems, one calendar, and one phone directory application. You should seek to standardize on major applications, which, coupled with synchronization tools, will enable you to survive in your embryonic client/server environment.

- A single, enterprise-wide directory for all user and network-related information is highly desirable. This should include names and addresses for users, servers, printers, and other network resources. It should support industry-standard application program interfaces (APIs), so that all applications can use its services. Synchronization programs would become a thing of the past. Interoperability would be improved. Support costs and administrative errors would be reduced. The bottom line is that multiple, incompatible directories are user and administrator unfriendly. You should avoid them wherever possible. Fight for X.500.

- Considerable skill is required in server administration. This includes hardware setup and maintenance, operating system setup and troubleshooting, application installation and support, local and remote management, and many administrative tasks. As a result, your staffing decisions must be made very carefully. Tools for automation of these tasks will become increasingly important to your Server Farm administration.

6

Network Infrastructure

Simply having the necessary networking infrastructure is holding some companies back from client/server computing.

[FORRESTER, 1993]

This chapter defines the complex client/server network, lists the major requirements, details the important components, and describes the IBM Boca Raton network. Next, network management requirements, activities, and tools are described. The IBM Boca Raton approach is detailed, and the future of client/server networks is explored. The chapter winds up with some critical success factors and the network administrator's pledge.

Defining the Client/Server Network

A computer network, or more simply a network, is a data communications system that interconnects computer systems. A network may be composed of any combination of **LANs**, **MANs**, or **WANs**. A LAN, or

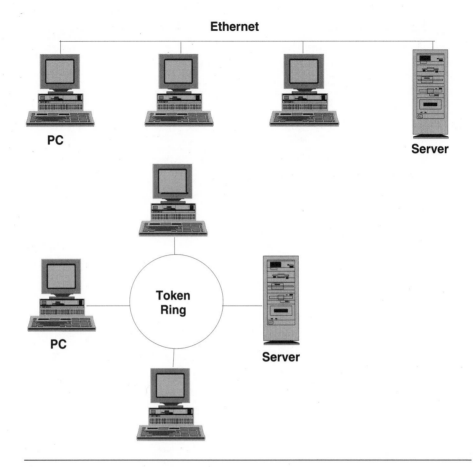

Figure 6.1   LAN—Local Area Network

Local Area Network (see Figure 6.1), is the interconnection of several personal computers and other hardware such as printers within a small local area (a room or the floor of a building). Designed originally as a means of sharing hardware and software among PCs, LANs are used as a general means of communications among PCs. A MAN, or Metropolitan Area Network, is similar to a LAN but covers larger geographic distances (up to 50 kilometers). A WAN, or Wide Area Network, is a network that spans long geographic distances, typically city to city.

A client/server network is a computer network in which client systems use the network to request services and data from network-attached server systems. Requesting services from a server system usually means running an application program on the server and, when the application is completed, having the server report results back to the client system. Chapter 1 discussed this in detail.

Network Requirements

The client/server trend has become a compelling new paradigm for large, complex computing environments. As a result, client/server network requirements are solidifying. Following is a basic list you should consider during when planning a migration:

- **Accessibility.** The network should provide connectivity to applications and data for on-site and off-site users. On-site accessibility is obvious. Off-site access either from a fixed station or a mobile system is becoming increasingly important.

- **Protocol Support.** It is important for a large network to support multiple protocols, such as SNA, NetBIOS, TCP/IP, and IPX, because many applications support only one or two of the major communications protocols. However, many major applications do support these and other protocols. IBM mainframe applications now support TCP/IP communications, in addition to its SNA protocols. It is becoming possible, and desirable, to standardize on a single communications protocol, such as TCP/IP.

- **Reliability.** This is an absolute requirement. If the network isn't operational, business is being held up. Redundancy of key network components and alternate data paths in case of failure are mandatory. Quality components and reliable equipment vendors are critical here.

- **Performance.** Given a stable network, it must perform well. The network must have reserve bandwidth capacity for peak demand periods. Response times are highly application and server dependent, but network transmission delays should be proportional to the amount of data transferred; that is, small requests should be nearly instantaneous, whereas large file transfers may take longer periods. A good rule of thumb is that applications should run no slower nor less reliably on the network than on a single computer system.

- **Security.** The network must be physically secure and impervious to unauthorized access, with confidential data transmission supported. Mobile clients and communications with suppliers or vendors heighten this need.

- **Cost-Effective.** The network has to provide added value above the cost to build and maintain it. Intelligent trade-offs need to be made to minimize costs while keeping characteristics such as reliability and performance acceptable to the users.

- **Manageable and Serviceable.** Faults and performance bottlenecks should be detectable for all network devices. A consolidated management station should receive these alerts and guarantee communication with network support personnel. An important consideration often overlooked is having both an **in-band** (in the network) and an **out-of-band** (a separate network, e.g., a public telephone network) fault communication capability for critical network components. Maintenance access to all network devices and connectivity ports should be straightforward. Network assets and configuration should be tracked and visible to network administrators. Network performance and operational statistics should be easily accessible for identification of potential bottlenecks and problems. Network usage should be measurable and reportable by using organization.

- **Extendible.** The network must be extendible to support new requirements. This can be as simple as the addition of a new LAN or as complex as providing additional bandwidth for multimedia applications. A sound, documented network architecture must be in place to satisfy this requirement. Given the rate and pace of change in internetworking products, this is highly challenging and requires considerable technical expertise.

Clarifying the Network Cloud

To understand how a complex client/server network can satisfy these requirements, we need to understand the components of the network and how they are combined to form a useful infrastructure.

Most LANs are set up to operate in a client/server mode, where each

PC on the LAN takes turns in accessing or storing information to a server system (see Figure 6.1). Two of the most common types of LANs are **Ethernet** LANs and **token-ring** LANs. An Ethernet LAN typically operates at 10 Mbps and the interconnections among the PCs are serial. A token-ring LAN typically operates at 16 Mbps, and the interconnections among the PCs form a ring.

LAN Cables

There are four major types of cable used to create LANs: unshielded twisted pair (UTP), coaxial cable (coax), shielded twisted pair (STP), and fiber-optic cable. UTP is inexpensive and can support the most common LAN transmission speeds (10 Mbps for Ethernet and 16 Mbps for token-ring). Coax is more expensive than UTP, but supports faster speed transmission. STP is fairly expensive but can support transmission speeds to 100 Mbps, making it a good choice for current and future speed requirements. Fiber-optic cable is the most expensive, but also the fastest, making it the cable of choice where high-speed communication is required [Derfler, 1993].

Network Data Formats

Data that is prepared by an application to be transmitted over a LAN is first broken up into groups of data bytes, called **frames**. When data is physically transmitted over a LAN, each frame will typically be broken up into one or more **packets**. A packet is a set of data bytes that are transmitted as a group across a network. A packet typically contains the address of the destination, the type of packet, and data information. If a large PC file is being transmitted from a client to a server, it will be broken up into several packets as it is transmitted and then reorganized into the file format when received.

Protocols

The well-defined format of the frames and packets, along with how they are sent and received, is called a **protocol**. There are many such protocols (actually too many). A protocol's data format refers to the bits of information added to transmitted data that permits its successful receipt. Examples are TCP/IP, NetBIOS, and IPX. Protocols are frequently described with reference to the standard protocol stack as defined in the OSI (Open Systems Interconnect) reference model (Figure 6.2). Each layer of the stack refers to a software layer (usually implemented as a service program) that adds protocol information to the actual data as it is being transmitted and removes protocol information from the packet as it is received. The protocol information helps identify the source, the destination, the protocol type, and the data. One can think of a packet being handed from one layer to another as it is moved down the stack, with each layer providing its own unique contribution. For example, the network layer will add network addressing information to a packet so that it can be routed to the correct network (see Figure 6.3).

Most protocol choices are made because of desired applications. If an application is limited to one or another protocol, that will dictate how it is installed and used on the network. This implies that a useful network must be prepared to support multiple protocols. However, to simplify network management, it is desirable to support only a single protocol stack. Today, we are seeing most important applications support the

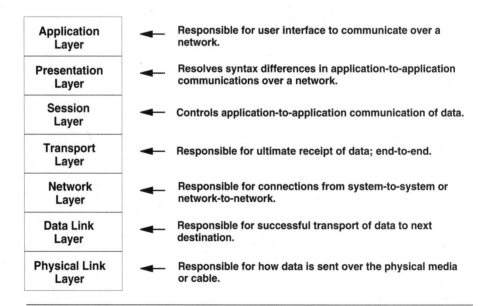

Figure 6.2 OSI Protocol Stack

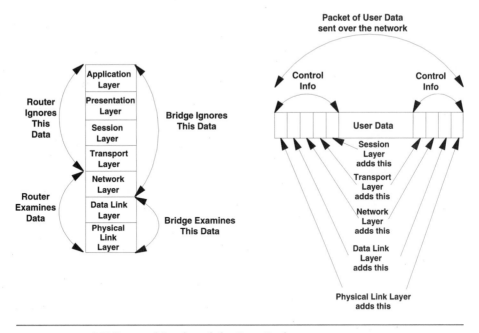

Figure 6.3 OSI Protocol Stack and the Data Packet

major protocol stacks, such as NetBIOS, TCP/IP or IPX. This provides the flexibility necessary to achieve a single protocol network.

The NetBIOS protocol is used for on-site communications by Lotus Notes, TaP/2, CallUp C/S, and NetDoor, IBM Boca's standard applications. NetBIOS is a very common high-level protocol for PC applications. One of its major disadvantages is that it typically uses the NetBEUI lower-level protocol to complete its communications and NetBEUI doesn't provide for a network identifier in the protocol. For an application using NetBIOS to communicate with an application running on a system on another (nonbridged) network, the NetBIOS frames of data must be **encapsulated** in a protocol that can be routed from network to network. For example, NetBIOS must be encapsulated within TCP/IP frames to send it over a LAN-WAN link. See "WANs" later in this chapter for an example. NetBIOS/NetBEUI can readily operate on a **bridged** network (such as the Boca Raton network), where the bridged LAN segments appear to be a single network to the protocol. This is also called transparent LAN bridging. See "Bridges" later in this chapter for details.

TCP/IP (Transmission Control Protocol/Internet Protocol), developed by the Department of Defense in the 1970s, offers an alternative approach to transparent LAN bridging in the form of routing data between **subnets** (or networks). A subnet is a general term to describe a set of systems that can communicate with one another directly (i.e., systems on the same network). Systems on different subnets require assistance by a routing device to transfer data between them. Therefore, TCP/IP offers the ability to segment parts of a complex network (i.e., create subnets) easily. This improves the ability to isolate problem areas, and hence improve network management. Beyond the site, TCP/IP can be used to support LAN-to-WAN connectivity as well, making it the protocol of choice for a complex, multisite network. In fact, TCP/IP is used to route other nonroutable protocols, such as NetBIOS, as was discussed earlier.

In IBM Boca Raton, TCP/IP is used for print file data transmission, CAD file application data transfer, Internet communication, some mainframe communications, and all AIX application communication. The SNA protocol is used for some PC- mainframe communications.

Hubs

Most LAN installations use **hubs** to interconnect the PCs. This simplifies wiring and maintenance. Figure 6.4 shows how all PCs connect to the hub directly. If the LAN is Ethernet, the hub is set up to connect the PCs serially. If the LAN is token-ring, the hub is set up to connect the PCs in a ring. The connection is made on the hub's **backplane** (circuit board).

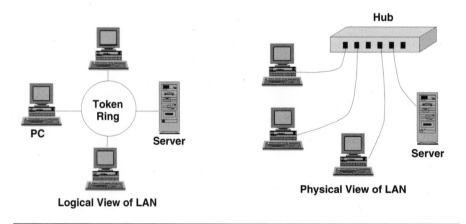

Figure 6.4 Hubs

The Boca Raton site uses IBM 8230 (Figure 6.5) today, and is considering investment in IBM 8260 (Figure 6.6) hubs for its LANs in the future. The Network Team just replaced a large number of older IBM 8228 hubs with 8230s. The 8228 is what is known as a passive hub, or a hub that just interconnects the attached PCs as a LAN. Active hubs, such as the 8230, interact with the network management system to report hub problems and can shut down network adapters that cause problems on the network (e.g., **beaconing**, or transmitting at an incorrect speed). The IBM 8260 Multiprotocol Intelligent Hub is under consideration not only because it can remotely manage and shut down errant adapters, it is also upgradable to high-speed **switching** (see "Switching Hubs" later in this chapter).

Bridges

In most cases, a LAN's PC clients will be in the same general area on a floor of a building and serve a specific department. Things get more complicated when several LANs must be interconnected to share information

Courtesy International Business Machines Corporation

Figure 6.5 IBM 8230 Controlled Access Unit (Hub)

Courtesy International Business Machines Corporation

Figure 6.6   IBM 8260 Multi-Protocol Intelligent Hub

across departments across a larger area. Within a single site, two approaches to interconnecting LANs are the most common. The first uses an approach called **bridging** to link two LANs such that clients on either LAN can transparently access the servers of both. Bridging several LANs together requires that they are all using the same physical layer protocol (e.g., token-ring or Ethernet). Typically, bridging is done by adding a PC with two LAN cards to the network and connecting each LAN to one of the cards. Bridge software on this bridge PC (or just bridge) keeps a list of client physical addresses on both LANs. When data from one LAN is to go to the other LAN, the bridge software intercepts it and passes it over to the next LAN (see Figure 6.7).

In IBM Boca Raton, the bridges are PS/2 386-based machines (Figure 6.8). To improve bridge throughput in congested bridges, the older technology network adapter cards were replaced with high-performance IBM 32-bit LANstreamer token-ring adapter cards.

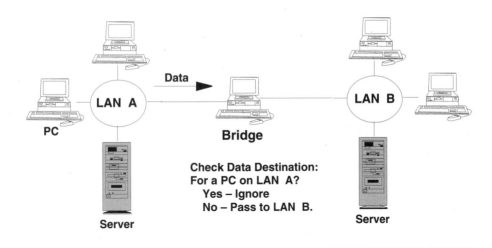

Figure 6.7 Bridge Example

Figure 6.8 Cables and Bridges in IBM Boca Raton

Routers

The second major approach to interconnecting LANs is called **routing**. Figure 6.9 shows two LANs connected to a system called a **router**. A typical router is a high-performance computing system, connecting two or more LANs, that runs router software. The router is more sophisticated in its handling of network data than a bridge. Routers recognize network-level (LAN-level) routing information. Routers can direct information along different paths in a large network through sharing information with other routers on the network (routers build routing databases to contain this information). This can relieve congestion in a large network dynamically. Routers can also perform protocol conversions to send data between dissimilar networks.

In IBM Boca Raton, several types of routers are used. RISC/6000 Model 320 systems and IBM 6611 Routers are used to route TCP/IP traffic on the IP subnets (see "The IBM Boca Raton Network" later in this chapter). Each will recognize packets destined for the other two IP subnets and route them accordingly. Other routers are used to connect the Boca Raton network to three other IBM sites—Raleigh, Atlanta and Austin—over a WAN.

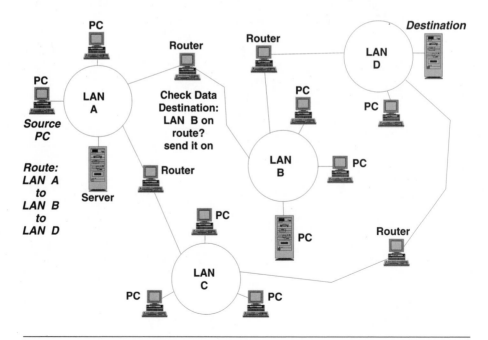

Figure 6.9 Router Example

An example of a router that does protocol conversion is the system used in Boca Raton that converts SLIP formatted data from/to the public telephone network to/from token-ring protocol on the site network for mobile client access.

Switching Hubs

From a networking perspective, a **switch** is a computer—controlled device that can direct (switch) all digital network bandwidth from one destination to another on demand. Switches, also called digital switches, have only recently appeared on the networking scene as optional features of advanced, intelligent hubs. The switching hub is used to interconnect one or more LAN segments and switch communications among them on demand. Several recent products apply switching to Ethernet LANs, token-ring LANs, and state-of-the-art **Asynchronous Transfer Mode (ATM)** networks (see "A Clearer Vision for the Future" later in this chapter for more details). By dynamically switching packets between connected LAN segments, "switching allows simultaneous transmissions among pairs of network segments, increasing overall network bandwidth by two or more times the bandwidth of individual LAN segments" [Faulkner, 1994]. Thus, switching offers improved performance to the limits of the LAN adapter to satisfy the demands of applications requiring large bursts of data. It does this without replacing existing adapters, wiring, or software, making switching hubs a compelling alternative if improved performance is required. The switching hub can be set up to perform dynamic bridging or dynamic routing between LAN segments. By employing a higher-speed (low-latency) approach to transferring packets, improved performance is realized on the network. Some of these advanced products perform routing between dissimilar LAN segments, such as Ethernet and FDDI.

Gateways

A **gateway** is formally defined as a program or system that converts and routes data from one application to another. The term *gateway* is frequently used interchangeably with the term *router*, but they are different. The router does not convert application data, while a gateway does.

An example of a true gateway is a system used to convert e-mail messages from one format to another to allow interoperability between two different e-mail applications. An example, discussed in detail in Chapter

5, is the IBM Mail LAN Gateway/2, which converts Lotus Notes e-mail to OfficeVision e-mail and vice versa.

Terminology Overlap

You should be aware that the terms *gateway, router, hub, switch,* and, sometimes, *server* are all used interchangeably in the trade literature! What is very confusing is that combination products sometimes combine elements of each of these terms. This is becoming increasingly common as this hot product area matures. It is important not to get hung up on the formal definitions, but to understand the basics of each.

For example, hubs and their features and options are growing by leaps and bounds. There are hubs that can accept bridges, routers, and switches as optional modules.

WANs

Beyond linking LANs to LANs at the same location, LANs can bridge to remote LANs over WANs. A WAN is a wide area network, or a network spanning long distances, typically city to city. Figure 6.10 depicts the interconnections. In this case, the WAN is a dedicated link between the two LANs. WANs can be set up by leasing dedicated telecommunication lines (private WAN) or purchasing a service from a WAN vendor, such as a long-distance telephone carrier (public WAN). The selection is based on the required bandwidth between the two sites and security considerations.

A typical dedicated WAN line will use T1 service (usually called a T1 line). T1 service is a digital data transmission service that can transport up to 1.544 Mbps. The next level of WAN service is called T3, a digital data transmission service that can transmit up to 44.746 Mbps, which incorporates 28 T1 circuits.

One of the oldest and most familiar lower-level protocol architectures over a public WAN is called **X.25**. It supports up to about 64 Kbps (thousand bits per second) transmission, making it very slow for today's internetworking needs. Data is broken up into X.25 packets and then transmitted over the WAN. Higher-level protocol frames, such as TCP/IP, are contained within the X.25 packets.

The next step up from X.25 is a public WAN protocol called **frame relay**. It is a simplification of the X.25 protocol that can operate at speeds

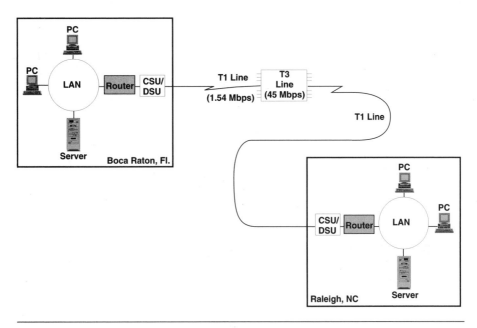

Figure 6.10 LAN-WAN-LAN

from 64 Kbps to 1.544 Mbps (note that frame relay can take full advantage of the available bandwidth in a T1 line). Therefore, it is ideal to interconnect two LANs over a WAN and is replacing X.25 commercial services. It is designed to provide high-speed packet transmission, very low network delay, and efficient use of network bandwidth.

IBM Boca Raton uses several private WANs—to communicate between other IBM sites and to the **Internet,** for example. The term *Internet* refers to the large and growing public-domain network developed by the Defense Department, which uses TCP/IP as its communication protocol. It is shared by universities, corporations and private individuals.

The IBM Boca Raton Network

First, the Network Team had to establish a robust and bandwidth-rich network to support a client/server application mix. Fortunately, the Boca site network has been built by a team of dedicated and knowledgeable network experts, second to none in the industry, the ISSC LAN Transport

Team. With foresight and careful planning, the team had already made the necessary investments so that by the end of 1993, IBM Boca had a robust site network. The network had adequate redundancy and capacity to support the anticipated additional workload of client/server applications with minimal extensions. Specifically, an additional site backbone was installed to provide an alternate data path for NetBIOS traffic. Other network extensions included upgrading bridges (PS/2 486 systems replaced 386 systems) and hubs (8230s replaced 8228s) to improve performance and manageability at key internetwork junctures.

The IBM Boca Raton site network combines most of the elements just described to create a multiprotocol, **source-route-bridged**, site-wide network, with worldwide links. Source-route bridging is a method in which the source PC discovers the destination PC's address and the addresses of all intermediate bridges along the route before sending any data. The source PC then places the address of all intermediate bridges along with the data so that each bridge along the path has precise routing information. Essentially, the many LANs on the site are interconnected by over 300 bridges in a hierarchical fashion to provide redundant pathways for the data traffic. However, there are trade-offs to this approach. First, the best routes are not always chosen, so the network congestion must be monitored by network administration carefully. Second, there is a seven-hop limit to any network path with the current token ring adapters (the new IBM LANstreamer adapter can handle up to 13 hops). See "A Clearer Vision for the Future," later in this chapter, for 1995 plans to improve the network.

Let's examine Figure 6.11, a simplified diagram of the IBM Boca Raton Network, to understand how it is organized:

1. Each building on the site has a token-ring LAN for each floor (called a floor ring!). The floor rings can be thought of as the lowest ring level in a hierarchical ring structure. They are operated at 16 Mbps. The physical wire is shielded twisted pair.

2. Each floor ring in a building has two bridges connecting it to the two sets of redundant campus token rings (could have been called building rings!). The campus rings are the second level in the hierarchy. Campus rings are wired with multimode optical fiber.

3. The two sets of campus rings (called the even and odd rings, based upon their number) provide redundant paths to the three site primary backbone rings—the third and highest level in the hierarchy.

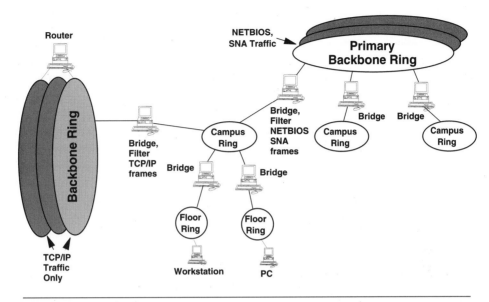

Figure 6.11 The IBM Boca Raton Network—Simplified View

Each campus ring has three bridges connecting it to one of the three primary backbone rings. With the campus rings connected in this fashion, there are several alternate paths for data to travel in case of failure or network congestion. The primary backbone rings are wired with multimode optical fiber.

Since bridges operate at the data link layer of the network protocol stack (Figure 6.3), higher-level protocol data is transparent to the bridge. Therefore, a bridged network can be used to support a multiprotocol environment, as long as the format of the data link and physical layers are the same. The Boca Raton network supports NetBIOS, TCP/IP, and SNA protocols across the same network. Once a packet arrives at its correct destination, it is recognized by the higher levels of the protocol stack software with its higher-level protocol information.

Besides connecting LANs, bridges can recognize the data content of a packet and disallow its entry to certain paths on the network. This is called **filtering**. On each even campus ring (one of the two redundant sets) of the IBM Boca Raton network, a bridge filters out non-TCP/IP packets, allowing all TCP/IP packets to flow to one of three TCP/IP backbone networks. This was done to guarantee adequate bandwidth for the

TCP/IP users, who frequently transmitted large CAD data files. It also avoids creating bottlenecks for non-TCP/IP users on the other backbones.

IBM Boca's Backbones

There are a total of six backbone rings on the Boca Raton site. The three primary backbone rings support NetBIOS and SNA traffic (data packets). Three support TCP/IP traffic. The third NetBIOS/SNA backbone was added in the second quarter of 1994 as the result of a performance modeling project initiated by the Site CIO (see "Performance and Performance Modeling" later in this chapter for details). The third backbone was a **collapsed backbone**. The Network Team purchased a router for this purpose. All campus rings are connected to ports on the router, and its backplane (internal circuitry) serves as the third primary backbone. The performance on this collapsed backbone is better than on a normal, wired backbone.

The three TCP/IP backbone networks are also called subnets. For TCP/IP, the subnet identifies the network for a set of **hosts**, or systems that can communicate. In this case, the systems are RS/6000 workstations and PCs. In Boca, the three TCP/IP backbones correspond to three subnets supporting a maximum of 4,096 host addresses. Each backbone has its own router (an RS/6000 system or IBM 6611) to send data from subnet to subnet and a **name server**. A name server is a system used in a TCP/IP network that converts TCP/IP network addresses into names and vice versa.

A "hot port" philosophy allows workstations to be moved from office to office within the subnet (ports connected to the same backbone) without administrator intervention.

IBM Boca's WANs

In the corporate environment, the entry and exit points of a site network need to be carefully managed. For leased WAN lines to other corporate sites, no special measures are required. For WANs communicating over shared or public media (e.g., the public telephone network), **firewalls** need to be erected to prevent unauthorized transmission or receipt of data over the WAN. A firewall in this context is a specialized server or servers that are isolated at the periphery of the site network and require special approval for access. This approval is for both external and internal users. One can say that the periphery of a private, site network is logically equivalent to the semipermeable membrane of a living cell. Only in certain circumstances does the cell allow material to flow in; in other circumstances the cell allows material to flow out!

Figures 6.12, 6.13, and 6.14 describe three separate examples of WAN firewalls erected at the Boca Raton site. The first example shows how IBM Boca users exchange information with vendors via Lotus Notes. A Notes database server with a modem is connected to the public telephone network. Vendors dial in to this server and, when properly logged on based on their authorization, may write or read data from a Notes database intended for site users. Similarly, site users access another Notes database server, where they write or read information intended for the vendor. At defined periods, the Notes servers replicate the database between the servers to complete the information exchange. A router is used as a firewall to only allow communication between the paired servers.

The second example shows how IBM Boca users access the Internet. The Internet is a vast network connecting university and business computer systems around the world. Data sharing and electronic communication via Internet is becoming commonplace for casual as well as business users. IBM Boca residents now can subscribe to Internet access on the network. An RS/6000 server has been installed that is the point of communication for Internet file transfer and e-mail. The user logs on using **telnet** (a standard TCP/IP logon program) to the special purpose server.

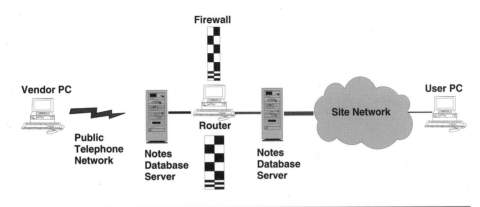

Figure 6.12 WAN Application 1—Vendor Data Exchange

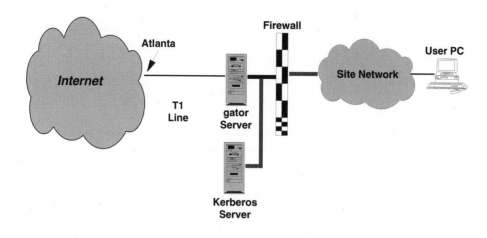

Figure 6.13 WAN Application 2—Internet Access

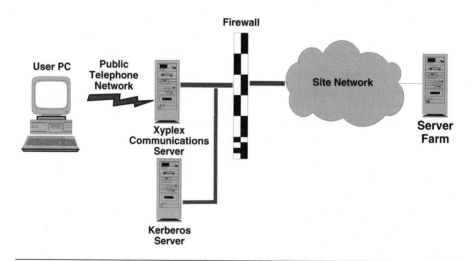

Figure 6.14 WAN Application 3—Mobile Client Access

While logged on, the user employs standard Internet data query tools (e.g., ftp) to search the worldwide Internet and gather information files to be stored in space allocated on the server. After logging off, the user can then issue a command (ftp) to the server, which transfers the information files to his PC or workstation. The Boca site uses a T1 link to Atlanta for high-speed Internet access.

The third example illustrates the **mobile client** access interface. Typically, a mobile client is a PC system with access to the site network, but not present on the campus (see Chapter 4 for details on mobile client). To gain remote access to the network, the user starts the logon process from his mobile client system to the **Xyplex communications server** over the public telephone network. The Xyplex communications server facilitates communication between the mobile client and the site network by converting TCP/IP packets on the site's token-ring network to TCP/IP packets for the public telephone network, in Serial Line Interface Protocol (SLIP) format.

Before granting the user communication privileges, the Xyplex communications server passes the user's ID to the **Kerberos** server for authentication. Kerberos is the name of a security system, developed at MIT. Kerberos checks that the client is known to it. If so, it will send a ticket to Xyplex, letting it know that it should expect a client to contact it soon. Kerberos next sends a packet to the client system that is encrypted with the user's password. Inside of that packet is the same ticket that was sent to Xyplex. The logon application on the client will prompt the user for his or her password and use it to decrypt the packet from Kerberos. At this point, the workstation is ready to contact Xyplex, which will, in turn, give the client access to resources on the network. If authorized, the user can freely interact with authorized site network servers [Malamud, 1992].

The IBM Boca Raton site utilizes several T1 lines to service interconnections to other IBM locations. The lines are used to communicate with several mainframe systems located there. SNA and TCP/IP are used to transmit data from and to the mainframe applications. Client/server traffic using NetBIOS protocol can also be transported over these lines. The NetBIOS protocol is **encapsulated** within SNA frames by a program called LTLW—LAN to LAN over WAN.

IBM Boca's Clients

Each PC or workstation on site is equipped with a 16 Mbps token-ring adapter card. When connected by cable to one of the more than 10,000 "plug 'n go" token-ring ports, the PC is able to communicate on the site network. It is recognized by its unique identifier on the token-ring card by other PCs on its LAN and by the network's bridges when it attempts to transmit data from LAN to LAN. Chapter 4 discusses Boca's clients in detail.

IBM Boca's Server Farm

The IBM Boca Raton Server Farm is a collection of IBM Personal System/2 and RISC System/6000 server systems, centrally managed by a team of server administrators. It is completely described in Chapter 5. From a network perspective, it is located near the major network **points of presence** (connection ports). This ensures that there is sufficient flexibility in attaching the servers to the network. Currently, the Server Farm is organized into six server groups, with each group connected to a single 16 Mbps token-ring LAN segment. Each of these six LAN segments is bridged to each of the three primary network backbone rings. If any of the servers in the Server Farm can be identified as providing service for a specific campus area, its server group will also be bridged directly to that associated campus ring. Figure 6.15 provides some statistics about the Boca Raton Network.

Computer networks have become the assembly line, warehouse, and delivery system for many organizations, so networks deserve all the management resources once lavished on the forges and furnaces of heavy industry [Derfler, 1993].

What Is a Network Management System?

A network management system is like a ring of secret agents who uncover facts about their environment and report the important facts

Token Ring LANs	166
Backbone	6
Campus	24
Floor	128
Miscellaneous	8
Token Ring Adapters	8,542
Bridges	320
Routers	6
Gateways	15

Figure 6.15 The IBM Boca Network Stats

back to their ring leader in a private code. In actuality, a network management system is composed of software **agents**, installed on all key network components (hubs, servers, bridges, routers, gateways, and clients) that report back to a common manager program in a network management protocol. The agents monitor network events (e.g., network traffic) and update a local database with accumulated information. When polled by the common manager, the agents transmit the accumulated information to the common manager program. The common manager will display network status and enable an administrator to perform his duties.

Most network management systems use a special communications protocol to transfer management information. The most common network management protocol is called **SNMP**, the Simple Network Management Protocol. It was developed for use in TCP/IP networks by the Internet Engineering Task Force (**IETF**). Its use is broad and growing among network component vendors. It is simple to create agents that use it, and it has relatively low overhead in terms of component performance impact. The next most common network management protocol is called **CMIP**, the Common Management Interface Protocol. It is part of the International Organization for Standardization (ISO) Open Systems Interconnect (OSI) specification. However, CMIP is difficult to program and has relatively higher overhead than SNMP. It is much less widely supported.

The Holy Grail of network management systems is to have one that can handle the diversity of today's network equipment or to have a "manager-of-managers" that can gather up the critical information from a set of subservient managers. This manager-of-managers or MOM would then present, on a single network management display, the status of all events of interest in the network.

Why Do You Need a Network Management System?

Simply stated, a network management system is required because keeping a complex, client/server network up and running with good performance is virtually impossible without it. There are too many complex components that must seamlessly work together on a continuous basis, so problems are inevitable. Given that a large business depends on continuing stable network operations, investment in a network management system is compelling.

A Business Research Group survey of 400 MIS executives and network administrators at Fortune 500 and mid-sized companies indicated increasing interest in enterprise network-management systems. Eighty percent of the survey's respondents plan to implement an integrated network-management system over the next two years [*PC Week*, March 1993].

Unfortunately, in today's rapidly growing client/server environment, no single network management system will, by itself, provide all the necessary functions. Interoperability and integration become top priority because the current network management tools are fragmented and the only "integration is provided by the human mind" [Caruso, 1990]. Existing network tools were developed piecemeal, and do not help with management of the total network. Either system redundancy or extra technicians have been previously employed to support complex networks [Adams, 1991].

Because of this lack of integration, it is difficult to recruit and retain qualified network management personnel. Therefore, staff costs are becoming an ever-larger percentage of the network support budget, running almost 30 percent of total expenses [Caruso, 1990]. Two thirds of the cost of a complex network is daily operation [Adams, 1991]. A major goal is to maintain end-user service without staff explosions, despite growth and technological changes [Terplan, 1992]. The IBM Boca Raton Network Team is composed of 11 members, 8 regular employees and 3 contractors. They are highly skilled and dedicated, and very hard to replace!

Because many vendor-specific network management systems exist with little integration, it is difficult to have any single point of operational control or platform to allow automation of management functions. Complex client/server networks use a mixture of vendor-specific management protocols. Heaven for the user would be to have a well-defined interface between the network manager and its elements, so that they can be bought from any vendor and managed as one network [Mazda, 1991]. In IBM Boca Raton, a large kit bag of software and hardware tools are employed to keep the network up and running. These will be discussed later in this section.

Industry standards groups are working to standardize network management. The OSI (Open Systems Interconnection) Management Framework formally describes network management with the following five major categories:

1. **Fault Management** is concerned with determining where a fault is in the network and quickly fixing it. The user wants fast and reliable problem resolution and to be informed of status promptly.

Faults need to be tracked and recorded in a database to ensure completed work and statistics for management review. Proper network design with redundant hardware components and network pathways avoid or minimize a fault's impact [Stallings, 1993]. Critical network components, such as intelligent hubs, mission critical servers, and routers, should provide remote management communication with both **in-band** and **out-of-band** communication channels, ideally. In-band means on the site network itself. Out-of-band means on another communications network (e.g., the public telephone network). This is the highest priority category.

2. **Accounting management** deals with tracking network usage for purposes of properly billing users for their fair share. The network management system must be able to specify the accounting data to be gathered, compute charges, and create reports. A key responsibility is determining if the network has been misused by analyzing system usage data. This can improve network upgrade planning [Stallings, 1993]. Asset management is an additional important requirement in this area. The network management system should be able to identify and track all network components (including client PCs and workstations). This should include software as well as hardware to form an inventory database. The creation of a continuously updated inventory database is important for configuration management as well.

3. **Configuration and name management** deals with the network management tools that start up or shut down all or part of a network. These tools must communicate with network components (hubs, bridges, routers, gateways, and servers) to change their configurations, based on network congestion or problems. The tools must maintain an accurate map of the complete network configuration. From the user's perspective, all of these activities should be behind the scenes. If configuration action is required, however, users need to be notified [Stallings, 1993]. A complete network inventory database is required to support configuration management. The database should identify when a system or software needs to be replaced, repaired, fine-tuned, or upgraded to a new operating system or application [Francis, 1993].

4. **Performance management** covers the ongoing evaluation of the network to monitor service levels, identify bottlenecks, and report on

trends to management. Key indicators are resource usage (storage space in a critical gateway), processing delays, and throughput measurements (that fraction of the network capacity that is actually used) [Terplan, 1992]. Performance management tools provide statistics to network administrators for problem resolution, such as adjusting routing tables (to minimize traffic congestion at an overloaded network juncture) or expansion of network resources [Stallings, 1993].

5. **Security management** is an area that is concerned with the security of the network at all levels. The security management tools must offer functions to generate, store, and distribute encryption keys to protect confidential user data, maintain and distribute user passwords for network access authentication, monitor for viruses and take corrective action, monitor and control access to network management data, and maintain security logs [Stallings, 1993].

Network Management in IBM Boca Raton

Of necessity, IBM Boca Raton must use a large number of network management applications and tools to manage the network. There are two major reasons for this. First, the products that make up the network are diverse, and no single management system supports all requirements. Second, network management technology for client/server, heterogeneous networks is relatively immature. There are pieces missing, so sometimes local tools must be developed or specific tools purchased to cover all the bases.

Figure 6.16 maps the major components of the IBM Boca Raton network to the five major network management categories. This is a good tool to understand the relative completeness of your network management systems, as well. The numbers in parenthesis in each table item cross-reference to one of the many network management applications in use in IBM Boca Raton. A brief description of each follows.

IBM Boca Raton's Network Management Applications

In IBM Boca Raton, multiple network management applications manage different parts of the network. Let's get the big picture by walking

	Faults	Accounting	Configuration	Performance	Security
PC Clients (OS/2, IBM PC)	User calls Help Desk. (21) (22)	Automated inventory. No charging based on usage. (24)	User controlled. Network installation for apps (pull), OS/2 (push). (31)	User controlled	Power-on password. Anti-virus program. (30)
Workstation Clients (AIX, RS/6000)	User calls Help Desk. (21) (22)	Manual inventory. No charging based on usage.	User controlled. Network software distribution (push) (32)	User controlled	Power-on password.
Servers - PS/2	Network based continuous monitoring. (17) (18) (19) (21)	Manual inventory	Remote startup, shutdown on alerts. Manual software maintenance. (18) (19)	Performance monitoring as required (OS/2 tools)	Checks invalid logons. Anti-virus program. Badge-locked room. (30)
Servers - RS/6000	Network based continuous monitoring. (20) (21)	Manual inventory	Remote startup, shutdown on alerts. Manual software maintenance. (20)	Performance monitoring as required (AIX tools) (20)	Check invalid logons and access levels. Badge-locked room. (20)
LAN Segments, Ports	Trace tools isolate breakage. (14) (21) (23)	Online database for cable drops. (28) (29)	See Hub section	Network based continuous monitoring (14) (21) (23) (24) (25) (27)	Standard security practices on site.
Hubs	Network based continuous monitoring.(8230 hubs only). (14)	Manual inventory	Remote startup, shutdown. (8230 hubs only) (14)	Network based continuous monitoring (8230 hubs only) (14)	Badge-locked room.
Bridges	Network based continuous monitoring. (14)	Automated inventory (26)	Remote startup, software maintenance, shutdown, and backup. (26)	Network based continuous monitoring. (14)	Badge-locked room.
Routers	Network based continuous monitoring. (15)	Manual inventory	Manual startup, shutdown, software maintenance.	Network based continuous monitoring. (15)	Badge-locked room.
Gateways (offsite WAN interfaces) to Mainframes, Internet, etc.	Network based continuous monitoring. (20)	Manual inventory	Remote startup, shutdown on alerts. Automated backup. (20)	Network based continuous monitoring. (20)	Firewall to prevent unauthorized access.

Figure 6.16 Network Management Map—IBM Boca Raton

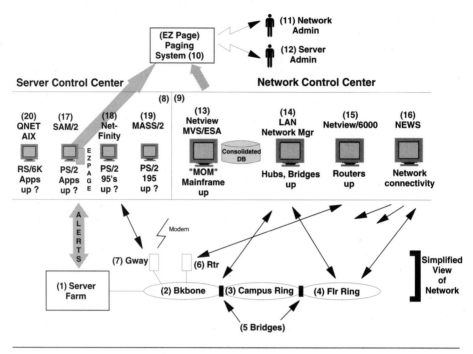

Figure 6.17   IBM Boca Raton's Network Management System

through Figure 6.17. At the bottom of the figure you see a simplified view of the network, consisting of the Server Farm (1), the backbone token rings (2), the campus token rings (3), and the floor token rings (4). At the juncture of the rings are the bridges (5), which interconnect the rings. The routers (6) are shown connecting to the backbone rings. The gateway systems (7) are also shown connecting to the backbone rings.

The Server Farm (1) is shown communicating information (alerts) to a set of four applications (see descriptions below) in the Server Control Center (8). They monitor the servers to determine if they and their applications are up and running. The Network Control Center (9) has three major applications (see the descriptions that follow) that monitor the network infrastructure (hubs, bridges, routers, connectivity) and a fourth that serves as the MOM as well as determining if the mainframes are up and running. Both the Server Control Center and the Network Control Center communicate with a paging system (10). Server alerts page the server administrator on call (11). Network infrastructure alerts page the network administrator on call (12).

IBM NetView MVS/ESA

The manager-of-managers (MOM) in the system is the mainframe-based NetView application (13), an IBM program product. NetView is the central collection point for network data. NetView screens are dynamic, indicating alerts (e.g., faults) as they arise.

With NetView MVS/ESA, alerts are viewed as they are collected. By using host applications such as Network Performance Monitor (NPM) and Service Level Reporter (SLR). the user can define and view reports for problem isolation and trending. Network operations personnel monitor the host-attached display and react to alerts.

IBM LAN Network Manager (LNM)

The LNM (14), an IBM program product, is the heart of the Boca LAN management system. LNM is a network management program and problem determination aid for a network that is composed of one or more IBM token-ring segments. LNM provides fault, configuration, and performance management for the intelligent hubs (8230, 8260), bridges, and LAN segments. It runs on OS/2 and communicates with NetView MVS/ESA. LNM allows user to monitor remote LAN segments, run path tests, display LAN configurations, and modify bridge parameters. LAN Network Manager is "widely regarded as the best network management tool for token-ring LANs" [Davidson, 1992].

Individual LAN segments are managed by LNM via communication with the network's bridges. IBM 8228 passive (nonintelligent) hubs are managed manually. IBM 8230 intelligent hubs are remotely managed by LNM.

IBM AIX NetView/6000

NetView/6000 (15) is a RISC- and AIX-based IBM program product whose primary focus is the management of network resources, using SNMP (SNMP is an industry-standard network management communication protocol). NetView/6000 includes several management applications, encompassing fault monitoring and diagnosis, performance monitoring, and network configuration applications. It passes data to NetView MVS/ESA. NetView/6000 provides an graphical user interface on the display console in the Network Control Center. It provides a dynamic graphical topology map of the network and allows access to network management applications and diagnostics facilities. It is used to monitor the routers and the TCP/IP name servers on the network.

Network Early Warning System (NEWS)

NEWS (16) is a locally developed application that confirms connectivity across the site network. The NEWS display is prominent in the Network Control Center, colorfully showing outages on the screen. NEWS is bottom-line oriented—it tells the network administrator if the **data-link layer** is up or down on rings in the network. The data-link layer is the layer in the OSI protocol stack just above the physical layer. All protocols provide a data-link layer. NEWS records any outages in a DB2 for OS/2 database and automatically generates a page for network administrators 24 hours a day if a problem is encountered.

SAM/2

The System Application Monitor/2 (17) is a locally developed application that monitors application activity on the PS/2 servers in the Server Farm. If SAM/2 determines that an application session is down, it will generate a page to the server administrators and notify the Help Desk. SAM/2 also monitors hard disk storage usage and will generate an alert if a high-water mark is exceeded.

IBM NetFinity

NetFinity (18) consists of two IBM program products (NetFinity Services and NetFinity Manager) that are designed to manage PC-based systems (Intel 386SX and higher processors). NetFinity Services provides configuration details and resource monitoring information to the NetFinity Manager. NetFinity Manager supports a remote management console to one or more PC systems (clients, servers) for system restart, system monitoring, and remote session. NetFinity is used to remotely manage the PS/2 Server 95s in the Server Farm. During normal working hours, server administrators monitor the NetFinity console in the Server Control Center. Outside working hours, server administrators are equipped at home with NetFinity Manager on their home PC for remote access.

NetFinity can also be used to gather PC inventory and configuration data in a central database and to provide Help Desk personnel with remote session capability for users with PC problems. Remote session capability means that the Help Desk support person can remotely view and control the calling user's PC to take corrective action if required. See Chapter 7 for a discussion of Boca's Help Desk support.

IBM MASS/2

The Maximum Availability and Support System/2 (MASS/2) system management software (19), an IBM program product, allows administrators to monitor, control, diagnose, and configure PS/2 Server 195 systems from a remote workstation. It uses the RMP (Remote Management Processor card) in the 195 for remote communications with its built-in modem.

QNET

QNET (20) and a suite of AIX-based locally developed tools monitor application activity on the RS/6000 servers in the Server Farm. If these tools determine that an application session is down, they generate a page to the server administrators.

The network administrator's kit bag is by no means exhausted! There are an additional set of tools that are required for a variety of administrative activities.

Network General's Sniffer

The Sniffer (21) is a powerful, user-friendly, network tracing and monitoring device. The Sniffer has been useful in tracking **broadcast storms** (an incorrect packet broadcast onto a network causes multiple systems to respond all at once, typically with equally incorrect packets, which causes the storm to grow exponentially in severity), locating problematic adapters, locating incorrectly configured adapters, and locating bandwidth hogs. The Sniffer product comes as a portable unit and as a remote unit with a console. The IBM Boca site has invested in portable Sniffers for use in shooting network problems.

Protect

Protect (22) is a locally developed application that plays a major role in preventing incorrectly configured workstations from adversely affecting the site's network. The Protect program continuously polls the network for unauthorized adapters and automatically removes them from the network when found. The primary use is to remove duplicate gateway addresses and name server addresses.

OS2ping

Every IBM Boca network support person carries a ping program with him when troubleshooting problems. The locally-developed OS2ping program (23) is used to search the network for a specified adapter address. OS2ping results determine network paths, connectivity, adapter type, performance, hop counts, and network capacity.

IBM LAN Station Manager (LSM)

LSM (24), an IBM program product, measures ring utilization and collects asset management data. Each LAN segment on site has a PS/2 running LSM reporting the relative utilization of the ring's bandwidth to the LAN Network Manager (LNM) (14) and Rupoll (25) applications. LSM is also installed on all PC client systems to report hardware and software configurations of each client to LNM. The data is stored in a DB2 for OS/2 inventory database.

Rupoll

Rupoll (25) is a locally developed application that works with LNM and LSM. Rupoll automatically polls specified ring segments for LSM devices at specified periods and stores the results in a DB2 for OS/2 database.

IBM LAN Bridge Manager/2 (LBM/2)

LBM/2 (26), an IBM program product, simplifies the software installation, backup, and configuration management of the site's bridges. This includes bridge code, filters, drivers, and configuration files. A network administrator can remotely manage hop counts, thresholds, and bridge passwords with LBM/2. All bridge configuration files are automatically backed up on one central server system by LBM/2.

IBM Trace and Performance (TAP)

The TAP program (27), an IBM program product, has two major capabilities: protocol tracing and bandwidth monitoring. It is primarily used on the site to monitor the available bandwidth on the site's backbones. Bandwidth usage is displayed in a speedometer type format that is easy to read from any spot in the Network Control Center. The measured bandwidth data can be printed for easy historical viewing.

Regional Information Database System (RIDS)

RIDS (28) is a mainframe database system that contains a record of each authorized network user and their respective network addresses (e.g., TCP/IP address and adapter address).

Boca Cable Tracking System (BCTS)

All cabling ports in user offices are labeled for problem determination. All port locations are cross referenced with office locations and stored in the central database called the Boca Cable Tracking System (29).

IBM AntiVirus/2

IBM AntiVirus/2 (30) is an internal, comprehensive antivirus program for DOS and OS/2 systems developed by IBM Research. It is installed on all PC-based clients and servers.

IBM NetView Distribution Manager/2

NetView DM/2 (31) is an IBM program product that is used to distribute OS/2 operating system code, operating system services, and applications over a network.

IBM SoftDist/6000

SoftDist/6000 (32) is an application used to distribute AIX operating system code and applications over a network.

The Network Support Process

The local Network Control Center staff of seven includes four problem resolution personnel, one designer, one planner, and one TCP/IP administrator. Additional support is provided as needed from the Southeast Region center in Raleigh, North Carolina.

The problem resolution personnel monitor the Network Control Center consoles. Figure 6.18 identifies each console. Figure 6.19 is an actual

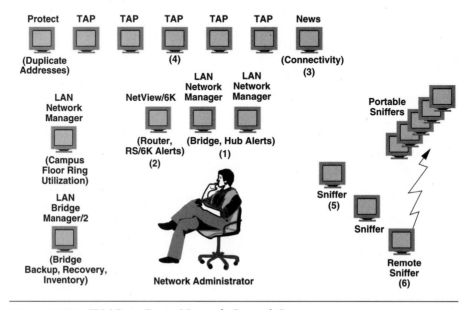

Figure 6.18   IBM Boca Raton Network Control Center

Courtesy International Business Machines Corporation

Figure 6.19 IBM Boca Raton Network Control Center Photograph

photograph of the center. There are two LAN Network Manager consoles (1), which display alerts from the network bridges and hubs, and utilization of the campus and floor rings. There is one NetView/6000 console (2), which displays alerts from the routers and AIX gateway systems. There is one NEWS console (3), which graphically displays network connectivity problems across the network. There are five TAP consoles (4), which display backbone utilization (the sixth backbone is a collapsed backbone). There are two local Sniffer consoles (5), which can diagnose problems on the site backbone rings. Finally, there is a remote Sniffer console (6), which can communicate with any one of the six portable Sniffers (stored in wiring closets across the site) to diagnose problems on the campus and floor rings.

If the network administrator sees an alert requiring attention on one of the Network Control Center application consoles, he first attempts to resolve the problem remotely. If remote action is not sufficient, a formal problem is opened in the Network Control Center database and forwarded to the specific owner of the network device for follow-up and resolution.

If a user is having network problems and needs assistance, he calls the Help Desk. The Help Desk attempts to resolve the problem with the user. If not resolved, the user's call is forwarded to network administration for resolution.

During off-hours, with no one monitoring the Network Control Center, an alert will generate a telephone page automatically to the network administrator on call. He or she will then come to the site to correct the problem. In the case of a PS/2 server alert, the server administrator will either come in or attempt to resolve the problem from her PC at home. If a user calls the Help Desk with a problem, the support personnel can dial a single number to reach the network support person on call (they rotate usage of a single cellular phone).

In addition to using the portable Sniffer when required, the network problem resolution personnel carry a special service diskette when they are troubleshooting a problem. It contains a set of network diagnosis applications that can identify connectivity problems and determine if systems are active or inactive on the network (e.g., OS2ping). Finally, each carries a radiophone (a telephone with walkie-talkie features) for voice communication and a pager.

Two common network administration problems are broadcast storms and **beaconing**. Broadcast storms, caused by a misaddressed packet of information, are a network manager's nightmare as they can negatively affect network performance. TCP/IP broadcast storms are minimized by installing an IP address range filter (a program that checks the address against a legal range) on the network's bridges. This means that if the IP address (network address in TCP/IP-speak) is not within the acceptable range, the bridge throws the packet away, thereby reducing the storm's severity. Similarly, NetBIOS broadcast messages can cause storms. Again, filters are used on the bridges to discard errant packets.

Beacons are most commonly caused by user PCs coming up on a token ring at the wrong speed (e.g., 4 Mbps vs. 16 Mbps). This brings the entire floor ring down and causes a beacon state. Violating adapters are immediately removed when connected to the network intelligent hubs (8230s). This is done by sending a special frame to the token-ring adapter that shuts it down. Violating adapters on nonintelligent hubs (e.g., 8228s) are much tougher to track down. This makes the case for the use of intelligent hubs quite compelling.

Although complex to manage with its broad set of tools, the IBM Boca Raton Network is very stable. This is a tribute to the dedication and skills of the network support team.

On a network level, the ability of the CPU to do work must be balanced with the ability of the network to deliver the work and take back results [Malamud, 1992].

Performance and Performance Modeling

The performance of a complex network is very challenging to measure and even more so to predict. The variables are many: physical wiring, internetwork architecture and connecting systems (hubs, bridges, routers, and gateways), servers' hardware and software, clients' hardware and software, the network operating system, the application mix, and the number of active users.

The operation of a complex network is very similar to the operation of a complex operating system on a single PC. In the design of the operating system, a great deal of attention is paid to the average time the system requires to perform services for its application programs, as this has a dramatic effect on the overall performance of the applications. These services include input/output (typically from the hard disk), the processing of application instructions, and memory management. Simply stated, applications should run on a network operating system as if running on a standalone system with a conventional operating system.

Some current network operating systems actually provide faster application support than a conventional operating system. For example, if a network file server has a very-high-speed hard disk coupled with a large amount of buffer memory to cache data, response time for a client system requesting data may be faster than getting the data from the client's own hard disk! This is yet another reason why client/server computing has become so popular. A secondary observation is that by providing shared access to data and applications without any loss of performance, client/server computing provides a cost-effective means to expand the resources of individual PCs.

Network management software plays a key role in real-time performance monitoring and management, as we have just seen. This is supplemented by specialized network Sniffers and analyzers that can be used to monitor network traffic.

As you plan a new network or plan to upgrade an existing one, a predictive **performance model** is useful to determine architectural and implementation limits of all network components. A performance model is a software program that describes the operation of a complex system and then simulates its operation for the purpose of determining performance characteristics and bottlenecks. This "what if" analysis can be used to identify bottlenecks or suggest alternative designs that simple specification analysis will not reveal. According to the Gartner Group [Gartner, 1993], the greatest increase in LAN network operations job function has occurred in performance modeling.

Van Kirk [1993] recommends that performance modeling focus on application impact. He points out that in a client/server environment, processing is split between client and server. "An application that performs most of its processing on the client may create what looks like a heavy utilization curve. In reality, the bulk of the usage occurs when users initially load the program"—at this point users will accept a long pause. However, a highly interactive application, that is, accessing a shared database, may need a "faster pipe."

An analysis of network bandwidth utilization in 1993 by the Boca Raton network administrators predicted that network utilization would grow substantially as the site's users migrated to client/server applications in 1994. The network backbones' average utilization during prime shift was 15 to 25 percent at that time. It was estimated that average utilization could be as high as 60 percent of the available bandwidth by June 1994. This was deemed to be too high for the current network, so enhancement alternatives were considered. The initial choices were to upgrade the site's backbone networks from 16 Mbps to 100 Mbps with **FDDI** (Fiber Distributed Data Interface, a 100 Mbps protocol for fiber-optic LANs) or ATM (Asynchronous Transfer Mode, a new very-high-speed switched communication protocol and supporting hardware). Because of the large investment involved (greater than $1 million in capital), the Network Team decided to invest in development of a network performance model to get a better prediction of bandwidth utilization growth.

The IBM Boca Raton site had an in-house team of experts available to tackle this assignment: the IBM PC Company's Performance Analysis organization, normally assigned to analyzing PC Company product performance (i.e., PCs and servers).

The top priority was to determine the backbone ring utilization and end-user response impact of the new client/server applications. Lotus Notes, as the replacement for OfficeVision e-mail was chosen to be primary application for analysis.

First, the SES Workbench simulation modeling application was selected to be the tool to perform the analysis. SES Workbench ran on AIX on an RS/6000, had built-in features to support a complex network, and had an easy to use GUI. After that, three efforts began in parallel.

1. A model of the IBM Boca Raton network was created on SES Workbench. The model considered the following network components: backbone rings, campus rings, a representative sample of floor rings, bridges, routers, servers, PCs, and external links.

2. The network bridge traffic data from the NetView mainframe database and carefully measured IBM Trace and Performance data were analyzed and reduced for input into the simulation model. This was the most challenging part of the entire project, because of the large volume of data requiring analysis.

3. A study comparing OfficeVision/VM e-mail traffic versus Lotus Notes e-mail traffic was undertaken. It concluded that for simple text messages, Lotus Notes e-mail traffic was equivalent to Office-Vision/VM traffic. This told the Network Team that, at least in the short run, they should not expect too much of an increase in e-mail traffic with the migration from OfficeVision to Lotus Notes. However, they would need to prepare for an increase in traffic as the users started to use the **rich text** features of Notes mail and databases. Rich text is a term describing the capability of a document or a part of a document to contain text, graphics, scanned images, audio, and full-motion video data. The use of rich text in Notes documents, including features such as multiple fonts and tables, greatly increase the data volume even as it increases the communication quality of the document.

After these tasks were completed, the model was run against the current traffic load on the network. It was valid to within 3 percent of actual measurements. By increasing the simulated traffic to the level anticipated with full use of Notes features, it was determined that with the simple addition of another site backbone ring, the network would continue to provide adequate performance. Therefore, the number of site backbones was increased from five to six in June, 1994.

In addition to providing the basis for a critical decision, the model established a base for future "what-if" analysis. The Network Team is now positioned to more easily project future network demands and measure the adequacy of alternative solutions.

Security is more than just protecting your own assets. It is a fundamental aspect of being a good corporate citizen. [Malamud, 1992]

The Challenge of Security Management in Client/Server Networks

Network security is concerned with controlling access to the network, antivirus protection, protecting the confidentiality of the network's data, and physical protection of the network assets. All businesses, large and small, must address these items seriously, if they use their client/server computing environment to process and store their critical business information. The risks of data loss, data corruption, and data theft are too great without well-defined security measures and processes. The following sections address each of the major aspects of network security.

Access Control

Access control is usually maintained by requiring users to supply their ID (identifier) and password prior to using the network. Passwords can be stolen and methodically attacked, but with the right controls (nontriviality, frequent changes) can serve as an effective access control barrier. A recommended secondary measure is the maintenance of access request logs by server administration for a well-defined period. If unauthorized access is suspected, this can help pinpoint the problem. Access control was much more straightforward in a mainframe-centric environment, where a single ID and password guarded access to all applications and data. In the typical client/server environment, there is no single gate of entry for user access control.

In IBM Boca Raton, the user first logs on to the network through his assigned **domain server** (OS/2 LAN Server establishes a set of servers as a domain with a specific server, called the domain server, handling user logons). Each application then separately prompts the user for an application-specific ID and password. However, users would clearly prefer the single ID, single password approach for the entire environment. As a secondary measure, all users are encouraged to employ the timed keyboard lockout feature of OS/2, which will automatically prevent access if no key is hit within a specified period.

More challenging than granting secure access to on-site users is granting remote access to users. More challenging still is exchanging information with vendors and suppliers, or communicating with them via e-mail, or exchanging files with worldwide Internet users. In the discussion regarding IBM Boca's WANs, examples of each was discussed. In conjunction with any remote access control measure you employ, a documented, well-defined process by which each extracompany link is approved and established is heartily recommended.

Antivirus Protection

A computer virus is a software program that replicates itself on computer systems by incorporating itself into other programs, sometimes for the purpose of damaging the integrity of the host computer system. Damage can be in the form of data corruption and data loss. Computer viruses are introduced into a client/server computing environment through inadvertent receipt and use of an infected program. Viruses can be detected by special-purpose programs that can recognize a virus' unique patterns in the software programs on a computer system. In IBM Boca Raton, the IBM AntiVirus/2 application is installed, which periodically checks both client and server computer systems' hard disk drives for the presence of harmful viruses. It is highly recommended that this become a standard practice to protect your critical business information.

Protecting Data Confidentiality

Data protection means encrypting data such that they is not interpretable by a casual or spying user. How the data are transmitted and the transmission medium dictate whether data should be encrypted, and, if so, how.

For transfer within a site network secure from unauthorized access, most user data can be transmitted without encryption. For confidential personnel or critical business information, software-based encryption methods should be employed.

The most commonly used method is called **DES** (Data Encryption Standard). DES is a widely used, government sponsored, data encryption method that scrambles data into a nearly unbreakable code for transmission over a network. The encryption key has over 72 quadrillion combinations and is randomly chosen. This is the method used by Lotus Notes if data encryption is selected for a Notes database. The encryption key is, of course, transmitted only to authorized users!

For transfer over a WAN, where complete access control is not assured, encryption of all data is common (and recommended). All data is encrypted on leased T1 communications links leaving the Boca Raton site. A high-speed DES encryptor/decryptor is installed at each end of the WAN [Davidson 1992].

Physical Security

Physical security is also more challenging in a client/server environment than a mainframe-centric one, but can be readily solved. Simply put, you should centralize all major network points of presence (campus ring and backbone ring ports), the network control center, bridges, routers, gateways, and the server farm in a secure room. This is precisely what was done at the IBM Boca Raton site. With a badge-lock door entry reader, only authorized people can visit the keys to the network kingdom!

A secondary problem is securing the client system assets spread across the site. Critical data can be strewn about on portable PCs and workstations. The solution is a consistent program of perimeter security, door locks, and user education.

A Clearer Vision for the Future

You should set near-term and long-term goals for a site network infrastructure. It should reflect an understanding of technology trends and what new technologies are ready for public consumption. Following are some broad goals to consider for the future.

Standards

Standards arising from the actions of standards-setting bodies, such as the **International Organization for Standardization (ISO)** or the **Institute of Electrical and Electronic Engineers (IEEE)**, are typically called open standards, or standards that offer every vendor access and level the playing field. An example is the OSI Reference Model, the standard for describing computer network architectures. Some de facto standards, or standards that arise from their widespread acceptance in the marketplace, also qualify as open standards. An example is the so-called **ISA** bus for PCs. It was originally published as the system bus for the IBM Personal Computer AT. ISA stands for Industry-Standard Architecture. Sometimes de facto standards are published by standards-setting bodies and become open standards. An example is the standard for Ethernet local area networks (IEEE 802.3), which was originally developed by Xerox.

Most vendors favor open standards because they are easy to duplicate, are defined by the interfaces of components (hardware or software), are stable and consistent, enable price-competitive products, and allow alternatives for customers. This is in contrast to proprietary standards which are controlled by a single vendor, costly to duplicate, and reduce customer alternatives [Gagliardi, 1994].

For much of its history, IBM has been in the enviable position of being able to establish de facto standards for information technology almost at will. With their mere introduction, new IBM products, data formats, protocols, and architectures have brought forth an onrush of add-ons, copies, and enabling applications. The most recent notable example was the IBM PC in 1981, which quickly displaced the Apple personal computer as the leading personal computer and established an industry. The introduction of the PS/2 family of personal computers with Micro Channel architecture marked the end of this era. Led by Compaq, a "Gang of Nine" refused to embrace Micro Channel and offered an alternative in the form of the EISA bus.

Recognizing the strong industry trends and customer requirements for multivendor solutions built on industry standard requirements, IBM has responded with its Open Blueprint. Open Blueprint is a framework for organizing products and applications in an open, distributed environment. It is also a guide for developers to provide function to integrate and operate with other products. Figure 6.20 shows the base framework in which IBM and other vendor products can fit. IBM's Worldwide Client/Server marketing is dedicated to providing services and multivendor solutions, based on open standards, for customers worldwide.

Six important areas for standards in information technology are **communication services, system management services**, database, software development tools, user interface, and operating systems [Tapscott, 1993]. It is important that you remain aware of the standards and their

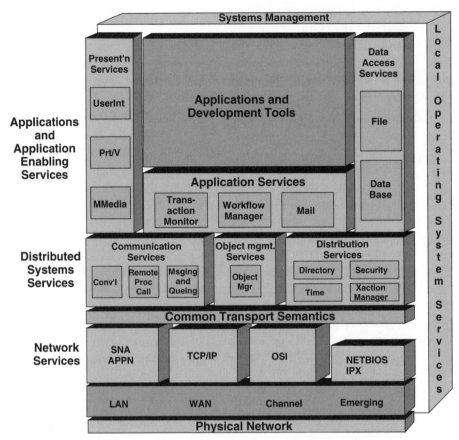

Courtesy International Business Machines Corporation

Figure 6.20 IBM's Open Blueprint

evolution in these areas to make critical decisions regarding products and services that become part of your client/server infrastructure.

The most fundamental standards that can affect the success of your client/server environment are the communication and system management services. The reason is simple—they affect *every* user and *every* support person in fundamental ways. Communication services means the software and protocols that move data across the network. Today's leading communication service for complex networks is TCP/IP, an industry standard communication protocol.

A higher-level, or next-generation, communication service is called the

Distributed Computing Environment (DCE). DCE defines a set of software services that simplify application development for complex networking environments and improves network data access and administration.

Network management services means software and hardware service tools that enable a network administrator to manage a network (e.g., diagnose and repair faults, measure performance, and resolve bottlenecks). The Simple Network Management Protocol (SNMP) is the de facto industry standard for communication of network status, problems, and so on between network components. It is widely supported by most network component vendors.

A Higher-Speed Network

Looking at the rapid changes occurring in networking technology, it appears that there will be an unending stream of new products capable of delivering higher and higher network bandwidth to users. Happily, this coincides with user requirements for higher bandwidth for applications using graphics and multimedia.

Figure 6.21 summarizes the IBM Boca Raton multimedia requirements for 1995. Lotus Notes, the primary e-mail application, will be increasingly used for transmission and storage of graphics, image, audio, and video data streams. It is estimated that this will double the network traffic impact in the coming years. Video-on-demand applications are planned to be used for delivering education to users desktops in the future. Each session requires a 1.2 Mbps compressed digital video data stream from a video server to a user's PC. (A single computer display image is 2.5 to 6 million bits. It must be refreshed 30 times per second to appear correct to the human eye. This requires 75 Mbps, at minimum, if the data is uncompressed! Therefore, only a portion of the screen is used and the data is compressed to reduce traffic.) This data must be delivered in real time to maintain the video image. Person-to-person videoconferencing from office to office is doubly demanding, requiring up to a 2.5 Mbps of network bandwidth to support real-time communications—this is over 15 percent of the available bandwidth in a 16 Mbps network for just one user-to-user session! Note that the Network Team has carefully limited the number of users for video-on-demand and videoconferencing due to the large portion of the network capacity required.

To meet this demand in your organization, you must focus on new networking products able to handle the new applications. One class of

Application	Function	Bandwidth Requirement	# Users
Lotus Notes	Groupware	Up to 2x current e-mail traffic	3,500
Video Servers	Video on Demand	1.2 Mbps per user session	1,500
Person-to-Person	Video Conferencing	2.5 Mbps per user session	20 Executives

Figure 6.21 IBM Boca Raton's Multimedia Requirements

new products that improve delivery of dedicated data streams to user PCs is the **switching hub,** as discussed previously. Some key features to consider when purchasing a hub are its performance when completely configured (some high-end hubs, like the IBM 8260, can support multiple, dissimilar LAN segments), upgradability to one or more switching technologies, and remote management (in-band or out-of-band) capabilities [McCusker, 1994].

Switching hubs make the current LAN cables more effective in delivering data to the user's systems at the speed capacity of the LAN adapter. However, this doesn't take into consideration the impact to the site backbone networks, which must handle an aggregate increase in overall network traffic due to new applications. To use the traditional plumbing analogy, the backbone pipe must be increased in capacity to handle the increased data flow from each of its contributing tributary LAN pipes. The answer must be new network devices that transmit data at much higher speeds.

The major technologies today supporting higher speeds networks include **FDDI** (Fiber Distributed Data Interface), **Fast Ethernet,** and **ATM** (Asynchronous Transfer Mode). FDDI is a mature protocol for 100 Mbps transmission over fiber-optic LANs. FDDI over UTP (unshielded twisted pair cabling) is a recent version that provides cost advantages over traditional FDDI, as it will run over less expensive cables. It is the conservative choice today for upgrading site backbone networks, as it is a mature technology with a large number of installed users. It is the high-speed protocol of choice where a collapsed backbone approach is infeasible. FDDI was a serious candidate to upgrade the Boca site's backbones in 1994. However, since the network performance analysis revealed that an additional 16 Mbps backbone was sufficient to tide the site over until

1995, the Network Team decided to wait for ATM product maturation and availability.

Fast Ethernet products operate at 100 Mbps. There are two competing approaches from different vendor camps. One is called 100VG-Any-LAN (IEEE 802.12); the other is called 100BaseX (IEEE 802.13). The protocols are still in the proposal stage to IEEE . Both require new adapters and hub upgrades, but will work over most existing cabling. Switching hubs, based on Fast Ethernet, are becoming available to provide even greater performance gains. Fast Ethernet is still an emerging technology and should be approached with caution at this time. However, because of the broad industry support for these new products, they should be seriously considered for future network upgrades and installations [Van Norman, 1994].

ATM is a **multiplexing** (assignment of the capacity of a data transmission media to several users) and switching technique that offers speeds from 25 Mbps to 1.2 Gbps over UTP or fiber-optic cables. A blizzard of products is available today from many vendors seeking to capture a share of this emerging market. This includes LAN adapters, switching hubs, and ATM switch products for WANs. ATM is still an immature technology. Many user installations are pilot tests only. However, ATM has a very bright future for both LAN and WAN network data transmission.

An ATM switching solution enables bandwidth to be dedicated between two devices without the data being visible to other devices. Devices can use this bandwidth with adapters of different speeds based upon application requirements. For example, a server may elect to use a higher-speed adapter than client workstations. ATM switching enables the guarantee of a specific quality of service for each connection.

Switching technology coupled to very-high-bandwidth media (e.g., fiber optics) is now emerging as the solution of choice for site backbones. In the near future, this same approach is expected to replace shared media solutions at all levels of the campus network; that is, dedicated bandwidth provided by high-speed switching will be the standard service to the client [*Infonetics*, January, 1994].

A major consideration in making a network upgrade decision is cost. A recent study [Van Norman, 1994] estimated the per port costs of several networking technologies (see Figure 6.22). The table illustrates a good approach to evaluating alternative technologies. It also points out the cost effectiveness of switching solutions over shared media solutions if high bandwidth is required.

A future IBM Boca Raton network design, in Figure 6.23, shows PCs

	Speed (Mbps)	1993 Cost per Port ($)	1993 Cost per 1 Mbps for 100 Users ($)
Standard Ethernet	10	250	25
Switched Ethernet	10	500	50
Fast Ethernet	100	500	5
Switched Fast Ethernet	100	1,000	10
FDDI over UTP	100	1,000	10
FDDI	100	2,000	20
ATM	155	9,000	58

Van Norman, "Client/Server Computing," Faulkner Information Services.

Figure 6.22   Cost Per Port Estimate

connected to intelligent hubs, which in turn connect to the next level of multiport, intelligent hubs. These hubs connect redundantly to a primary and a backup high-speed ATM switch, replacing the site's backbone rings. The site's campus rings would be collapsed onto the backplane of multiport routers and eliminated. The floor rings, with 170 to 220 drops per ring, would be segmented into several rings with fewer PCs on each. Product availability and bandwidth demand would determine when and if the Network Team introduces switching technology to the client systems.

A More Reliable Site Network

Network reliability doesn't just come from individually reliable components. It must be built in to the design. Key attributes includes modularity, redundancy, and manageability.

Modularity means that the network is separable into well-defined subnets. If there is a problem in a subnet, it can be isolated with little or no impact to the rest of the network. This is more difficult to perform with the current IBM Boca Raton network design. It is essentially a web of LAN segments interconnected by intelligent bridges, making it difficult to isolate a particular section. This approach effectively supports the nonroutable protocol NetBIOS, which is heavily used on the site—the LAN web appears to be a single network to the protocol. By dropping NetBIOS support, and standardizing on TCP/IP, the way is paved to create a

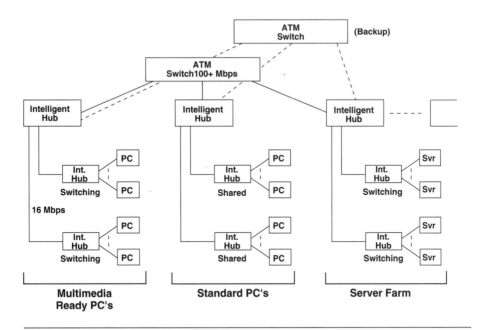

Figure 6.23 A Future IBM Boca Raton Network Design

subnet-based design in which each subnet is connected by a router to the rest of the network. The routers would transfer traffic effectively between subnets. In the event of a network fault, the offending subnet could be shut down without impacting the remainder of the network. Since most WAN (off-site) traffic uses TCP/IP, this would mean that a single communication protocol could be used for almost all traffic, a highly desirable goal. This simplifies network management and client and server software support by eliminating the complexity of an additional protocol (Net-BIOS).

Redundancy means that critical network components have a hot backup or are fault tolerant. This should include all hubs, bridges, gateways and routers. Uninterruptible and **conditioned** power is a must for your network components as well. The most important feature of line conditioners is that when power returns after an outage, power to the attached devices is kept off until the power system has settled. The line conditioners will also remove any electronic noise, line sags, line spikes, and brownouts.

A manageable network is a network with intelligent components able to communicate with the network management system. Passive or dumb components (e.g., an 8228 hub) have been eliminated in IBM Boca Raton. Your plan for a manageable network should include a plan to replace all dumb components with intelligent ones. An associated critical requirement is the availability of agents for these devices that all speak the same communication language, either SNMP or CMIP. A secondary requirement is for intelligent devices to support *both* in-band and out-of-band communications for alerts and remote management.

Where is my MOM?

I mean my Manager-of-Managers, of course. By investing only in devices that support a single management-communication protocol, the way is paved for a MOM to visit (and stay) at your site.

The goal is to have a single MOM receiving alerts, presenting status on a single display in the network control center, and allowing administrator action to be taken. Agents installed on all critical network components (e.g., bridges and routers) should report alerts back to the MOM, based on predetermined events and thresholds being reached (e.g., congestion at a bridge is excessive). The system should have the ability to attach to other applications that will automatically analyze traffic data to identify potential problems like network bottlenecks. Other applications should be able to analyze data trends, making recommendations to resolve potential problems. Applications should place all data in one central database combining availability, utilization, assets, and performance information. The MOM should be able to page network administration personnel based on predetermined thresholds and outages.

Based on recent IBM Networking Systems announcements, a suite of network management products will soon be available to support SNMP for communications on all devices in the IBM Boca Raton network. This will allow the site to standardize on SNMP in the future.

As the site network evolves to SNMP-managed devices, IBM NetView/6000 will become increasingly important. NetView/6000 has the ability to manage 8260 hubs, ATM products, routers, name servers, and TCP/IP hosts.

Another step is to move to an application like the internally developed **Global Service Coordinator (GSC)** as the IBM Boca Raton site MOM. GSC is an application that runs on the NetView/6000 application platform on an RS/6000. It receives events (a change in the state or status of a server or service detectable by any monitoring application) from network management applications, such as NetView/6000. GSC offers great flexibility in how it then communicates with network administrators. A graphical display interface is presented on the network console in the Network Control Center. E-mail messages can be sent. Alphanumeric pages can be initiated. Furthermore, this can be set up to repage or seek alternate administrators, if problems are not responded to within a defined period of time.

Higher-Speed Remote Communications

As bandwidth demands impact on-site networks, there is a similar impact on communication channels between sites (WANs) and between mobile users and their home site. Groupware applications, such as Lotus Notes, are designed to share information across these intersite communication channels. Depending on your organization's workflow, geographic dispersion, and need for current information, WAN data bandwidth requirements should be part of overall network planning.

According to Forrester Research [Callahan, 1993], frame relay is the protocol of choice for near-term public WAN solutions. Frame relay is a WAN service protocol for high-speed, long-distance digital data packet transmission. It is a simplification of the X.25 protocol but faster. Therefore, it is ideal to interconnect two LANs over a WAN and is replacing X.25 commercial services. It is designed to provide high-speed packet transmission, very low network delay, and efficient use of network bandwidth. From 64 Kbps to 1.544 Mbps speeds are defined. If greater WAN bandwidth is required, private WAN services (i.e., private leased high-speed lines) should be purchased. T1 and T3 services provide 1.54 Mbps up to 44 Mbps speeds.

The most volatile and exciting area of personal computing today is mobile computing. Many new technologies are reaching maturity this year and next that must be considered to improve your mobile environment. These include faster protocols, such as **PPP** (Point-to-Point Protocol) and **ISDN** (Integrated Services Digital Network), and wireless communication protocols such as CDPD. PPP is an underlying (physical-level) protocol for TCP/IP transmission over standard telephone lines. It is faster than the aging SLIP. ISDN is a standard protocol for integrating different types of data streams on a single digital network, such as data, video, and voice. It is just recently being offered by the telephone carriers of the world for faster data transmission over entirely digital telephone lines (most local public telephone connections use analog communication). Typical speed offered is 57 Kbps. Availability across the United States is still a limitation for this technology. A pilot project using ISDN for mobile client communications is underway in Boca Raton at this time.

Wireless communication offers challenges in availability of service, cost, performance, and security for the network administrator. There are a hodge-podge of wireless technologies exploding onto the market today: analog cellular, digital cellular, radio, satellite, and so on. Unfortunately, different protocols make it confusing to reach people with different devices. Services based on the cellular phone communications services appear to have the most promise. **CDPD** (Cellular Digital Packet Data) is a wireless communication protocol transporting digital data packets at 19.2 Kbps across idle channels on cellular telephone networks. However, despite the backing of the cellular industry, CDPD is still not widely available for wireless, mobile computing use. The same is true for other wireless services. Wireless communications charges are much higher than wired phone communications charges. Securing wireless communications means encrypting all transmissions, impacting performance and ease of use. Luckily, the Network Team has not been bombarded with user requests for service, so there are no firm plans to establish wireless communications for Boca mobile users in the near future! Unless there is a compelling business case and user demand, you should watch and wait too.

DCE

The **Distributed Computing Environment (DCE)**, as defined by the Open Software Foundation (OSF), is a major emerging software technology that offers compelling value for the large, complex network. DCE provides a comprehensive, integrated set of service programs that supports transparent communications and resource sharing across a complex network. These software services are to be used by client/server application developers to create robust, secure client/server applications. They are:

- **Security Services,** based on MIT's Kerberos, for user password authentication procedures.

- **Directory Services,** which provides a common naming convention for resources on the network. It provides a single naming model throughout the distributed computing environment, enabling users to identify network resources by name. With this universal naming system, users can locate and access servers, files, disks, or printers without specifying their physical location in the network [Faulkner, 1994].

- **Remote Procedure Call Services,** a communications mechanism that enables subprograms to execute on several servers in the network while an application is running.

- **Time Services,** which synchronizes all network resources

- **User Data Privacy Services,** which allows access to the DES encryption standard.

- **Data-Sharing Services,** including the Distributed File System, which provides a consistent interface to link files and data directories between workstations on the network.

- **Threads Services,** which enables programmers to develop concurrent programs, improving application performance with multiple processing of simultaneous requests (a thread is a single flow of control within a process or application program, analogous to a task in a multitasking program) [Faulkner, 1994].

DCE works transparently on applications on both LANs and WANs. It connects various hardware and software systems, applications, and databases. Its goal is to provide true multivendor interoperability. For a fee, OSF licenses DCE to member and nonmember companies to port to their own operating systems.

If (and this is a big if) all client/server application providers utilized DCE services in the creation of their software, there would be considerable end-user and network administrator benefits. First, by centralizing user authentication procedures, users could use a single ID and single password across all applications. Administrators would have a single, centralized repository for security information. Common naming for all network resources would improve usability and, again, simplify network administration. Remote Procedure Call services could be used to load balance application processing among server systems. Common time services would ensure a single time reference for scheduling and time stamping. Access to the DES algorithm would standardize encryption across the network.

Critical Success Factors

Your network infrastructure is the plumbing of your client/server computing environment. It supports your users, their clients, and their servers. Following are some critical success factors to consider as you ponder this important investment.

- **KISS.**   You should Keep It Simple, Stupid! There is beauty, and more important, manageability in keeping the network simple. A simple topology lends itself to reliability, performance, and easier debugging when things to go wrong.

- **Expandability.**   Your network design must offer room for future expansion. It must be able to evolve as technology changes (modularity helps here). Redundancy should be built in.

- **Technology.**   State-of-the-art technology is desirable, but bleeding-edge is not. If you use predictive modeling, it will help you avoid leaping too far into advanced technology that may not really be required.

- **Standards.**   Standards-based products are preferred, because they support interoperability. Your new products must be interoperable with the existing environment and other vendor's equipment. Think DCE!

- **Interoperability.**   "The vendor's network architecture is the starting point for a user's network architecture" [Malamud, 1992]. There are major advantages to sticking with a single vendor. However, you should be prepared to select from several vendors, but insist on interoperability.

- **Reliability.**   You should seek to minimize or eliminate single point of failure areas, in particular at the network backbone. Redundant equipment is desirable for this purpose. Multiple diverse routing paths for physical media is preferred. Spares should be available for all critical equipment. Maintenance contracts should exist for all critical equipment.

- **Management.**   Prepare your network for debuggability. Test tools must be available for this purpose. The network management system must be able to alert support personnel in the event or in anticipation of failures or outages. It must include distributed probes on critical systems and automated data gathering and analysis.

- **Planning.** Assume improvements in network technology and increasing bandwidth demands will require your network to be upgraded every two to three years. Funding for upgrades and technology testbeds will be required to maintain a successful network. The network design should provide extra capacity to avoid unnecessary upgrades.

- **Modeling and Simulation.** This is a critical tool to help you predict potential problems before they impact day-to-day operations. Modeling can be used to analyze network optimization as well as testing changes to the network before actually implementing them. The result will be better network operation.

Now, Take the Network Administrator's Pledge!

Please repeat after me: I (fill in your name) will provide the user with an efficient, cost-effective network environment with 100 percent availability, 100 percent of the time. I will work in a proactive mode, predicting problems and resolving them before any impact to my customer. When problems do arise, they will be resolved by automation where possible, they will be resolved remotely where possible, and they will be resolved expeditiously.

You have now joined a large and growing community of client/server network administrators (for better or for worse!).

7

Communication, Education, and Support

Training for . . . professionals is a continuous process, not an event; constant validation and assessment are required to assure skills are available when needed.

[IBM CONSULTING GROUP, 1994]

This chapter will first discuss the communications process necessary to win the hearts and minds of users migrating to client/server computing. The development of a just-in-time user education process will be presented. Next, user support for the client/server environment will be explored, including Help Desk and Tools. The chapter winds up with some critical success factors.

Winning Hearts and Minds

The move to client/server computing is a culture shock to large organizations used to mainframe-based applications and workflow. Careful communication and demonstration is required to win users' hearts and minds.

Human intellectual inertia is a barrier as well. The new standard applications with GUI interface require initial education, active practice, and ongoing support. A shift in daily operations and applications is hard for many people to adapt to quickly. Also, many users will be engaged in hot projects, preventing them from migration.

Once beliefs are changed, intellectual inertia can be overcome. Once quality, stable tools are delivered, the transition to a client/server computing environment can occur smoothly.

Communications/Education Team

The Communications/Education team should be staffed with strong communicators and writers at the outset of any major migration. Its primary responsibility should be to develop and execute a communication plan, drawing upon the expertise of the migration project leaders and its team members. Its education delivery responsibility is discussed in "Education Delivery" later in this chapter

The Communication Plan

The Communication plan should address (1) user community analysis, (2) strategy, (3) deliverables, and (4) the schedule of execution. Let's take a closer look at each of these items.

User Community Analysis

Within any large working population there are specific groups that require a special communication focus. Executive management is especially important for early buy-in and participation. A clear and effective overall strategy statement and business plan presentation is the critical deliverable here. In IBM Boca Raton, the Communication Team's first order of business was to create the presentation with a set of clear visuals and deliver it to all site executives. This process was in addition to the business case justification presentations to gain financial backing.

Next the CIO department and suppliers of service, that is, the members of the rollout teams, need to be solidly behind the new environment. They need to become early adopters of the tools, despite missing pieces, bugs, and performance problems. They also need to become an empowered team to execute the migration plan under time and budget constraints.

In IBM Boca Raton, the CIO hired a consulting company to run a team-building session prior to the start of the rollout. The two-day session brought together the CIO department members, ISSC leaders, IBM Education and Training leaders, and representatives from major user organizations. The session focused on defining goals, surfacing motivations, and crafting plans of action. One major value of the session was in forging an early rapport among these different groups. Another major value of this communications activity was to motivate the attendees to be solidly behind the migration effort.

A third, perhaps surprising, group that needs special attention is the site's secretaries. This was briefly discussed in Chapter 3. In Boca Raton, a key to winning the hearts and minds of the site's executives and managers was to gain the acceptance and active use of the new client/server applications by the secretaries. In many cases, the secretaries were delegated mail and calendar responsibilities by the manager that they supported. If the secretary could adapt to the new tools, the manager's way was paved. As a result, secretaries were the third major group to be introduced to the new environment, receive education, and new upgraded client systems. If your site has similar relationships between secretaries and managers, this approach is highly recommended.

Unless your site has other special groups requiring early or special attention, the remaining users should be handled on a department by department basis, according to their rollout schedule. At the IBM Boca site, this meant that approximately 8 weeks prior to rollout, a user-focused strategy presentation was delivered to the target department and its manager. It also included details of the rollout process and how each user would be affected.

Communication Strategy

Based on your user community analysis, a clear communication strategy can be built. It should have both a top-down and bottom-up approach. Top-down means gaining executive backing. Bottom-up means gaining grassroots user community support. The former allows the migration to start, the latter makes sure it succeeds. The following three-point communication strategy was used successfully in IBM Boca Raton:

1. Win early executive-level and critical user group support through focused, personal communication.

2. Win broad user support through frequent positive communication deliverables, user feedback mechanisms, demonstration of productivity and cost gains, and consistent quality responsiveness.

3. Win user support department by department with focused communication prior to and after departmental rollout.

Communications Deliverables

Communications deliverables are the documents, presentations, and programs "delivered" to the users in the execution of your communication strategy. They must be timely, highly accurate, sensitive to your audience, and consistent. Following is a suggested list of communications deliverables with a recommended delivery schedule:

- **Executive memos** to all managers and all users should be published at migration kickoff and key checkpoints during the rollout. They should be used to introduce new policies, procedures or new applications or tools. Either the CIO or the highest-ranking site executive should sign the memo.

- **Internal articles, newsletters, or technical reports** should be published at least bimonthly to all users. On-line softcopy and hardcopy versions should be provided to assure the widest possible distribution. In IBM Boca Raton, a Lotus Notes database was used for softcopy publication. Newsletters to users were produced monthly.

- **Well-advertised public presentations,** open to all site users, should be held monthly to present migration status. In IBM Boca Raton, monthly brown-bag lunchtime presentations were conducted, two longer format half-day sessions were conducted, and flyers with key client/server rollout facts were handed out in the site cafeteria on two occasions.

- **The strategy and rollout details** should be presented to each department well prior to their rollout date (8 weeks preferably). This is valuable for setting expectations properly and handling individual concerns and questions. In IBM Boca Raton, many such area meetings were held over the course of the rollout. This contributed greatly to an understanding of the information exchange necessary with the Client Rollout Team, in particular.

- **Postrollout feedback sessions** should be conducted with a regular sample of departments. These provide valuable feedback to all team members. In IBM Boca Raton, monthly postmortems were conducted during the rollout.

- **Conduct frequent CIO Council meetings.** Attendees should include the CIO, service support leaders, and user representatives. Rollout status and upcoming events (checkpoints and decisions) should be on the agenda. In IBM Boca Raton, CIO Council meetings were conducted twice a month.

- **Establish on-line databases for user communication.** Using Lotus Notes, the IBM Boca Communications/Education Team created an Important Bulletins database for critical user information, a Hints 'n Tips database for user advice on the new applications, and a Usability Issues database where users could make suggestions and get quick action (user problems were handled with the HelpPlus database, to be discussed in the Help Desk section). Each of these were part of the standard applications desktop provided to each site user.

- **Create a user's guide.** As each user received his or her new or upgraded system, a bright yellow folder containing a set of hard-copy deliverables was presented. It included a customized user's guide, copies of recently published internal articles, and critical details about the installation (IDs, network addresses, etc.). The user's guide, called the Client/Server Office Solution Guide, was nurtured over months by the Communications/Education team to include OS/2 basics, application basics, comparisons versus legacy applications, and key contacts. It was also available as a Lotus Notes database for on-line access. Its purpose was to supplement the education process (see "Just-In-Time Education" later in this chapter).

- **Consider a custom poster or calendar** for all site users with a client/server theme. In Boca Raton, a client/server 1994 calendar was created, customized with "Using What We Sell," and distributed to all users in December 1993.

- **Develop focused groupware.** In a large organization, there are many teams with unique work processes, as well as processes that affect the entire user community. With a powerful groupware development platform such as Lotus Notes, focused groupware applications can be quickly developed. Like seeds planted in a garden, these applications sprout and blossom to create compelling examples of productivity for all to see. Chapter 3 discusses this in more detail. The migration leadership should identify a set of key business application areas that are candidates for initial groupware development. Internal or external groupware experts should then set up short, focused group meetings with each business area to understand requirements and suggest a groupware application solution. If the reaction is positive, a prototype application should be created for evaluation. If accepted, the final application should be quickly deployed. In many cases, the prototype *is* the final application! This activity ties back precisely to the Information Sharing Cycle so important to business reengineering, as discussed in Chapter 1.

Just-in-Time Education

Training staff and users is vital to the success of a client/server rollout. A rollout is costly to fund and costly in impact to the employees undergoing training. A survey of Fortune 1000 companies estimated that almost one third of the total cost of client/server application acquisition and successful deployment was retraining expenses [McFadden, 1994].

Education Audience Analysis

The key audiences that should be addressed are the CIO team, the information technology support staff, the site's secretaries, the executives, and the general users.

The first audiences that must be educated in the new environment are the CIO team and any information technology support staff. It is assumed that the CIO team brings strong motivation and significant computer user experience to the table. It is further assumed that the information technology support staff brings skill and experience in client/server technology, support, and application development, but may require education in specifically selected user applications. (If not, you selected the wrong supplier!) If an inexperienced, internal information technology staff is employed, you should either consider outsourcing or postponing the migration. The bedrock support for a client/server infrastructure requires knowledge, skill, and experience across a broad set of technical areas.

The site's secretaries will most likely require early, specialized education. In IBM Boca Raton, a dedicated internal educator developed a complete education module and documentation for the site's secretaries.

Because of their time demands, you should consider customized education for executives and managers. The education delivery schedule was very flexible in IBM Boca Raton, so this was not done.

Client Rollout Education Requirements

Education requirements for a client/server rollout are:

1. **Effectiveness.** Skills must stick with the user after education.

2. **Timeliness.** If education occurs in close time proximity to client system delivery, it is more likely that lessons will stick with the user.

3. **Convenience.** Education should last long enough to transfer critical skills but not so long as to impact current work assignments. Scheduling should be flexible to accommodate individual user requirements, but not violate the timeliness requirement.

4. **Affordability.** The cost of education must be within budget limits.

Education Delivery Alternatives

The major education delivery alternatives are video tapes, Computer-Based Training (CBT), and classroom instruction.

Videos can be very cost-effective if used with groups, but offer no customization or Q&A (question and answer) interaction. If used as a supplementary delivery mechanism for individual applications or available on a long-term basis during steady state, they can be valuable.

Interactive CBT packages are very good for individual study. Recent packages incorporate CD-ROM and motion video technology for improved quality and interactivity. For a large-scale rollout, lack of individualized Q&A and lack of customization may be an obstacle, as it is for videos. Also, some packages are quite expensive (up to $2,500) and may actually cost more than classroom instruction. However, CBT delivery should be seriously considered for both rollout and steady-state if it is cost effective.

Traditional classroom instruction coupled with hands-on interaction is the best alternative for a large-scale rollout. The opportunity for individualized Q&A and local customization makes this a standout. However, this can be a costly selection. A high-quality instructor can cost over $2,000 per day. Assuming a 20 student class, this is a $200 daily charge per student. Don't forget to throw in the costs of class materials and technical and administrative support.

IBM Boca Raton needed to educate its client/server users in the critical standard applications, Lotus Notes (groupware and e-mail) and TaP/2 (calendar). The CallUp C/S and NetDoor applications were sufficiently self-teaching that no upfront classroom time was deemed necessary for them. IBM Education and Training was selected to develop a customized, hands-on, one-day class combining both applications. The customization allowed the Communications/Education team to familiarize the student users with standard, but local, Notes databases that would come with their new system. With outstanding teamwork among the Communications/Education Team, IBM Education and Training, and the users' focal points, classrooms and classes were scheduled to coincide with the client rollout. Users were able to take the one-day Notes and TaP/2 class within two weeks of receipt of his new or upgraded system. Figure 7.1 is a photograph of the actual classroom used in Boca Raton.

Over 60 percent of the site's users were OS/2 familiar. For the remaining 40 percent, the Communications/Education Team again worked with IBM Education and Training to develop a customized, one-day OS/2 class. Users were scheduled up to two weeks ahead of receipt of their new or upgraded systems to ensure that they would still be able to use legacy applications to do their job as soon as the system was installed. In IBM Boca Raton, the user guarantee was to provide continuity of access to legacy applications to minimize loss of productivity.

Delivering Advanced Education

As users digest the new applications, become comfortable with them, and develop expertise, advanced courses should be available to enrich their

Courtesy International Business Machines Corporation

Figure 7.1   Client/Server Classroom

use of the applications. A key objective for IBM Boca Raton was to educate at least ten percent of the users in Lotus Notes application development.

If you are investing in a groupware application with similar rapid application development features, percolating this application development skill in your organization will pay rich dividends in user satisfaction and productivity. The IBM Boca Raton approach was to maintain a center of competence and consulting in the CIO department to nurture and guide these fledgling skills.

User Support

User support means that if a user has a question or a problem, he or she has a quick and cost-effective means to get an answer or resolve his problem. To support a large organization (500 or more users) using client/server tools requires an organized approach to user support. This organized approach is usually called a **help desk**. A typical help desk includes a centralized staff of experts, a user-friendly voice response unit, a centralized problem tracking database, a well-managed user-communication process, a well-defined service-level agreement on responsiveness, and a communication process for network and server status.

A centralized staff of application and system experts should be ready to answer questions and solve problems for a well-defined portion of the working day. The trend is to provide 24-hour-a-day, 7-day-a-week support. The staff should treat each and every user with patience and respect. According to a recent *PC Week* survey, the most important attributes of a help desk support staff from a user's perspective are (1) technical expertise, (2) speed in responding to reported problems, (3) attitude of, and (4) consistency of phone support [Schneider 11/93].

An intelligent phone service interface for users, sometimes called a **Voice Response Unit (VRU)** is the first point of user contact for the help desk. A single, easy-to-remember phone number should be available for users to call and receive support. The VRU should offer a menu of choices to speed users to either automated responses (e.g., status of a common server) or an application expert.

A central database should be used by support personnel to enter and track problems through to resolution while referencing user profile information. This is useful to ensure problem closure, measure responsiveness, identify recurring problems, and identify users personal information and problems history quickly. Help desk staff should obtain a standard set of information from the caller (name, location, problem description, etc.).

A process for identifying users, classifying and recording their problems, seeking additional expertise if necessary, communicating results to the users, and closing their problems must be defined. Seeking additional expertise may involve contacting backup support personnel or visiting the user's office for hands-on support. This can be handled by information technology or CIO team members identified to the help desk staff as on-site support personnel.

A well-defined policy of responsiveness (or service-level agreement; see Appendix E for a sample) based upon problem severity is key. For example, a showstopper problem should be resolved within 24 hours. A serious problem with a workaround should be resolved within 72 hours. A minor problem with a workaround should be resolved within 7 days.

A well-defined process for communicating network and server status among support, network administrators, server administrators, and the users is a must. Ideally this is an automated process linked to the network management system of alerts (see Chapter 6).

The following facilities are less common, but should be sought out as part of comprehensive help desk system:

- **User direct access** to the central problem database for entry, review, and update. This will reduce the load on the help desk and increase user satisfaction.

- **On-line query capability** of a comprehensive information database for support personnel and users. This can be considered to be a "self-help desk" application.

- **Remote client system access by support personnel** to correct user problems. The NetFinity application for Intel-based systems provides this capability when NetFinity Services is installed on the user's system and the NetFinity Manager is installed on the support person's system.

- **Expert system** assistance to support personnel. An expert system is an application capable of rapid searching of an expert **knowledge base** to derive an answer to a complex question or problem. A knowledge base is a database containing rules (or rules of thumb) about a complex subject based on experience or simple reasoning (e.g., "If the program returned an '0C1' return code, it is defective").

Help Desk Benefits

User productivity and user satisfaction are the most important benefits of a well-run help desk. Some secondary benefits come from downstream uses of help desk data accumulation. By analyzing the problem database, problem areas of the network or problem applications can be identified. This can help in replacement and new purchase decisions.

Staffing Requirements

Help desk staff should have good technical expertise and good telephone communication skills. Good communication skills means patience and understanding with frustrated and, sometimes, angry users.

Computing the number of staff required is based on the expected volume of calls, which is dependent on the number of users. A baseline can be achieved by measuring call volume and average call duration for a defined period (e.g., 5 to 10 days). Dividing call volume by the number of users derives a calls-per-user factor. This factor can then be applied to predict call volume as the rollout proceeds and new users are added to the total. The predicted length of an average user call helps determine the number of calls per day a support person is expected to handle. The call volume can then be used to estimate the number of personnel required. It is a good idea early on in a rollout to estimate high in case there are startup problems encountered [Faulkner, 1994].

Beyond the Help Desk

Network-based software installation and backup/recovery applications are an important part of a comprehensive user support solution. Both of these areas have been discussed in prior chapters in detail. Each aids in recovery situations that can occasionally plague users and should be considered when investing in user support.

IBM Boca Raton's Help Desk and HelpPlus

The Boca Raton client/server Help Desk facility, supported by ISSC in Raleigh, North Carolina, was set up in January 1994. It supports the client/server standard applications (Lotus Notes, TaP/2, Callup C/S, Net-Door) and OS/2. As new applications and tools are added to the client/server environment, the skills of the technical support staff of eight are upgraded to handle them. Users have a single number to reach the help desk, are prompted for their serial number by the VRU to speed identification, and have a "fast-path" number to get to the client/server application experts.

HelpPlus is an internal, OS/2 front-end to the Help Desk's Problem database, system status information, and on-line self-help database. HelpPlus is available to all users for on-line problem status determination, new problem creation, system status updates (automatically communicated via the network management system) and a self-help database for on-line query. Figure 7.2 shows the HelpPlus icons.

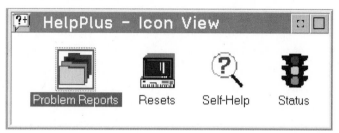

Courtesy International Business Machines Corporation

Figure 7.2 HelpPlus Icons

Critical Success Factors

Communication, education, and support sometimes take a back seat to the more concrete aspects of information technology, such as the clients, servers, and network hardware. However, without substantial financial and intellectual investments in these areas a client/server migration will fail. Following are some key success factors to be considered along with your communication, education, and support investments:

- An appreciation of **diffusion theory** (the theory of how ideas diffuse or spread through a large population) is important. An interesting case study regarding the inability of primitive people to accept boiling water as a remedy to kill germs in contaminated water is instructive. Because the germs were invisible, the people simply did not believe that they existed and refused to boil their water prior to drinking! This is analogous to the difficulty that many mainframe users have in identifying the compelling values of client/server computing. Changing the primitive people's beliefs required diffusing success stories throughout the community. The same is true of changing the beliefs of mainframe users.

- Don't underestimate the educational requirements of the CIO department and support staffs. Technology is changing rapidly, and falling behind can mean going out of business.

- Handling User Problems 101: During a complex client/server rollout, all information technology support personnel are tested to their maximum. Users can be irate, irrational, and rude. They can be right and wrong. Calm, careful follow-through as each problem hits (and they will!) is required to survive and satisfy the customer.

This is where the true teamwork of the user support organization is tested. When systems are up and running smoothly, everyone can relax. But when systems are down, mail is late or (worse) lost, productivity is impacted, days never end, and the pressure is on. It is easy to blame teammates and the users in these situations. When the users start to call the CIO directly and scream, it is the wise and prudent user support leader who gets the facts, listens to both sides carefully, and responds evenly. Such a leader accepts blame when appropriate and educates the user when not. This is not a sometime thing, it is an everyday thing.

- Handling User Problems 202: The truly skilled support team has the dedication to get down to a root cause of a complex problem. The client/server environment is complex. A complex server application is many-layered—operating system, network operating system, multiple drivers, application code, and so on. The temptation will always be there to just "reboot" (power-down and then power-up) the server and get things going again. This is the easy way out. A crack support team will always discover the root cause, communicate it to the responsible party, and have the problem permanently fixed.

8

Measuring Results

This chapter looks at the important measurements you need to successfully manage a complex, client/server environment. The measured results of the IBM Boca Raton migration are presented as examples. The chapter ends with some overall critical success factors for the prospective client/server migrater.

User-Related Measurements

Measurements can be broken into two broad categories: user-related and service-related. User-related measurements are measurements that are the results of user surveys and user activity tracking. For example, the results of a user satisfaction survey fit within the user-related category. The number of users completed in a client rollout is another example. User-related measurements identify status, problems, and trends in the user community. Status measurements identify progress or nonprogress for which action may be taken. Sometimes problems and trends are resolved by improving user communication and education. Sometimes they imply an underlying problem with the client/server infrastructure.

User Satisfaction Survey

Your users' overall satisfaction with the client/server environment is a key concern. In IBM Boca Raton, the mainframe environment had fairly mature user survey applications. For the client/server environment, a new survey application was written that was delivered by a Lotus Notes e-mail message to all site users on a monthly basis. Data was automatically accumulated into a central database for statistical computation. The survey asks for the customer of the system to rate (on a scale of 1 to 5, with 1 being very satisfied, 5 being very dissatisfied) their overall satisfaction with the systems, and their satisfaction (1 to 5) with four specific characteristics of the system. Write-in comments were supported as well. The results consistently showed that over 95 percent of survey respondents were satisfied with the new client/server environment.

Productivity Surveys

This is an often forgotten survey activity that is especially important in being able to justify your ongoing investment in information technology. It can be combined with a satisfaction survey but is better executed by one-on-one interviews. In IBM Boca Raton, the development of Lotus Notes databases across the site will be tracked to compare the resultant workflow improvements versus prior processes for productivity gains.

Education Feedback Survey

An effective education program jump-starts the user into the new environment. It avoids future problems, relieves pressure on the help desk support personnel, and leads to improved user satisfaction. Every user should be required to take a posteducation survey. Analyzing this information leads to improved courses and better instructors. In IBM Boca Raton, a 5-point rating system was used for a few short questions. These included, How good was the instructor? How effective was the course? Did you achieve a true skills transfer? and so forth. The results over several months averaged 1.9, where 1 is the highest and 5 is the lowest rating. Write-in suggestions were encouraged. This information resulted in key changes and improvements in educational plans. For example, short-course alternatives were introduced for the more technical users midway through 1994 in response to their feedback.

Client Migration Status

Keeping track of the client rollout rate and tracking to plan is a vital statistic. Failure to manage this effectively can waste precious dollars and create user dissatisfaction with delayed service. Figure 8.1 shows the progress made in the office client cumulative installations during 1994. The graph shows the original plan (which was too aggressive), the revised

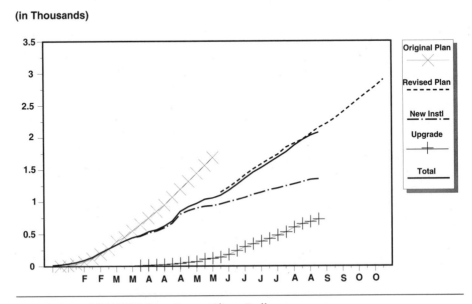

Figure 8.1   1994 IBM Boca Raton Client Rollout

plan, and the actual installs tracked through August 1994. By carefully tracking this data, the number of installation contractors required was determined, thereby controlling costs.

Application Tracking

Tracking application installations is heavily dependent on the client roll-out and should track as such. Figures 8.2, 8.3, and 8.4 show cumulative

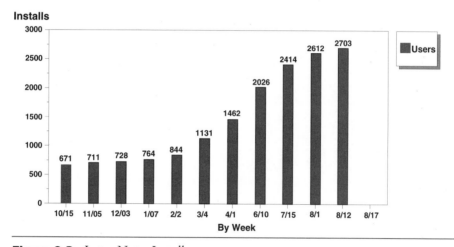

Figure 8.2   Lotus Notes Installs

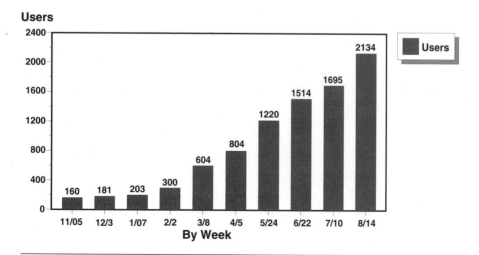

Figure 8.3   TaP/2 Installs

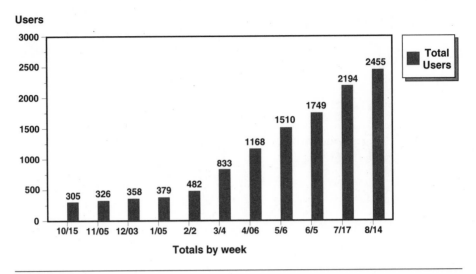

Figure 8.4 Net Door Installs

user ID assignment for three of the standard applications—Lotus Notes, Time and Place/2, and NetDoor—through August 1994, in Boca Raton, respectively. Failure to track with client installs indicates a breakdown in the installation process.

Figure 8.5 shows that the number of mobile client installs is shown to be increasing well on a month to month basis. This was expected to lag considerably behind the office migration due to its late availability (July 1994). Early users were part of the beta testing program for mobile client installation.

Two other interesting, related statistics should be tracked at a minimum. Network licenses versus average daily use should be tracked if an application sharing program such as NetDoor is used. This identifies the optimum number of network licenses to purchase. Notes Mail activity measurements should be acquired by investigation of the users' mail databases. This will give a measure of the rollout's success.

Legacy Exodus Tracking

If your client/server migration is based on user rolloff from the mainframe, you should track key statistics to identify trends. Figure 8.6 shows the increasing use of Notes as the primary e-mail application alongside

People

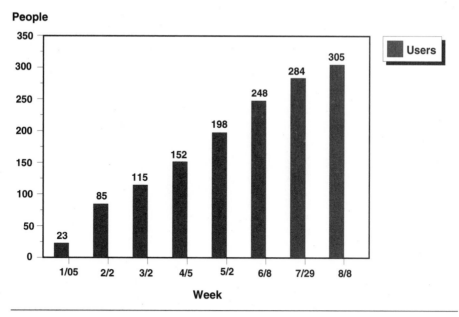

Figure 8.5   Mobile Client Installs

the number of users who have terminated their use of OfficeVision, in IBM Boca Raton. A related statistic is the ratio of OfficeVision IDs deleted divided by the total target populations (the sunset ratio). It is to be expected that these statistics will track to the client rollout but be several weeks behind due to a mandatory user break-in period. If the trend is too slow or stalled, it is time to ramp up your communication program to the users or get tough and just turn off the legacy service (with adequate warning)! The latter step should be undertaken only if your communication program is unsuccessful.

Service-Related Measurements

Service-related measurements are measurements of the client/server environment. For example, the availability and throughput statistics for a LAN segment is a service-related measurement. Service-related measurements identify problems and trends in the underlying client/server infrastructure. Targets for service-level measurements are typically included in

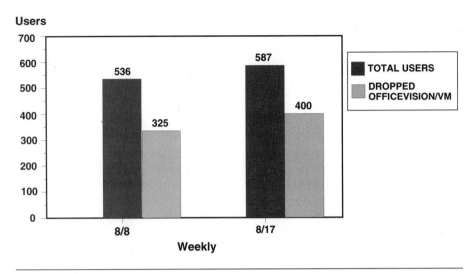

Figure 8.6 Lotus Notes as Primary E-Mail Application

an agreement with a supplier of service (Appendix E provides a sample). It is important to understand these targets and incorporate them into any measurement system used.

Network Measurements

Statistics for both network availability and bandwidth utilization by LAN segment should be gathered and summarized weekly for CIO inspection. Figure 8.7 shows some sample data from the Boca Raton site network's bandwidth utilization report. The data is based on a periodic polling of all LAN segments in the site network. The first column identifies the LAN segment, or token ring. The second column reports the average utilization of the LAN segment for the given week. The third column reports the number of times the LAN segment was polled when its utilization was less than 20 percent. This will be relative to the total number of times the segment is polled during the week (column 6). Columns 4 and 5 identify utilization rates of less than 40 percent and 60 percent, respectively. Network availability statistics should help you identify trouble spots in the network, such as overloaded segments or unreliable

LAN Segment Number	Average Utilization	Utilization <20%	Utilization <40%	Utilization <60%	Number of Records
504	3	727	0	0	727
57D	10	717	10	0	727
5D1	26	41	629	50	720
B51	32	531	169	25	725

Figure 8.7 Sample Network Utilization Report

bridges or routers. Bandwidth utilization statistics should help you predict when network upgrades are in order.

Server Farm Measurements

Measurements for server downtime and percentage availability per day for each server is important. This will help identify unreliable or overloaded servers. Armed with this information, you can take action to replace systems, upgrade systems, or just balance workload. Figure 8.8 provides a sample of data from IBM Boca Raton's server measurements.

Week of:	June 13 to June 19, 1994				
Date	Server	Time Down	Time Up	Downtime (Minutes)	% Available/ Day
June 16	BCR1	3:08	3:41	33	97.71
	BCR2	2:07	2:41	34	97.64
	BCR3	10:13	10:30	17	
		13:56	14:11	15	
		16:55	17:02	7	97.29
June 17	BCR0	9:10	15:01	351	75.63

Figure 8.8 Sample Server Availability Data

IBM Mail LAN Gateway/2 Throughput

This was a critical barrier to success. It was estimated that as the migration proceeded, mail traffic would continue to build between OfficeVision and Notes until over two-thirds of the users were fully migrated. Based on the project user population, it was estimated that peak weekly traffic through the gateway could exceed 100,000 mail messages. Based on the capacity of a single PS/2 server (300 messages/hour), it was estimated that at least 10 servers were needed to handle the prime working hours from Monday through Friday (300 messages/hour for 8 hours yields 2,400 messages per prime shift per server; multiplied by 10 servers, yields 24,000 messages per day; multiplied by 5 working days, yields over 100,000 messages transferred). Figure 8.9 shows the weekly measurements versus the projected traffic. Luckily, the cumulative total remained considerably below the estimated traffic, resulting in acceptable throughput for the users.

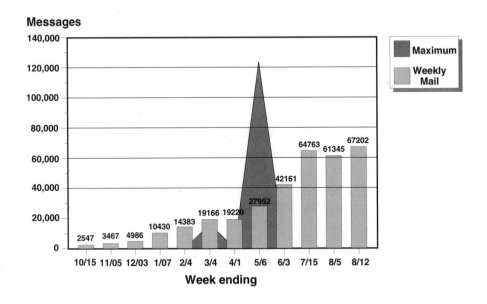

Figure 8.9 IBM Mail LAN Gateway/2: Messages Per Week

Help Desk Statistics

Problems in help desk support can crater the best of user information technology environments. All calls and problem reports should be tracked, entered into a database, and analyzed weekly to identify problems and trends. Important things to measure are the total number of calls per week, calls closed by the first point of contact (sometimes called level 1 support), calls closed by the second point of contact (usually called level 2 support, employing a higher degree of technical skill), and those calls resulting in a problem report being opened up requiring additional activity and follow-up. By tracking and analyzing this information, weaknesses in applications, network components and support staff can be identified.

Problems come in different severities, and their resolution should receive differing response priority. This should be spelled out in your service-level agreement with your supplier of services and tracked. For example, a showstopper problem might have a 3-hour turnaround time specified in the service level agreement, whereas a minor problem might have a 5-day turnaround time.

Figure 8.10 lists the help desk tracking data for a 3-week period in July and August, 1994 at IBM Boca Raton. It shows that most calls were closed by the first point of contact (Level 1), with about 20 percent being turned into problem reports requiring additional support investigation.

Week	7/17/94	7/25/94	8/1/94
Actual Calls	158	172	271
Closed at Level 1	78	74	77
Closed at Level 2	2	3	1
Problem Report Created	20	23	22
Problem Solved According to Turnaround Time Plan	44	22	42
Problem Solved Outside of Turnaround Time Plan	2	8	1
Problem Open	11	10	14

Figure 8.10   Sample IBM Boca Help Desk Statistics

Communicating Measurements

Measurements need to be made visible to be useful. They should be made visible to the support staff immediately so that corrective action can take place if a problem is identified. They should be made visible in summary form to the client/server leadership (CIO, supplier, or service leader) to aid the planning and investment processes. A CIO analytic database, updated weekly, is the recommended approach. Measurements should also be made available to users to gain their understanding, and, at times, their tolerance if outages occur (and they do occur). This can be done through the CIO database or periodic mail messages.

Critical Success Factors

Ready or not, it is time to wrap up. Following are some success factors that cut across all aspects of establishing a client/server computing environment for your users.

- **Have a Documented Strategy.** You should create a clear and simple statement of your migration strategy. It should have a clear and elevating goal. It should include a clear statement of productivity. Broaden the strategy over time to include technology goals. These should be consistent with business requirements and strategies. Validate the strategy through periodic reviews of all major development and administrative projects. Quarterly updates and approval cycles will maintain strategy quality and user acceptance.

- **Build a Financial Model.** Gather and consolidate *all* information technology expenditures into a comprehensive (spreadsheet-based) financial model (see Appendix C). Insist on detailed, granular charges from your supplier of service as you build the model. Extend the model to project "business-as-usual" versus client/server expenditures. Calculate the return from the client/server startup costs as you would any regular business investment. Use the results in justifying the project to management. Maintain the model on an ongoing basis to validate your investment.

- **Win Minds and Hearts.** Win your management's minds to get the money for the migration. This is the first major barrier that must be overcome. A positive business case and a solid strategy are the keys. Next win the user community's hearts. Early team building, a solid communication plan, forming a user council, and diplomacy are important.

- **Build a Skilled and Empowered Team.** Because the skill requirements are so broad, it is hard to gauge the strength of your team up front. Use the staffing example in Chapter 2 versus your project scope as a guide. If you are starting from scratch, hire an experienced supplier of service to get going . A CIO department with a core of technical and leadership skills to direct the supplier will be your eyes, ears, and brains. The team leaders should be empowered to make all technical decisions and most business decisions without any higher-level approval.

- **Think Vanilla, Offer Sprinkles.** You will be faced with a varied array of user demands, requirements, and requests. You cannot satisfy them all. Common nightmares are: Should multiple e-mail applications be supported? Should alternative operating systems be supported? How much server disk storage space should be offered to each user? and on and on. Supporting a single product or establishing a one-size-fits-all policy is simple, easy to communicate, and cost-effective (this is vanilla). The hidden cost of supporting alternatives is enormous: support staff education, installation, user education, license fees, and on and on. Use cost as your main defense with your users in offering only vanilla, but accept exceptions for sound business reasons (these are the sprinkles). For example, IBM Boca Raton supports Ami Pro for OS/2 as its standard word processor, but gave its lawyers WordPerfect because they required it to deal effectively with their external colleagues.

- **Here and Now, Invest; Tomorrow, Test.** You will be faced with a multitude of technical choices and alternatives at every turn. Should we buy a switching hub or a standard hub? Should we go ATM or FDDI? Should we invest in bridges or routers to expand our network? Should we wait for XYZ Company's new application, currently in beta test? A good rule of thumb is to invest only in tried and true technology today to guarantee your operation and test new technology to gain confidence for tomorrow's investment. A serious mistake is to bank on an emerging technology to solve an immediate problem. Regarding software, never mistake a beta test for a finished product. Never make important information technology plans based on availability of a promised new software application by a specific date.

- **Pilot First, Deploy Second.** Managing change is a major challenge. New features or functions should be introduced gradually to the user community. Always run a pilot test with a representative user sample first, before general availability.

- **Be a Standards Bear.** You should avoid proprietary, single-vendor solutions. The client/server revolution is being built with open, industry-standard products. Educate yourself and your staff in the major client/server standards and why they are important to your organization.

- **Measure, Measure, Measure.** Invest in methods to gather measurements automatically, with the ultimate goal of creating a living database from which to evaluate your progress in making client/server computing a reality.

Appendix A:

Products and Internal Tools

For each chapter in the book, the referenced and related products (both IBM and non-IBM) used at the IBM Boca Raton site are listed alphabetically, followed by the internally developed tools.

Chapter 2: Migration Management

- **CA-SuperProject:** An OS/2-based project planning and scheduling application from Computer Associates that supports PERT analysis.

Chapter 3: Applications

- **IBM Address Book Synchronization/2 Version 1.0:** Provides a unidirectional host-to-LAN address book synchronization from IBM CallUp Version 1 Release 3, and custom address books for enterprises who are using Lotus Notes or cc: Mail LAN Mail environments. This OS/2 32-bit program provides LAN-based users of IBM's OS/2 2.0 and 2.1, the host-to-LAN address book synchronization required to exchange mail across the enterprise, including synchronization for the IBM Mail LAN Gateway/2 Release 2.

- **IBM AIX Configuration Management Version Control Products (CMVC):** The IBM Configuration Management Version Control Server/6000 and the IBM Configuration Management Version Control Clients allow software developers to better manage their software development process with comprehensive software library control and problem tracking.

- **IBM CallUp:** an easy-to-use, multi-function online VM office directory application. Its functions store, maintain, and provide access to information about the employees and services of an organization. CallUp can be used to provide office directory application support for IBM OfficeVision/VM.

- **IBM C Set ++ for AIX/6000:** A productive application development environment for C and C++ application developers. It includes a C compiler, a C++ compiler, and other tools.

- **IBM Database 2 (DB2):** IBM's relational database management system for MVS environments.

- **IBM Database 2 AIX/6000 (DB2/6000):** IBM's relational database management system for IBM RISC System/6000 workstations.

- **IBM Database 2 OS/2 (DB2/2):** IBM's relational database management system for OS/2-capable systems. It supports access to OS/2 database servers from OS/2, DOS, and DOS Windows database client PCs.

- **IBM Network Door/2 (NetDoor):** The NetDoor program product provides access to tools, applications, and documentation that are already installed on OS/2 file servers on a local area network. Using the OS/2 LAN requester or TCP/IP, a user can access these programs as if they were installed on his or her own workstation.

- **IBM Personal Application System/2 (PAS/2) Version 3.0:** provides multi-function, data analysis solutions for the business professional in an office environment, fully exploiting the advanced facilities of OS/2 Version 2. When installed on a PC, IBM Personal AS/2 Version 3 is able to operate across a LAN or WAN if connected. This provides access to a wide range of data on host systems and personal computers, including access to DB2/2 and DB2.

- **IBM Publishing Systems BookMaster:** A Document Composition Facility (DCF) Generalized Markup Language (GML) program product that provides a rich set of GML tags for creating complex document layouts. BookMaster is a host-based solution for high-volume in-house publishing. It is based on the GML application used to create most of the IBM Corporation product support documentation.

- **IBM Time and Place/2 (TaP/2):** A client/server network-based calendar application that includes individual and group scheduling, to do lists, calendar printing, and delegation of control for update purposes. Vendor Independent Messaging is supported with communications with other applications such as Lotus Notes.

- **IBM Time and Place Connectivity/2:** A LAN-based bidirectional calendar connectivity program. It allows users of the Time and Place/2 time management product, as well as OfficeVision/VM, to perform interactive bidirectional view, free-time search, and calendar update operations in the LAN and mainframe environments.

- **Lotus Notes:** A workgroup application for sharing information and building business applications with integrated e-mail. Lotus Notes runs on OS/2 clients and servers, as well other operating system platforms.

- **Lotus SmartSuite for OS/2:** the Ami Pro word processor, the Freelance Graphics business graphics application, and the 1-2-3 spreadsheet for OS/2.

- **IBM CallUp C/S:** An internally developed application used to provide directory services in a LAN environment. CallUp C/S allows users to perform searches against person directories, service directories, and department directories. It also provides "reports-to," "show department," and "fuzzy search" functions. It uses IBM DB2 for OS/2 as the directory repository, which can be automatically synchronized with the IBM CallUp database on VM.

- **DLIST:** An internally developed application that converts an OfficeVision/VM distribution list to a Lotus Notes Group on a user's PC. An SNA and a TCP/IP version exist.

- **DNAMES:** An internally developed application that converts an OfficeVision/VM nickname file to entries in the Lotus Notes Personal Name and Address book on a user's PC. An SNA and a TCP/IP version exist.

- **DOCS2LN:** An internally developed application that converts OfficeVision/VM documents to a document in a Lotus Notes database on a user's PC.

- **DWSCRIPT, DWSOS2:** Internally developed GML/Script document compilers for DOS (DWSCRIPT) and OS/2 (DWSOS2).

- **OV2LNOTE:** An internally developed application that converts an OfficeVision/VM notelog to a Lotus Notes database on a user's PC. An SNA and a TCP/IP version exist.

Chapter 4: Client Rollout

- **IBM Advanced Interactive Executive Operating System (AIX):** IBM's version of the UNIX operating system developed for the RS/6000 family of systems.

- **IBM Communications Manager/2:** IBM's premier communications manager for OS/2 PCs. It contains the communications functions from Extended Services for OS/2. It includes 3270 terminal emulation and conversion of 5250 terminal emulation to Presentation Manager interface.

- **IBM Network Transport Services/2:** Provides programming interfaces (NetBIOS, token-ring, and Network Driver Interface Specification [NDIS]) necessary for OS/2 2.0 LAN enablement where the OS/2 LAN Server is not required. NTS/2 provides NDIS-compliant LAN Adapter Protocol Support (LAPS), a suite of network communication software.

- **IBM Operating System/2 Version 2.1:** A 32-bit operating system for OS/2, Windows 3.1, and DOS applications. Features include Adobe Type Manager, True Type fonts, and a range of 32-bit display drivers. All industry-standard networking protocols are supported. Multimedia features are built in. PCMCIA interfaces are supported.

- **IBM Personal System/2 Models 56 and 76:** Micro Channel desktop personal systems featuring 80486 processors, up to 64 MB of memory, a wide range of hard disk storage options, 3 slots, 3 drive bays, and XGA graphics.

- **IBM PS/ValuePoint:** A family of personal computer systems powered by a wide choice of processors ranging from a 486SX-25 to a 486DX2-33/66. Features include VESA local bus technology and SVGA local bus video.

- **IBM RISC System/6000:** A family of high-performance client and server workstation systems based on the POWER RISC architecture. It is designed to address the computing needs of engineering/scientific users as well as those of commercial applications.

- **IBM TCP/IP 2.0:** Provides TCP/IP support, including NFS (Network File System), XWindow System, including FTP (File Transfer Protocol) using OS/2 Presentation Manager (FTPPM). IBM TCP/IP 2.0 is interoperable with IBM's TCP/IP products for VM, MVS, DOS, and AIX.

- **IBM Token-Ring Network 16/4 Adapter II:** A token-ring adapter for IBM PS/2 systems with Micro Channel architecture. An ISA bus version is available as well. Maximum speed is 16 Mbps. It connects to unshielded and shielded twisted pair cable (UTP/STP).

- **ACPM/ALMCOPY:** An internally developed PC-to-mainframe data copy application.

- **IBM AntiVirus/2:** An internal, comprehensive antivirus program for DOS and OS/2 systems developed by IBM Research.

- **PCPRINT:** An internally developed PC application that allows users to route OV/VM print files to their office printers.

Chapter 5: The Server Farm

- **ADSM:** ADSTAR Distributed Storage Manager. ADSM is an IBM program product for enterprise-wide storage management for the network. It provides automatic backup and archive services to multivendor workstations, personal computers, and LAN file servers. Versions for AIX on RS/6000, VM and MVS on S/390, and OS/2 on PCs are available.

- **IBM 4039 LaserPrinter:** A network-attachable, 10-page-per-minute, 600 by 600 dots per inch, laser printer. The LaserPrinter supports PCL5 or PostScript and can be upgraded to print in duplex mode.

- **IBM Enterprise Systems/9000 (ES/9000):** A series of IBM water-cooled mainframe systems, ranging in capability from single-processing, 32 MB, 16-channel systems to 10-way multiprocessing, 512 MB, 64-channel systems. A large library of MVS-, VSE-, DPPX-, MUMPS-, and AIX-based systems and application software is available from IBM and third-party software suppliers.

- **IBM LANstreamer MC 32 Adapter:** A full 32-bit token-ring adapter for Micro Channel systems. It has the highest frame capability of any IBM token-ring adapter. Maximum transmission speed is 20 Mbps, with a 40 Mbps burst mode. It supports unshielded and shielded twisted-pair wiring.

- **IBM Mail LAN Gateway/2** (IMLG/2): An OS/2 application that allows incompatible electronic mail systems, such as Lotus Notes and cc:Mail, to communicate with each other, with System Network Architecture Distributed Services (SNADS) office platforms like Advantis' IBM Mail Exchange service offering, and through NJE to products such as OfficeVision/VM.

- **IBM Maximum Availability and Support System/2 (MASS/2):** System management software that allows administrators to monitor, control, diagnose, and configure PS/2 Model 195 and 295 Server systems from a remote workstation.

- **IBM Multiple Virtual Systems/Enterprise System Architecture (MVS/ESA):** A high-performance, multitasking operating system for IBM's S/390 mainframe systems. MVS/ESA supports many applications, include the IBM program product DB2.

- **IBM NetFinity Manager and IBM NetFinity Services:** NetFinity is a highly flexible, low-cost tool to help users with hardware and general systems management functions. It is designed to manage systems based on Intel Architecture for 386SX equivalent, or higher, personal computers. NetFinity is comprised of NetFinity Services and NetFinity Manager.

- **IBM NetView Distribution Manager/2 (NetView DM/2):** An application to control the distribution and installation of software and data to OS/2 systems across a network.

- **IBM OEM Personal/370 Adapter/A (P/370):** A coprocessor for selected Micro Channel Architecture Personal System/2 (PS/2) computers. It adds a standalone S/370 processor function to a PS/2 computer running Operating System/2 (OS/2). This creates a personal workstation that can run S/370 applications concurrently with OS/2 applications

- **IBM OS/2 LAN Server 3.0:** A network operating system that provides capabilities to interconnect IBM PS/2's and PCs on token-ring and Ethernet networks, and manage the sharing of network resources. It is a program that resides on a server system that runs IBM OS/2 as its base operating system.

- **IBM Personal System/2 Server 95:** an upgradable Micro Channel floorstanding system intended as a file and database server for large networks. Processor complex can be upgraded from an Intel i486DX2-50Mhz processor to an Intel Pentium 66 Mhz processor. Main memory can be upgraded from 8 MB of RAM to 64 MB of RAM. Internal hard disk storage can be upgraded from 1 GB to 8.4 GBs. Disk storage is controlled by high performance SCI and

SCSI-2 controllers. The Array models feature a RAID 5 controller that supports on-line spare and hot-pluggable hard disk drives.

- **IBM Personal System/2 Server 195:** An upgradable, fault-tolerant server designed to combine high levels of performance with a convenient migration path to the high-end Server 295. IBM designed the Server 195 for use in large networks requiring high-powered application servers with some of the Server 295's fault tolerance. These networks could then upgrade their Server 195s as needed. The Server 195 is equipped with a single 50 Mhz 486DX CPU, 256 KB of Level 2 (L2) cache memory, 32 MB of error checking and correcting (ECC) memory (expandable to 128 MB), 400 MB of internal storage (expandable to 9 GB), and two SCSI disk channels that utilize 32-bit RISC processors. Additionally, the Server 195 includes 8 expansion slots (one 16- and seven 32-bit slots), 10 half-height storage bays, and VGA graphics support.

- **IBM Print Services Facility/6000 (PSF/6000):** A print server application that runs on AIX and uses TCP/IP for communication. Features include centralized network printer control, print spooling, accounting, security, and job separation. Supported printers include IBM's family of IPDS laser printers and PPDS printers, as well as Hewlett-Packard's LaserJet printers.

- **IBM SAA Distributed Database Connection Services/2 Version 2 (DDCS/2):** Provides PC application access to enterprise data. OS/2 users can easily access host relational databases, just as they would with a local LAN server, with DDCS/2. It provides for central host database storage while maintaining subsidiary database servers on the LAN and supports host downloads of data to LAN database servers in incremental "snapshots" to preserve host resources for other tasks.

- **IBM SoftDist/6000:** An IBM product (available only as a PRPQ) used to distribute AIX operating system code and applications over a network. It has been superseded by NetView DM/6000.

- **IBM System Performance Monitor/2:** Provides an integrated set of performance data collecting, recording, graphing, reporting and analyzing functions that enable performance management of OS/2 Version 2.0 critical system resources on IBM and non-IBM PC hardware. SPM/2 also supports remote data collection from IBM OS/2 LAN Servers and IBM OS/2 LAN Requesters.

- **IBM Virtual Machine/Enterprise System Architecture (VM/ESA):** The VM operating system for the IBM S/390 series of mainframe processors. VM/ESA supports OfficeVision/VM and many other mainframe applications.

- **SAM/2:** The System Application Monitor/2 is a locally developed application that monitors application activity on the PS/2 servers in the Server Farm. If SAM/2 determines that an application session is down, it will generate a page to the server administrators.

Chapter 6: Network Infrastructure

- **IBM 6611 Router:** A multiprotocol, multiport router with bridging, routing, and data link switching functions to receive and transmit multiple protocols from one LAN to another. The data link switching function encapsulates SNA and NetBIOS frames into an IP datagram for transport over a WAN. Communications adapter support includes token-ring, Ethernet, SDLC, and other serial communications adapters.

- **IBM 8228 Multistation Access Unit:** A passive wiring concentrator (hub) that supports up to eight LAN stations via device attachment ports. Also known as a MAU.

- **IBM 8230 Controlled Access Unit:** An intelligent token-ring network wiring concentrator (hub). IBM 8230 hubs are the next step up from 8228s for token-ring LANs. They have on-board intelligence and can be managed with IBM LAN Network Manager. Each 8230 has one controlled access unit (a CAU) and up to four lobe attachment modules (LAM) with 20 ports each. This gives a maximum of 80 ports per 8230. The CAU controls the ports on each LAM. 8230s automatically shut down beaconing ports. This corrects one of the major flaws in the older technology 8228. LAN Network Manager can be used to manage the 8230s.

- **IBM 8260 Multi-protocol Intelligent Switching Hub:** The high-end member of the IBM intelligent hub product family. The 8260 can handle up to 8 Ethernet, 17 token-ring, or 8 FDDI networks in one

17-slot hub. It is able to integrate emerging ATM technology. It supports IBM 8250 modules for full forward compatibility.

- **IBM LAN Bridge Manager/2 (LBM/2):** an IBM program product that enables distributed installation, setup, and management of IBM token-ring bridge program products. It simplifies the software installation and management of LAN bridges including bridge code, filters, drivers, and configuration files. Additionally, an administrator can remotely manage hop counts, thresholds, passwords, etc. All bridge configuration files are automatically backed up to one central server.

- **IBM LAN Network Manager for AIX (LNM for AIX):** Works with the AIX NetView/6000 program to enable effective management of the LAN resources of a network. The functions of the LNM for AIX are integrated into the AIX NetView/6000 interface, enabling management of the physical resources in a multiprotocol network from a single workstation.

- **IBM LAN Network Manager:** LNM is a network management and problem determination aid for a LAN that is composed of one or more IBM token-ring segments. LNM provides fault, configuration, and performance management capabilities for hubs, bridges, LAN segments, PCs, and adapters. It runs over OS/2 and communicates with host NetView. LNM uses a form of CMIP for communication. It uses the OS/2 query manager database for data storage and retrieval.

- **IBM LAN Station Manager:** LSM is a network management application that automates asset management data collection and measures ring utilization over a network. When used in conjunction with the IBM LAN Network Manager application running on a server, LSM will pass PC and user information to a DB2/2 for OS/2 database for subsequent analysis.

- **IBM NetView/6000:** An AIX-based network management platform that runs on RS/6000 systems. It manages network resources using SNMP. It includes several management applications, include fault monitoring and diagnosis, performance monitoring, and network configuration applications. It integrates with IBM's host NetView product. NetView/6000 provides an graphical user interface that provides a dynamic graphical topology map and access to network management applications and diagnostics facilities.

- **IBM NetView MVS/ESA:** IBM's host-based network management platform for the MVS/ESA operating system. NetView MVS/ESA provides a centralized management point for all resources in an enterprise, with emphasis on operational status and automation. NetView MVS/ESA provides an integration/consolidation point for other resources.

- **IBM Token-Ring Network 16/4 Trace and Performance Program and Adapters (TAP):** This hardware-software combination provides valuable information for debugging application software, capacity planning and network reconfiguration. It analyzes trace data, measures media usage and collects ring-station traffic statistics.

- **Network General Sniffer:** The Sniffer, a product of the Network General company, is a tool for complex network problem determination. The Sniffer is a powerful, user-friendly tracing and monitoring device. Trace analysis is enhanced by the use of artificial intelligence features. Filters can be set up to find and store very specific types of traces.

- **SES Workbench:** A performance modeling application for complex networks from Scientific and Engineering Software Inc. It runs on the RS/6000 with AIX.

- **Xyplex Communications Server:** A communications server from Xyplex Inc. for TCP/IP networks. Remote clients using TCP/IP (SLIP or PPP) can communicate over the public telephone network to access an internal LAN-based network.

- **Boca Cable Tracking System (BCTS):** An internally developed central database containing all network port locations cross-referenced with office locations.

- **EZPAGE:** An internally developed, OS/2-based application that receives alerts over a network and generates appropriate telephone pages.

- **Global Service Coordinator (GSC):** An internally developed application that provides centralized service of network problems on an AIX, RS/6000 system. GSC can receive alerts from NetView/6000, LAN Network Manager, and other network management systems. It consists of a server and a graphical client.

- **Network Early Warning System (NEWS):** NEWS is a locally developed application that confirms connectivity across the site network at the data-link layer. NEWS records any outages in a DB2/2 database and automatically generates a page for network administrators 24 hours a day.

- **OS2ping:** Every network support person carries a ping program with them when troubleshooting problems. The locally developed OS2ping program is used to search the network for a specified adapter address. OS2ping results determine network paths, connectivity, adapter type, performance, hop counts, and capacity.

- **Protect:** A locally developed application that plays a major role in preventing incorrectly configured workstations from adversely effect the site's gateways. The Protect program continuously polls the network for unauthorized adapters and automatically removes them from the network when found. The primary use is to remove duplicate gateway addresses and name server addresses.

- **Rupoll:** A locally developed application that works with LNM and LSM. Rupoll automatically polls specified ring segments for LSM devices at specified periods and stores the results in a DB/2 for OS/2 database.

- **Regional Information Database System (RIDS):** An internally developed, mainframe database system that contains a record of each authorized network user and their respective network addresses (e.g., TCP/IP address, adapter address).

- **QNET:** QNET and a suite of AIX-based locally developed tools monitor application activity on the RS/6000 servers in the Server Farm. If these tools determine that an application session is down, they generate a page to the server administrators.

Chapter 7: Communication, Education, and Support

- **HelpPlus:** An internally developed application that provides OS/2 desktop-based user problem reporting, server status, and self-help.

Appendix B:

Glossary of Terms

Client/Server promises the packaging of knowledge from information, not information from data.

[DATAQUEST]

10Base-T   IEEE standard for twisted-pair Ethernet (10 Mbps, baseband, 500 meters).

100VG-AnyLAN   A version of the Fast Ethernet protocol suite, currently in the proposal stage, that can transmit data over all common cabling systems at 100 Mbps. The 100VG-AnyLAN proposal uses a Demand Priority method to grant individual device access to the network, an approach that is superior to CSMA/CD, the traditional Ethernet method.

100-BaseX   A version of the Fast Ethernet protocol suite, currently in the proposal stage, that can transmit data over most common cabling systems at speeds of 100 Mbps. 100-BaseX uses the traditional Ethernet CSMA/CD method to grant individual device access to the network.

802.2   IEEE standard for logical link control.

802.3   IEEE standard for the CSMA/CD (Ethernet) network access method.

802.5   IEEE standard for the token-ring network access method.

ACL   Access Control List. Data that controls access to a protected object. An access control list specifies the privilege attributes needed to access the object and the permissions that may be granted.

Accounting Management (AM)   One of the five standard network management functions. AM facilities calculate the amount of network time used by each segment of the network and facilitate a billing system for the usage of resources [Modiri, 1991].

ACK   Acknowledge. A network packet acknowledging the receipt of data.

ACSE   Association Control Service Element. The method used in OSI for establishing a call between two applications. Checks the identities and contexts of the application entities, and could apply an authentication security check.

ADMD   Administration Management Domain. An X.400 Message Handling System public service carrier. The ADMDs in all countries worldwide together provide the X.400 backbone. See *PRMD*.

AFS (Andrew File System)   A distributed Network File System for Very Large Scale Networking (VLSN).

Agent   A portion of a network management system that reports information about conditions and accept commands to alter the state of one or more managed objects. Typical commands are GET, SET, CREATE, DELETE, and ACTION.

AIX   IBM's version of UNIX, available on the PS/2, RISC System/6000 and other platforms. AIX on the RISC System/6000 is based on OSF/1 and meets 1151 of the 1170 elements of SPEC1170.

Alert   A network management term for data sent from a network management agent to a manager indicating that some action is to be taken or a problem has occurred.

Alias   A name, usually short and easy to remember, that is translated into another name, usually long and difficult to remember.

Alpha test   The first test of a software application or operating system performed by an external, volunteer organization.

Andrew File System   See *AFS*.

ANSI   American National Standards Institute. The U.S. standardization body. ANSI is a member of the International Organization for Standardization (ISO).

API   Application Program Interface. A functional interface supplied by the operating system or by a separately orderable licensed program that allows an application program written in a high-level language to use specific data or functions of the operating system or the licensed program.

APPC   Advanced Program to Program Communication. An API embodied in SNA LU 6.2 that supports synchronous program-to-program communications. It is the SNA implementation of CPI-C.

AppleTalk   A networking protocol developed by Apple Computer for communication between Apple Computer products and other computers.

Application Layer   The topmost layer in the OSI Reference Model, providing such communication services as electronic mail and file transfer.

Application Server   A server system that runs application code in response to a client system's request.

Archie   An Internet application for locating publicly available files using anonymous ftp.

ARP   Address Resolution Protocol. A method to translate an IP address into a MAC (Media Access Control) address.

ASCII   American Standard Code for Information Interchange. A 7-bit code representing 128 discrete characters without using a shift code. It defines 96 printable characters (A through Z in upper- and lowercase, 0 through 9, and punctuation marks) and several control characters (carriage return, line feed, and backspace). An eighth bit called a parity bit is sometimes added for error-checking. IBM developed an Extended ASCII with eight bits per characters for the IBM Personal Computer in 1981. The lower 128 characters (0 through 127) are standard ASCII; the higher 128 characters (128 through 255) are for international punctuation and other special characters.

ASN.1   Abstract Syntax Notation One. The language used by the OSI protocols for describing abstract syntax. This language is also used to encode SNMP packets. ASN.1 is defined in ISO documents 8824.2 and 8825.2. Also see *Basic Encoding Rules*.

Async   Asynchronous. Operating without precise clocking. Also, a method to transmit data that sends a single character at a time.

ATM   Asynchronous Transfer Mode. A method of high-speed data transmission that can dynamically allocate bandwidth to multiple data streams of different types by breaking each stream into 53-byte cells (5-byte header, 48 bytes of data) of information. It is intended to support many different types of traffic on a single network (e.g., voice, video, and data). ATM is planned to be used as a basic data transport technique for high-speed WAN and LAN applications. Operating speeds are from 25 Mbps to 155 Mbps for individual connections today. Gigabit range transmissions are predicted within the next five years.

Attribute   A term used for a data item for a network management system or a directory service (such as X.500). An attribute consists of a type identifier along with one or more values.

Authentication   Verifying that a data transmission from a person (or a process) is indeed from that person (or process).

B-ISDN See *Broadband ISDN*.

Backbone That portion of a network used to interconnect major subnetworks. For example, the cable used to connect the networks of two buildings on a site could be called a backbone.

Backplane A board in a hub or router that contains one or more buses that carry all network communications, enabling internetworking among the various modules that directly connect different LAN segments. The backplane is analogous to a PC bus to which various interface cards are connected.

Bandwidth The amount of data that can be transmitted across a particular network. Token-ring has a 16 Mbps bandwidth. Technically, bandwidth is defined as the difference, in Hertz (Hz), between the highest and lowest frequencies of a transmission channel.

Baseband A network technology that uses a single frequency for data transmission. All communicating stations participate in every transmission.

Baud The number of modulations of an analog signal in one second, typically referring to data transmission speed over a telephone line.

BBS See *Bulletin Board System*.

Beacons, Ring Beacon When a token ring has a hard failure that brings it down, the ring enters the beacon state. Ring beacons are most commonly caused by user machines coming up on a ring at the wrong speed.

BER Basic Encoding Rules for ASN.1.

Berkeley Software Distribution (BSD) UNIX operating system and its utilities developed and distributed by the University of California at Berkeley. "BSD" is usually preceded by the version number of the distribution; e.g., "4.3 BSD" is version 4.3 of the Berkeley UNIX distribution.

Beta test The second major test phase performed on an unreleased version of a software application or operating system by an external volunteer or internal organization. Since beta test follows alpha test, it is assumed that the software is basically stable and will only have a few minor bugs left. It is a very common practice in the PC software industry for software vendors to recruit a large number of external volunteers to participate in a beta test of an update to an existing application or the release of a new one.

Big-endian A format for storage or transmission of binary data in which the most significant bit (or byte) comes first. The reverse convention is called little-endian.

BOC Bell Operating Company. A more common term is RBOC for Regional Bell Operating Company. The local telephone company in each of the seven U.S. regions.

Bps   Bits per second. The rate of data transmission across a network.

Bridge   A device that transparently interconnects two LANs that use the same logical link control protocol but may use different Media Access Control (MAC) protocols. This is performed in a manner transparent to higher levels on the protocol stack. Only data destined for the other LAN is transferred. Bridges can usually be made to filter packets, that is, to forward only certain traffic. Related devices are repeaters, which simply forward electrical signals from one cable to another, and full-fledged routers, which make routing decisions based on several criteria.

Broadband   The multiplexing of multiple independent network data streams onto a single cable. This is usually done using frequency division multiplexing. Broadband technology allows several networks to coexist on a single cable; traffic from one network does not interfere with traffic from another because the "conversations" happen on different frequencies in the "ether," rather like the commercial radio system.

Broadband ISDN (B-ISDN)   Digital data transmission standard to handle high bandwidth applications, such as video. The architecture supports wide-area transmission at speeds of 51, 155, and 622 Mbps per channel. Eventually 2.4 Gbps will be supported. Fiber-optic cable is required.

Broadcast   A packet delivery system in which a copy of a given packet is given to all hosts attached to the network. Example: token-ring.

Broadcast storm   Condition when an incorrect packet is broadcast onto a network, which causes multiple systems to respond all at once (typically with equally incorrect packets, which causes the storm to grow exponentially in severity).

Brouter   A combination bridge and router device that transmits data between networks at both the data link and network layers.

Bulletin Board System (BBS)   A computer, and associated software, that typically provides electronic messaging services, archives of files, and any other services or activities of interest to the bulletin board system's operator. Although BBSs have traditionally been the domain of hobbyists, an increasing number of BBSs are connected directly to the Internet, and many BBSs are currently operated by government, educational, and research institutions [Kochmer, 1992].

Cable   The wires used to interconnect one or more network components. Cable types include twisted pair, coaxial, and fiber optic.

CAE   Common Application Environment. The formal standards adopted by X/Open, together with the X/Open specifications.

CASE (Computer-Aided Software Engineering)   Software products that aid software developers with data modeling, library management, and code generation.

CAU   Controlled Access Unit. A term used by IBM to describe its intelligent hubs, such as the 8230.

CCITT   International Consultative Committee for Telegraphy and Telephony. A unit of the International Telecommunications Union (ITU) of the United Nations. An organization with representatives from the PTTs of the world. CCITT produces technical standards, known as "Recommendations," for all internationally controlled aspects of analog and digital communications.

CDE   Common Desktop Environment. CDE was defined by COSE and is a consistent set of APIs for the desktop that will run across the systems of the COSE members. It is modeled on IBM's OS/2 Workplace Shell and has been submitted to X/Open for planned adoption in 1994 in the UNIX environment.

CD-I   Compact Disk–Interactive. A format developed by Philips Consumer Electronics Co. for recording and playing interactive multimedia program on 120-mm optical (compact) disks.

CDDI   Copper Distributed Data Interface. FDDI over shielded or unshielded twisted-pair copper wire.

CDPD   Cellular Digital Packet Data. A wireless communication standard transporting digital data packets at 19.2 Kbps across idle channels on cellular telephone networks.

CD-R   Compact Disk–Recordable. A 120-mm optical (compact) disc on which data can be recorded once and read many times.

CD-ROM   Compact Disk–Read-Only-Memory. CD format for text, graphics, and hi-fidelity stereo sound.

CD-ROM XA   CD-ROM eXtended Architecture. CD enhanced format that supports concurrent audio and video. This was originally supported by Sony, Philips, and Microsoft.

Channel Service Unit (CSU)   When paired with a DSU, or Data Service Unit, the CSU/DSU interconnects a LAN bridge or router with a WAN.

Checksum   A calculated value that depends on the contents of a packet. This value is sent along with the packet when it is transmitted. The receiving system computes a new checksum based upon the received data and compares this value with the checksum of the packet. If the two values are equal, the receiver is assured that the data was received correctly.

CID (Configuration, Installation, Distribution)   An IBM architecture that supports electronic code distribution. An application that is CID-enabled is set up to be electronically distributed over a network.

CIO (Chief Information Officer)   The individual responsible for management of a business unit's information technology infrastructure, ongoing investments, and ongoing support.

Circuit   A direct data stream between two systems on a network.

Circuit switching A communications paradigm in which a dedicated communication path, on which all packets travel, is established between two hosts. The public telephone system is an example of a circuit-switched network.

Circuit-switched service A category of long-distance telecommunication service in which the equipment dials a connection, transfers data, and hangs up when it completes the transmission [Derfler, 1993].

CISC Complex Instruction Set Computer. A computer whose processor is designed to sequentially run variable-length instructions, many of which require several clock cycles, that perform complex tasks and thereby simplify programming.

Client A computer or process that accesses the data, services, or resources of another computer or process on the network.

Client/server computing A computing model in which clients' systems (usually intelligent PCs and workstations) run user applications. The applications use a combination of their resources and a portion of the storage and computing resources of one or more server systems (e.g., high-performance PCs) to perform useful work. The application portion on the client requests server resources by communicating over a network.

Client/server network A computer network in which client systems use the network to request services and data from network-attached server systems.

CLNP Connectionless Network Protocol. The OSI protocol for providing the OSI Connectionless Network Service (datagram service). CLNP is the OSI equivalent to Internet IP, and is sometimes called ISO IP.

CLTP Connectionless Transport Protocol. Provides for end-to-end Transport data addressing (via Transport selector) and error control (via checksum), but cannot guarantee delivery or provide flow control. The OSI equivalent of UDP.

CMC Common Mail Calls. A proposed cross-platform standard from the X.400 API Association. It defines a messaging interface to applications. It is supported by IBM, Microsoft, Novell, Lotus, and Hewlett-Packard.

CME OSI-compliant Conformant Management Entity.

CMIP Common Management Interface Protocol Standard, ISO IS 9596-1. A definition of control blocks that define transmission of network management information. It is part of the Organization for Standardization (ISO) and Open Systems Interconnection (OSI) specification.

CMIS Common Management Interface Service, ISO IS 9595. The set of services provided by the common management information service element.

Collapsed backbone A collapsed backbone is formed when the midplane/backplane of a box (hub, bridge, router) is used as the backbone. The performance on a collapsed backbone is often better than on a normal backbone.

Communication services The software and protocols that move data across the network.

Compiler A computer program that converts source programs (e.g., C or FORTRAN) into executable (or binary) programs.

Compound document A document or a part of a document that contains text, graphics, scanned images, audio, and full-motion video data.

Concentrator Another term for a hub.

Confidentiality A term used in computer security to mean encryption of transmitted data.

Configuration and Name Management (CM) One of the five standard network management functions. CM facilities enable a network manager to exercise control over the configuration of a communication subsystem by allowing the a manager to close down nodes at will should a fault occur or workloads change [Modiri, 1991].

Connectionless service A data transmission service in which each frame of data can be broken up into one or more independent packets, each containing both a source and destination address. The packets may be delivered out of sequence or dropped. Sometimes called datagram service. Examples: LANs, Internet IP, ordinary postcards.

Connection-oriented The model of interconnection in which communication proceeds through three well-defined phases: connection establishment, data transfer, and connection release. Examples: X.25, Internet TCP and OSI TP4, ordinary telephone calls.

CORBA Common Object Request Broker Architecture. A set of specifications to enable objects to transparently make requests and receive responses across a computer network.

Corporate network Connects two or more geographically distant sites, where each site connects several hundred users.

COS Corporation for Open Systems. A vendor-sponsored organization that intends to deal with today's pressing network integration problems and solutions. Among the members of COS are AT&T, DEC, IBM, and the U.S. government.

COSE Common Open Software Environment. An open standards acceleration organization. Unusual in that it met entirely electronically. COSE was incorporated within OSF in March 1994.

CPI-C Common Programming Interface—Communications. Isolates applications from the networking protocols used to implement the end-to-end data-exchange facilities. CPI-C has been selected as the conversation API for X/Open (TCP/IP) and AIX/OSF, and is rapidly becoming an industry standard.

CPU   Central processing unit. The part of a computer system that executes instructions.

CSMA/CD   Carrier Sense Multiple Access with Collision Detection. The media access control method employed by Ethernet networks.

CSU   See *Channel Service Unit*.

CUA   Common User Access. A worldwide IBM standard defined for the screen interface for end users. It is part of IBM's Systems Application Architecture.

Cyclic Redundancy Check (CRC)   A number derived from a set of data that will be transmitted. By recalculating the CRC at the remote end and comparing it to the value originally transmitted, the receiving node can detect some types of transmission errors [Malamud, 1992].

DAE   Distributed Application Environment. An IBM family of programs that offer client/server computing spanning IBM and non-IBM hardware and software.

Daemon   An event-triggered program, equivalent in function to an agent.

DASD   Direct Access Storage Device. A hard disk is an example.

Data Model   Describes the data that a computer process works with and produces.

Datagram   A data packet transmitted through a network with prior connection being established between the source and destination systems.

Data Link Layer   Layer 2 of most network architectures. Defines the method to transmit data between two network entities across a single physical connection or a series of bridged connections.

Data Link Switching   See *DLS*.

Data Service Unit (DSU)   When paired with a CSU, or Channel Service Unit, the CSU/DSU interconnects a LAN bridge or router with a WAN.

DBMS   Database Management System.

DCE   (1) Data Circuit-terminating Equipment, a device used in X.25 networks that accepts/starts calls. (2) The Distributed Computing Environment, which is a definition of networking support programs as provided by the Open Software Foundation (OSF). It defines the interface from a workstation to a network and includes a naming service, a remote procedure call, and a distributed file system (also called an Andrew File System or AFS).

Decision Support Systems (DSS). Software products that provide services, such as an interactive query of a database, or functions, such as statistical routines, that give meaning to information. DSS presents the information to the end users.

DECnet   Digital Equipment Corporation's proprietary network architecture.

Dependent display terminal   Typically a combined CRT display and keyboard device connected to a network that transmits keystrokes to a multiuser system running a desired application. The multiuser system returns updated user interface screens to the terminal. These were most commonly employed by mainframe multiuser systems. A similar use is currently employed in client/server networks with the X-Windows architecture.

DES Data Encryption Standard. A widely used, government-sponsored, data encryption method that scrambles data into an unbreakable code for transmission over a public network. The encryption key has over 72 quadrillion combinations and is randomly chosen.

Dictionary/Directory An inventory of data resources that controls the totality of data elements within an application and that serves as the repository of all descriptive information about each data element, including location information.

Digital Switch See *Switch*.

Directory In DCE, the directory contains information about resources, services, objects and users on the network. This makes it simple to find each of these things by using only the name and makes it possible for each component to be moved in the network as business or technology dictate without needing to change applications.

Distributed computing A type of computing that allows computers with different hardware and software to be combined on a network to function as a single computer to share the task of processing application programs.

Distributed database A collection of several different data repositories that looks like a single database to the user.

Distributed Directory Services A DCE service that provides a single naming model throughout the distributed computing environment, enabling users to identify network resources by name. With this universal naming system, users can locate and access servers, files, disks, or print queues without specifying their physical location in the network [Faulkner, 1994].

Distributed Relational Database Architecture See *DRDA*.

Distributed services Permits transparent sharing of files and other system resources among systems.

DLS Data Link Switching. An IBM network protocol used to encapsulate nonroutable protocols (e.g., NetBIOS) across a WAN within the routable TCP/IP. Introduced by IBM on the 6611 product.

DME Distributed Management Environment, developed by the OSF, defines a set of APIs for writing applications to manage distributed computing environments.

DNA DEC's Digital Network Architecture for telecommunications.

DNS Domain Name System. The distributed name/address mechanism used in the Internet.

Document compiler A software program that translates a document and a set of tags into final printed output. The IBM document compiler, BookMaster, used tags of the form :P. and :H1, where :P. indicated the start of a paragraph and :H1 indicated a new title for a page.

Domain (1) That part of a network in which the data processing resources are under common control. (2) In TCP/IP, the naming system used in hierarchical networks.

Domain controller A designated server in a client/server network responsible for control of a set of data processing resources, such as a group of file servers or printers. Clients will gain access to these resources by logging on to the domain controller.

Dotted decimal notation The syntactic representation for a 32-bit integer that consists of four 8-bit numbers written in base 10 with periods (dots) separating them. Used to represent IP addresses in the Internet, as in 192.67.67.20.

Download The transmission of data from a mainframe to a PC or from a server to a client. See *Upload.*

DRDA Distributed Relational Database Architecture. IBM's architecture for allowing relational databases on a network to interconnect and share data.

DSAP Destination Service Access Point. The network (MAC) address of the destination of a data transmission.

DSA Directory System Agent. The software that provides the X.500 Directory Service for a portion of the directory information base. Generally, each DSA is responsible for the directory information for a single organization or organizational unit.

DSOM Distributed Systems Object Method. A complete implementation of CORBA. DSOM works transparently with SOM.

DSU See *Data Service Unit.*

DUA Directory User Agent. The software that accesses the X.500 Directory Service on behalf of the directory user. The directory user may be a person or another software element.

DTE Data Terminal Equipment. The user's terminal device used in X.25 networks.

EBCDIC Extended Binary Coded Decimal Interchange Code. An 8-bit code defining 256 different characters used on IBM mainframes.

EDA Electronic Design Automation. A set of software tools that aid electrical engineers in designing VLSI chips and printed circuit boards.

EDI Electronic Data Interchange. A computer sends required data in electronic form over telecommunication lines directly to the receiver's computer [Tapscott, 1993].

EIA Electronic Industries Association. A standards-making body recently renamed Telecommunications Industries Association (TIA).

Electronic mail   E-mail. A system that allows users to send messages on a network.

Empowered team   A team of workers who are able to make any and all decisions necessary to accomplish their mission and are accountable for the results.

Empowerment   A management approach to give technical professionals more autonomy and decision-making power in the organization.

Encapsulation   The technique used by layered protocols in which a layer adds header information to the Protocol Data Unit (PDU) from the layer above. As an example, in Internet terminology, a packet would contain a header from the physical layer, followed by a header from the network layer (IP), followed by a header from the transport layer (TCP), followed by the application data.

Encryption   The manipulation of data in order to prevent any but the intended recipient from reading that data. There are many types of data encryption that are the basis of network security.

Ethernet   A 10 Mbps standard for LANs, initially developed by Xerox, and later refined by Digital, Intel, and Xerox (DIX). All hosts are connected to a coaxial cable where they contend for network access using a Carrier Sense Multiple Access with Collision Detection (CSMA/CD) paradigm. Adopted as an IEEE standard (802.3).

Event driven   An application that can respond to events occurring in its environments (such as a keystroke or a message from another application).

Fast Ethernet   An emerging new set of protocols that can transmit data over most conventional cables at 100 Mbps. Two versions are in the proposal stage: 100VG-AnyLAN and 100-BaseX.

Fault Management (FM)   One of the five standard network management functions. FM facilities alert a network manager when a fault is detected. Provides isolation, examines error logs, accepts and acts upon error detection notifications, traces faults, and corrects faults arising from abnormal operation [Modiri, 1991].

Fax (Facsimile)   A machine that scans a paper form, converts the image to a coded stream of bits, and transmits it over the public telephone network. See *Group III Standard.*

FCS   Fiber Channel Standard. A draft ANSI standard that provides a fiber-optic replacement for the SCSI, IPI, and HiPPI copper channel standards.

FDDI   Fiber Distributed Data Interface. A high-speed (100 Mbps) protocol for fiber-optic LANs.

Federation of databases   A set of internally consistent database and all tied together by another database "designed to meet the needs of senior management" [Vaskevitch, 1993].

File Server A server system that stores files created by application programs and makes them available for sharing by clients on the network.

Filtering When applied to a network bridge, filtering refers to the recognition of the type of a data packet and redirecting it to another path on the network or rejecting it.

Firewall When applied to a large site network, a firewall is computer-controlled boundary that prevents unauthorized access to the network for transmitting and receiving data.

Flame To express strong opinion and/or criticism of something, usually as a frank inflammatory statement in an electronic message.

Fractional T1 A WAN service that provides one or more 64 Kbps channels of a T1 line.

Frame A set of data bytes transmitted or received by the data link layer of the network protocol stack. A frame will consist of a header, information, and trailer bytes. When physically transmitted, it may be broken up into one or more packets.

Frame Relay A WAN service protocol for high-speed, long-distance digital data packet transmission. It is a simplification of the X.25 protocol on a faster channel. Therefore, it is ideal to interconnect two LANs over a WAN and is replacing X.25 commercial services. It is designed to provide high-speed packet transmission, very low network delay, and efficient use of network bandwidth. From 64 Kbps to 1.544 Mbps speeds are defined.

FTAM File Transfer, Access, and Management. The OSI remote file service and protocol.

FTP File Transfer Protocol. A protocol (and program) used with TCP/IP to send files over a network.

Full Duplex Transmission The transmission of data across a network in both directions at the same time.

Full-period service A category of telecommunication service that provides a dedicated circuit for data transmission for a single customer.

Gateway A program or system that converts and routes data from one application to another. E-mail programs typically contain gateways so that they can exchange messages with other messaging programs and services.

GML Generalized Markup Language. A document tagging language used to create formatted documents when interpreted by a document compiler such as BookMaster.

G.O.D. Architecture Global Operations Directorate approach to inter-network management in which a single management interface protocol is supported by each installed device. Impractical because of the large installed base of diverse equipment [Herman, 1991].

Gopher A distributed information service that makes available hierarchical collections of information across the Internet. Gopher uses a simple protocol that allows a single Gopher client to access information from any accessible Gopher server, providing the user with a single "Gopher space" of information. Public-domain versions of the client and server are available.

GOSIP (Government OSI Profile)   The subset of the OSI protocols endorsed by the U.S. government.

Group III Standard   A standard for compressed transmission of fax data developed by the CCITT. It specifies a format of 203 horizontal dots by 98 vertical dots per inch in standard resolution mode, or about 1,400,000 dots, or pixels, for a page of text.

Groupware   A new classification of application software that allows users to conveniently share data across a telecommunications network.

Guardbanding   A term used to describe an engineering practice of designing the parts of a system to operate with sufficient tolerance in a performance band, such that the system will operate successfully even if new parts are substituted.

GUI   (GOO-ee). Graphical User Interface. A pictorial way of representing to a user the capabilities of a system and the work being done on it.

Half-duplex transmission   The transmission of data across a network in which only one side can send at a time.

Header   The portion of a packet, preceding the actual data, containing source and destination addresses, and error checking and other fields. A header is also the part of an electronic mail message that precedes the body of a message and contains, among other things, the message originator, date, and time.

Help Desk   A user problem support service. A staff of application and infrastructure experts are available by phone to resolve user problems in real time.

Hierarchical routing   The complex problem of routing on large networks can be simplified by reducing the size of the networks. This is accomplished by breaking a network into a hierarchy of networks in which each level is responsible for its own routing.

HiPPI   High-Performance Parallel Interface is a draft ANSI standard that provides high bandwidth, point-to-point transmission for the efficient transfer of large blocks of data over copper wires. It provides a point-to-point transmission with a peak data rate of 800 Mbps for 32 bit bus and 1.6 Gbps for 64 bit bus. The distance limitation is 25 meters.

Hop   A term used in routing. A path to a destination on a network is a series of hops, through routers, away from the origin.

Host   In the TCP/IP sense, a computer that allows users to communicate with other host computers on a network. Individual users communicate by using application programs, such as electronic mail, and ftp. Also, used to refer to a large computer system, such as a mainframe.

HSM Hierarchical Storage Manager. A data backup system that stages data on different storage devices typically based on frequency of use.

HSSI High Speed Serial Interface. The physical-layer interface between a DTE and a DCE at speeds in the SONET STS-1 range.

Hub A central point for the cables attached to one or more network interface cards on a LAN.

IAB Internet Activities Board. The technical body that oversees the development of the Internet suite of protocols (commonly referred to as TCP/IP). It has two task forces (the IRTF and the IETF), each charged with investigating a particular area.

ICMP Internet Control Message Protocol. The protocol used to handle errors and control messages at the IP layer. ICMP is a part of the Internet Protocol (IP).

IEEE Institute of Electrical and Electronic Engineers. A professional society and standards-making body.

IETF Internet Engineering Task Force. Part of the IAB, a volunteer group of engineers responsible for Internet standards development.

IMLG/2 The IBM Mail LAN Gateway/2 product, which runs on OS/2 and provides mail gateway service between OfficeVision/VM and Lotus Notes, among other applications.

Information Technology (IT) The computing and networking systems used by a business to process and store its information (data).

Information technology architecture The underlying framework that defines and describes the technology platform required by a business to attain its objective and achieve a business vision [Tapscott, 1993].

Information warehouse The totality of functions that make informational data available to end users by providing a mechanism for taking control of the information in an organization in a systematic manner.

Internet A set of connected networks. The term *Internet* refers to the large and growing public-domain internetwork developed by DARPA that uses TCP/IP. It is shared by universities, corporations, and private individuals. To be on the Internet you must have IP connectivity, i.e., be able to telnet to or ping other systems. Networks with only e-mail connectivity are not actually classified as being on the Internet.

Internet Address A number that identifies a host in an internet. It is a 32-bit address assigned to hosts using TCP/IP. See *Dotted decimal notation.*

Interoperability The ability of unlike systems to work heterogeneously. Computers of different sizes and brands can communicate together— sharing resources, information, and software applications [Tapscott, 1993].

IP Internet Protocol. The network-layer protocol for the Internet protocol suite.

IP datagram   The fundamental unit of information passed across the Internet. Contains source and destination addresses along with data and a number of fields that define such things as the length of the datagram, the header checksum, and flags to say whether the datagram can be (or has been) fragmented.

IPng   IP next generation. Under development by the IETF IPng committee, IPng is intended to upgrade the current IP to greatly increase the number of networks and nodes beyond the current 4 billion addresses, plus other enhancements to support future high-speed internetworking requirements.

IPX   Novell's Internetwork Packet Exchange network communication protocol.

I/S   Information Systems. The in-house information systems organization that provided mainframe system installation, support and application development until 1992 in Boca Raton.

ISDN   Integrated Services Digital Network. A standard architecture, specified by CCITT, for integrating different types of data streams on a single network, such as data, video, and voice. It is just recently being offered by the telephone carriers of the world.

ISSC   Integrated Systems Solutions Corporation. The IBM subsidiary that provides information system services to external and internal IBM customers. It absorbed the Boca Raton I/S services organization and now provides support in Boca Raton.

ISO   International Organization for Standardization

Kerberos   The security system of the MIT Athena project. It is based on symmetric key cryptography.

LAN   Local Area Network. The interconnection of several personal computers and other hardware such as printers. Designed originally as a means of sharing hardware and software among PCs; now used as a general means of communications between PCs.

LAN adapter   Moves data to and from a personal computer's memory to transmit and receive data over LAN cable.

LAN segment   See *Segment.*

LAPS   LAN Adapter Protocol Support. A suite of network communication software for OS/2. It includes the NDIS-compliant protocol and network adapter drivers.

Layer   Communication networks for computers may be organized as a set of more or less independent protocols, each in a different layer (also called a level). The lowest layer governs direct host-to-host communication between the hardware at different hosts; the highest consists of user applications. Each layer builds on the layer beneath it. For each layer, programs at different hosts use protocols appropriate to the layer to communicate with each other. TCP/IP has five layers of protocols;

OSI has seven. The advantages of different layers of protocols are that the methods of passing information from one layer to another are specified clearly as part of the protocol suite and that changes within a protocol layer are prevented from affecting the other layers. This greatly simplifies the task of designing and maintaining communication programs.

Legacy applications   Widely-used applications developed for large mainframe systems.

LIN (LAN Internetwork)   Multiple LANs interconnected within an organization.

Little-endian   A format for storage or transmission of binary data in which the least significant byte (bit) comes first.

LON   LAN Outer Network. Remote users who participate in the LAN by dialing into the network.

Local Area Network (LAN)   See *LAN*.

Logical LAN   One or more physical LANs that are bridged together, representing a single name space to any client within the logical LAN. May be physical LANs connected with a split bridge across a WAN, or may be all local to increase the size of the logical LAN beyond the size allowed on a single physical LAN.

Logical Link Control (LLC)   The upper portion of the data link layer, as defined in IEEE 802.2. The LLC sublayer presents a uniform interface to the user of the datalink service, usually the network layer. Beneath the LLC sublayer is the MAC sublayer.

LPRMON   A printer monitor utility supplied with IBM TCP/IP 2.0.

LU 6.2   Logical Unit 6.2. A peer-to-peer (system-to-system) communication protocol that supports program interoperability developed by IBM as part of SNA. Also called APPC.

MAC   Media Access Control. The process by which systems on a network control access to the network cable.

MAC address   The hardware address of a device connected to a shared media.

Mail gateway   A machine that connects two or more electronic mail systems (especially dissimilar mail systems on two different networks) and transfers messages between them.

Mainframe   A large computer system, such as a IBM System/370 or System/390 architecture computing system running either the MVS or VM operating system. See *Host*.

MAN   Metropolitan Area Network. A LAN-like network that covers larger geographic distances (up to 50 km), possibly crossing public rights-of-way.

Managed Object   Managed element of a network. "The managed object forms an abstract representation of a resource looked at from the perspective of management. It may be a physical item, such as a multi-plexer, or it may be logical, such as a connection. The managed object contains attributes, each attribute having a value" [Mazda, 1991].

Management console   A display terminal which provides the status of one or more network entities and sometimes the ability to respond to network events, such as faults.

MAPI   Messaging Application Program Interface. A standard software interface for message interchange provided by the Microsoft Corporation.

MAU   Multistation Access Unit. Used for token-ring networks to centrally connect one or more devices. Also called a hub or concentrator.

Media   Material that stores or transmits data. Network cable, magnetic tape, and diskettes are examples of media.

Message Integrity Checks (MICs)   Methods to ensure that a transmitted message has not been tampered with.

MHS   Message Handling System. A server-based application to process electronic mail messages.

MIB   Management Information Base. A rigorously defined database for network management information. It is the conceptual repository of management information within an open system. It consists of the set of managed objects, together with their attributes. Standard, minimal MIBs have been defined, and vendors often have private enterprise MIBs.

Middleware   Any set of software routines or functions that allow two dissimilar programs to interoperate. The term typically refers to software that supports client/server database applications that transparently allow clients to access data from one or more database servers.

MIS   Management Information System.

Mobile client   A client system with access to the enterprise network, but not present on the site. This includes truly mobile notebook systems as well as desktop systems permanently stationed at a user's home.

Modem   A device that converts binary information into on-and-off analog tones that can be transmitted over analog telephone lines. The original modem operated at 300 bits per second. Today, the most common speed is 9,600 bits per second. Up to 57,600 bits per second is the maximum today. Since they typically connect to a computer or terminal, an RS232C communications interface is used [Derfler, 1993].

MOM Architecture   Manager-Of-Managers architecture, in which a hierarchy of network managers is established and each network management system communicates with a common protocol to a MOM. Difficult to maintain, as administrators must support multiple management systems [Herman, 1991].

Mosaic   An application, with a GUI interface, that supports easy browsing of information on the Internet. In addition to standard binary and text files, Mosaic supports multimedia information. It was developed by the Software Development of the National Center for Supercomputing Applications at the University of Illinois.

Multicast A special form of broadcast in which copies of the packet are delivered to only a subset of all possible destinations. See *Broadcast.*

Multimedia The combination of text, graphics, image, sound, and video in a single application or data stream.

Multi-mode fibers Optical fibers that have larger cores than single-mode fibers and so can use a variety of light sources and connections. They cannot be used for long-distance transmissions.

Multiplexing Fixed assignment of the capacity of a data transmission media to several users.

MVP Architecture MultiVendor Management Platform architecture, in which each device and management system use a common set of management services, protocols, and databases [Herman, 1991].

MVS IBM's Multiple Virtual System operating system for mainframe computers.

Name resolution The process of mapping a name into the corresponding address, typically a TCP/IP address.

Name server A server system used in a TCP/IP network that converts TCP/IP network addresses into names and vice versa. An example of a TCP/IP name is bocaraton.ibm.com, which is recognizable and can be used for e-mail purposes. It corresponds to a unique number that is the actual network address. The name server performs the conversion on request.

Named Pipes An interprocess protocol used by OS/2, LAN Manager, and LAN Server to communicate between server and client.

NDIS Microsoft's Network Driver Interface Standard defines a standard interface between network communication software (i.e., redirector software) and the network interface card (LAN adapter).

NetBEUI (net-boo-ee) Microsoft's NetBIOS Extended User Interface. Client software that redirects application software requests for service across the network.

NetBIOS Network Basic Input Output System. Client software that redirects application software requests for service across the network. Originally developed in 1984 as a high-level programming interface to the IBM PC Network i n 1984, it quickly became a de facto session layer standard for the LAN industry. Most major LAN vendors support NetBIOS.

Network A computer network is a data communications system that interconnects computer systems. A network may be composed of any combination of LANs, MANs, or WANs.

Network address   The network portion of an IP address. For a class A network, the network address is the first byte of the IP address. For a class B network, the network address is the first two bytes of the IP address. For a class C network, the network address is the first three bytes of the IP address. In each case, the remainder is the host address. In the Internet, assigned network addresses are globally unique.

Network architecture   How systems are to be interconnected in a network.

Network cable   The media that carries the digital network signals.

Network interface card   See *LAN adapter.*

Network layer   The OSI layer that is responsible for routing, switching, and subnetwork access across the network environment.

Network licensing   A method of purchasing usage rights to an application over a network in which only the number of simultaneous users determines the number of licenses required to be purchased.

Network management services   Software and hardware service tools that enable a network administrator to manage a network (e.g., diagnose and repair faults, measure performance, and resolved bottlenecks).

Network Operating System (NOS)   A family of programs that run on networked computers. Some programs provide the ability to share files, printers, and other devices across the network.

NFS   Network File System. A network service that allows a system to access data stored on a different system as if it were on its own local storage. Part of the ONC standards developed by Sun Microsystems.

NIC   Network Interface Card. Another term for LAN adapter.

NMS   Network Management Station. The system responsible for managing a (portion of a) network. The NMS talks to network management agents, which reside in the managed nodes, via a network management protocol. See *Agent.*

NOC   Network Operations Center. Any center tasked with the operational aspects of a production network. These tasks include monitoring and control, troubleshooting, user assistance, and other similar tasks [Jacobsen, 1991].

NSAP   Network Service Access Point. The point at which the OSI Network Service is made available to a Transport entity. The NSAPs are identified by OSI Network Addresses.

Null modem   An RS232-C cable that allows two DTEs to communicate directly.

Object   A set of programs or subroutines, called methods, and data, called variables, that model something in the real world.

Object Identifier   An OSI concept for hierarchical naming that provides a handle by which to refer to objects. By assigning each node in the hierarchy a value unique among its sibling nodes, a node can be identified by the concatenation of the values assigned to those nodes in the path from the root node down the tree to the identified node. This facilitates "walking the MIB" functionality by an Agent or network management application [McCloghrie, 1989].

Object-oriented design A method of software development in which code and related data are developed and treated like a self-contained object. A critical feature of the tools that support this method, called inheritance, is the ability to create new objects by referring to existing objects.

Object request broker The mechanism that allows objects to communicate with each other over a network.

OC-n Optical Carrier-n. SONET hierarchy for fiber-optic transmission.

SONET Level	Rate (Mbps)
OC-1	51.84
OC-3	155.52
OC-9	466.56
OC-12	622.08
OC-18	933.12
OC-24	1,244.16
OC-36	1,866.24
OC-48	2,488.32

ODI Novell's Open Data-Link Interface defines a standard interface for network communication software to interface with a network interface card (LAN adapter).

Office client An office client is a PC with e-mail, calendar, phone directory, network connectivity, and, optionally, word processing, spreadsheet, and business graphics applications installed in an office.

OfficeVision An IBM VM application that supports electronic mail, calendar, documents and file management. Also known as OfficeVision/VM, OV or OV/VM.

OLE Object Linking and Embedding. A compound document architecture controlled by Microsoft.

OLTP Online Transaction Processing. Near-real-time handling of incoming transactions by a computer system.

OMG Object Management Group. A standards-setting body for object-oriented design.

ONC Open Network Computing. A distributed applications architecture promoted and controlled by a consortium led by Sun Microsystems.

Open Blueprint IBM's direction for distributed products and solutions. It is a structure for customers to organize products and applications in an open, distributed environment. It is also a guide for developers to provide function to integrate and operate with other products.

Open System   An abbreviation of the IEEE definition is "A . . . set of . . . standards . . . that . . . accomplish interoperability and portability of applications, data and people." The ISO definition is similar. Many UNIX vendors define an open system as a UNIX system.

OS/2   Operating System/2 for the Personal System line of computers. OS/2 extended edition provides multitasking, common communications interface, integrated relational database, and query functions.

OSF   Open Software Foundation. A not-for-profit organization that develops and delivers open technology to its members. There are several hundred members of OSF, including Apple, DEC, HP, Hitachi, IBM, ICL, Lotus, Microsoft, Motorola, Novell, and Xerox. OSF delivers five technologies: OSF/1, DCE, DME, Motif, and ANDF.

OSI   Open Systems Interconnect. Standards developed by ISO for an open network environment. The OSI Reference Model is an abstract model defining a seven-layer architecture of functions, with protocol standards defined at each layer.

OSI Reference Model   A seven-layer structure designed to describe computer network architectures and how data passes through them. Developed by ISO in 1978. Also see *International Organization for Standardization.*

Out-of-band   A communication channel other than the primary network that is carrying the data. For example, critical network management alerts should be communicated on a separate channel to guarantee their receipt.

OV   See *OfficeVision.*

OV/VM   See *OfficeVision.*

Packet   A set of data bytes that are transmitted as a group across a data network. A packet typically contains addressing and data information.

Packet-switched service   A type of telecommunication service that breaks up data into packets for transmission.

Packet switching   The transmission of data in small, discrete switching packets for the purpose of making more efficient use of physical data channels.

Palladium   Print management technology developed at MIT with IBM, Digital, and Hewlett-Packard. This is a complete set of end-user functions to submit and control printing in an open distributed environment.

Parallel Disk Array (PDA)   A storage system in which a set of small hard disks appear to be a single, fast hard disk to the operating system or application. See *PDA, RAID.*

Paradigm   A pattern, example, or model.

PASC Portable Applications Standards Committee. The new name for POSIX, based on the realization that it is more than UNIX.

Parity bit An extra bit appended to data for error-checking purposes. Based on the number of zero and one bits transmitted, either a zero or one parity bit is appended so that the sum of the one bits is either always odd (odd parity) or always even (even parity).

PBX A telephone switching system, purchased by a business, that interconnects telephone extensions to the public network.

PC Personal Computer.

PCI Peripheral Component Interconnect local bus. A standard internal connection in a PC for data transfer to peripheral controller components.

PCMCIA Personal Computer Memory Card International Association bus. A standard external connection that allows peripherals adhering to the standard to be plugged in and used without further system modification.

PCS Personal Communication Services. Future wireless communication service operating at radio frequencies of 120 Mhz in the 2 GHz range to provide a transport for data and voice.

PDA See *Parallel Disk Array.*

PDU Protocol Data Unit. A formally defined data structure to contain protocol information to be passed between entities. This is the OSI term for a packet.

Peer-to-Peer Communication Network communication between entities at the same network protocol layer.

Performance Management (PM) One of the five standard network management functions. PM facilities evaluate the behavior of network and layer entity resources and effectiveness of communication activities. PM can also adjust operating characteristics and generate network utilization reports by monitoring a station's performance [Modiri, 1991].

Performance model A software program that describes the operation of a complex system and then simulates its operation for the purpose of determining performance characteristics and bottlenecks.

PERT analysis Program Evaluation and Review Techniques. A method of deriving plans of action from a set of individual tasks. PERT analysis is used to identify critical paths in a complex plan.

Physical layer This OSI layer provides the procedures for transferring a single bit across a physical media.

Physical Media Any means in the physical world for transferring signals between OSI systems.

Ping Packet internet groper. A program used to test reachability of destinations by sending them an ICMP echo request and waiting for a reply. The term is used as a verb: "Ping host X to see if it is up!"

Platform   A product, design, or architecture upon which applications, other products, or designs can be built.

Points of presence   A term for connectivity ports in a network.

Port   The abstraction used by Internet transport protocols to distinguish among multiple simultaneous connections to a single destination host.

Portability   Provides the freedom to run application programs on computers from many vendors without rewriting the program code.

POSIX   Portable Operating System Interface. The "X" at the end denotes that POSIX is a UNIX-type specification. POSIX is a set of interfaces involved in applications portability to systems.

PostScript   The de facto printer language in the client/server computing environment. Developed by Adobe Systems Inc., it is capable of printing varied fonts, graphics, image, and color.

PPP (Point-to-Point Protocol)   Proposal for multiprotocol transmission of datagrams over serial (point-to-point) links (RFC 1171/1172). Can be used as the underlying protocol for TCP/IP transmission over telephone lines, for example. It is seen as the successor to SLIP. PPP is based on HDLC.

Print server   A server connected to the network that completes printing requests by clients on the network.

Private WAN   A private, usually leased line, WAN service. Private WAN services, such as T1 and T3, offer high-speed data transmission from 1.54 Mbps to 44 Mbps.

PRMD   Private Management Domain. An X.400 Message Handling System private organization mail system.

Protocol   A formal definition of information interchange. In networking terms, protocol refers to the bits of information added to transmitted data that permit its successful receipt.

Protocol stack   Usually used to refer to the OSI seven-layer protocol stack. Implies the bits of information added to transmitted data as it is passed from level to level by a well-defined series (stack) of software subroutines to guarantee its successful transmission over a network.

Proxy   The mechanism whereby one system represents another system in responding to protocol requests. Proxy systems are used in network management to avoid having to implement full protocol stacks in simple devices, such as modems.

Public WAN   A WAN service offered by a vendor in which data traffic from several customers is interleaved.

Pull installation   The delivery of software over a network to a computing system initiated by the user of the target computing system.

Push installation   The delivery of software over a network to a computing system either initiated by network administration or automatically initiated by another application.

RAID   Redundant Array of Inexpensive Disks. A de facto standard that defines how 2 or more inexpensive hard disks can be combined to provide enhanced fault tolerance or performance in a computer system. RAID level 0 defines disk mirroring. RAID level 5 defines data striping across multiple disks with checksum data.

RBOC   Regional Bell Operating Company. See *BOC*.

Redirector   Client software that accepts requests from application programs and routes them across the network for service.

Redirection   A function performed by a network operating system, such as IBM's OS/2 LAN Server program, to give access to a resource on a network (such as a server hard disk) as if it was on the client's system.

Remote client   A term used to describe the service to a remote workstation to share data and applications located on a common WAN/LAN server. The remote client approach supports small single-server networks but does not scale well to support large or distributed environments.

Remote node   A term used to describe the service to a remote workstation interacting with an on-site communications server. The device driver within the LAN-attached communication server enables the server to take incoming data off a WAN and put it onto the LAN and vice versa. This approach can easily accommodate growth in the number of remote LAN users.

Remote Procedure Call (RPC)   The DCE communications mechanism that enables subprograms to execute on several servers in the network while an application is running. A message from the client application is sent to the remote server, requesting its services. The RPC can be represented by a program written in any computer language.

Repeater   A communication device that simply amplifies network traffic at the physical layer for further transmission of that amplified signal.

REXX   An IBM-developed programming language, available for several operating systems (including VM and OS/2), used to create applications involving high-level manipulation of operating system resources.

RFC   Request for Comment. Documents created by Internet researchers on computer communication.

Rich text   A term describing the capability of a document or a part of a document to contain text, graphics, scanned images, audio, and full-motion video data.

Rightsize   The action of a large business to move from an exclusive mainframe-centric computing environment to a best-fit-of-technology computing environment, where a mix of PCs, workstations, PC servers, workstation servers, minicomputers, and mainframes interoperate in a client/server computing network.

RIP Routing Information Protocol. Early BSD UNIX routing protocol used within a small network.

RISC Reduced Instruction Set Computer. A computer in which the processor's instruction set is limited to constant-length instructions that can usually be executed in a single clock cycle.

RMON Remote Network Monitoring MIB. An extension to SNMP that defines a set of standardized management objects for remote network monitoring.

Route The path that network traffic takes from its source to its destination. Also, a possible path from a given host to another host or destination.

RPC See *Remote Procedure Call.*

ROSE Remote Operations Service Element. A protocol used in OSI Message Handling, Directory, and Network Management application protocols.

Router A device that is used to interconnect networks and intelligently route data traffic based upon the transmission protocol employed. A router is preferred in TCP/IP internetworks because of its ability to support the complex networks in which the protocol is typically employed. Individual LANs or groups of LANs can be treated as a logical subnetwork by a router within a larger, more complex network. Routers are devices that terminate data link or logical link protocols, making it possible for routers to match protocols from LAN to WAN.

RS232C Established by the Electronics Industries Association (EIA) in 1969, RS232C is a standard defining the electrical signaling and cable connection characteristics of a serial port, the most common type of communications circuit used today. DTE (Data Terminal Equipment) and DCE (Data Communications Equipment) classes of equipment are defined. Most Personal Computers have DTE ports. The connection is typically a 25-pin D-shell with a male plug on the DTE end. The DCE end is a female plug. IBM abbreviated the plug to a 9-pin D-shell with the introduction of the PC AT in 1984. An RS232C connection includes several independent circuits sharing the same cable.

RS/6000 RISC System/6000. IBM workstation systems employing the Power RISC chips, typically used for computer-aided design activities.

RSR Remote Site Recovery. The existence of a remote data center capable of assuming data processing operations in the event of a catastrophic failure in the main center.

RTF (Rich Text Format) A standard for encoding text and graphics developed by Microsoft.

RTL Register Transfer Logic. An intermediate form of digital logic design description used by electrical engineers in the simulation of digital designs.

QMF Query Management Facility. A data query utility that is part of IBM DB/2 database systems.

SAP Service Access Point. An address in a network where service is provided. An SSAP, or source SAP, is the source address of a service request. A DSAP, or destination SAP, is the destination address of a service request. These addresses are typically network-unique numbers placed in data frames to ensure successful delivery of information.

SCSI Small Computer Systems Interface. An industry-standard high-speed interface typically used for hard disk storage device attachments to PC or workstation systems.

Security Management (SM) One of the five standard network management functions. SM facilities provide for the protection of the network resources. SM includes authorization facilities, access controls, encryption, authentication, maintenance, and examination of security logs [Modiri, 1991].

Segment A LAN's physical elements, a term typically used when the LAN is part of a complex network. Sometimes the term *LAN segment* is used.

Server A system on a network that provides services to a requesting system, or client.

Server farm An area reserved for a large number of server systems with raised floor (to avoid wiring clutter), enhanced cooling, uninterruptible power, and centralized console-based management.

Session The logical stream of data between two programs over a network.

Shared Media a term used to describe a typical multidrop LAN (e.g., Ethernet or token-ring) in which the connected PCs or workstations share the bandwidth of the media.

SGML Standard Generalized Markup Language. An industry-standard document tagging language used to create formatted documents when interpreted by a document compiler.

SIDF System-Independent Data Format. A media format standard for data backup that is part of the SMS standard.

Single-mode fiber Optical fibers used for long-distance transmissions.

SLIP Serial Line Interface Protocol. A protocol for IP data transmission over serial lines (RFC 1055), such as telephone circuits or RS-232 cables interconnecting two systems. SLIP is now being replaced by PPP. See *PPP*.

SMAE Systems-Management Application Entity. An application entity whose purpose is system management.

Smalltalk   An object-oriented language developed in the early 1970s by Xerox at its Palo Alto Research Center (PARC).

SMAP   System-Management Application Process. An application process participating in systems management.

SmartIcons   The term used to describe application-specific icons in Lotus Development applications, which are smart because they simplify or automate tasks within an application when selected. SmartIcons can be created by users, depending upon the application, to create a more customized environment.

SMDS   Switched Multi-megabit Data Service. A high-speed, long-distance digital data transmission protocol suite. Transmission of data is via datagrams. It is similar to frame relay services in that it can be used to interconnect LANs over a high-speed WAN.

SMI   Structure of Management Information standard, ISO IS 10165-1 and 4. The definition of the contents and organization of network management information to be contained in the MIB. It is described using ASN.1.

SMP   Symmetric MultiProcessing. A computer architecture in which tasks are distributed among two or more processors.

SMS   Storage Management Services. A set of standards for data backup, including application programming interfaces and data formats, created by an industry consortium led by Novell Corporation.

SMTP   Simple Mail Transport Protocol that utilizes TCP/IP. It is a widely used e-mail protocol developed for the Internet. (RFCs 821, 822).

SNA   IBM's mainframe-based Systems Network Architecture.

SNMP   Simple Network Management Protocol. Issued in August 1988, SNMP includes a minimal but powerful set of facilities for monitoring and controlling network elements using a simple structure of management information (SMI), MIB, and the protocol.

SNMPv1   The common acronym for SNMP after SNMPv2 was produced.

SNMPv2   SNMP Version 2. Proposed in December 1992, SNMPv2 includes security enhancements, interoperability with SNMPv1 products, and RMON concepts to support management of a hierarchy of networks.

Socket   A service interface to the Internet; a process opens a socket, identifies the network service required, binds the socket to a destination, and then transmits/receives data.

SOM   Systems Object Model. A rich, language-neutral technology for building, packaging, and manipulating objects. It can be used easily by both object-oriented programming languages and procedural languages.

SONET   Synchronous Optical Network. A standard for high-speed— 51.84 Mbps (OC-1) to 2.488 Gbps (OC-48)—Data transmission over a fiber-optic network. It is being used for telephone networks today. It is planned to be the platform technology for ATM data transmission services over a WAN.

Source program The high-level language text form of a computer program (e.g., C or FORTRAN source). Also called source code.

Source routing A protocol in which a sender node specifies the internetwork route to its destination in the data frame. This was originally developed by IBM for its token-ring networks.

Source-routing bridge A bridge that requires the transmitting station to completely specify the route for data in advance.

Spanning tree bridge A bridge that discovers a spanning tree path through a network by exchanging frames of data with neighboring bridges.

SPX Novell's Sequential Packet Exchange network protocol.

SQL Structured Query Language. A standard computer language that is used to describe requests for information from a relational database.

STA Spanning Tree Algorithm. An algorithm that determines a connection among a set of nodes in the form of a spanning tree. An STA algorithm will be used by a root bridge to create a nonlooping path among all of the bridges of an internetwork.

Starlan A LAN technology, developed by AT&T, that uses a star or bus topology.

STP Shielded Twisted-Pair cable used for LAN cabling.

Structured Wiring System A system of reliable network cabling as specified by the Electronic Industries Association and Underwriter's Laboratories. It provides a standard way to wire a building for different network types. A main distribution frame connects all interior wiring as well as providing connectivity from outside sources (e.g., telephones).

Subnet A set of networking nodes wherein each node can communicate directly to every other (e.g., a LAN). A set of subnets form a network (e.g., a routed internet of LANs).

Subnet address The subnet portion of an IP address. In a subnetted network, the host portion of an IP address is split into a subnet portion and a host portion using an address (subnet) mask.

Subnetwork A collection of OSI end systems and intermediate systems under the control of a single administrative domain and utilizing a single network access protocol. Examples: private X.25 networks, a collection of bridged LANs.

SVGA Super VGA. A de facto industry video graphics standard offering up to 1024 by 768 resolution and up to 256 simultaneously displayed colors.

Switch From a network perspective, a computer-controlled device that can switch digital network bandwidth from one destination to another on demand.

Switched Ethernet   A digital switch that connects network segments together while supporting the Ethernet protocol.

Switched Media   A term used to describe a networking environment in which all the bandwidth is delivered from a digital switch over the media to a receiving system (e.g., ATM).

System architecture   The principles of design used for a system.

SystemView   IBM's network management system based on System/390 systems as primary hosts.

T1   A digital data transmission service that can transport up to 1.544 Mbps. Digital communication is full-duplex. The bit stream can be viewed as 24 channels of 64 Kbps that are multiplexed on the aggregate 1.544 Mbps stream.

T3   A digital data transmission service that can transport up to 44.746 Mbps, incorporating 28 T1 circuits.

TCP   Transmission Control Protocol. A transport-level protocol for connection-oriented data transmission. It is the major transport protocol in the Internet suite of protocols providing reliable, connection-oriented, full-duplex streams. Uses IP for delivery.

TCP/IP   The set of applications and transport protocols that IP to transmit data over a network. TCP/IP was developed by the Department of Defense to provide telecommunications for internetworking.

Telnet   The virtual terminal protocol in the Internet suite of protocols. Allows users of one host to log into a remote host and interact as normal terminal users of that host.

Terminal emulator   Software that allows a PC or workstation to emulate (appear as) a dependent display terminal to a host computer system.

Text editor   A simple text and word processing application typically used by computer programmers to create and edit their source programs.

Thick Ethernet (10-base-5)   Ethernet physical medium (wiring) in which a doubly shielded, 50-ohm coaxial cable is used.

Thin Ethernet (10-base-2)   Ethernet wiring in which a single-shielded, 50-ohm coaxial cable is used.

Thread   A single flow of control within a process, where a process is an application program with one or more concurrently executing threads. A thread is to a process as a task is to a multitasking program.

Total Quality Management (TQM)   An approach to managing a business in which business processes and team organizations are focused on a constant cycle of quality and cost improvements leading to improved profitability.

TQM   See *Total Quality Management.*

Twisted-pair Ethernet (10Base-T)   Ethernet wiring in which an unshielded pair of entwined wires is used.

Token-ring   A LAN protocol that uses token passing for media access control and connects systems on a cable ring. A master card on the token ring initiates a free token. When a LAN adapter with data to send (source) receives this free token, it replaces the token with its data and sends it to the next LAN adapter on the ring for relay. When the target LAN adapter of the data receives it, an acknowledgment is sent back to the source, which then initiates a new free token.

Transceiver   Transmitter-receiver. The physical device that connects a host interface to a local area network, such as Ethernet. Ethernet transceivers contain electronics that apply signals to the cable and sense collisions.

Transport layer   A network service that typically provides end-to-end communication between two systems on a network while hiding details of the underlying data transmission.

Tunneling   Tunneling refers to encapsulation of protocol A within protocol B, such that A treats B as though it were a data link layer. Tunneling is used to get data between administrative domains that use a protocol that is not supported by the internetwork.

Twisted Pair   A wiring system used to connect telephones to distribution panels or to connect LANs. A pair of insulated wires are twisted together to avoid noise pickup, forming a single cable.

UDP   User Datagram Protocol. A transport protocol in the Internet suite of protocols. UDP, like TCP, uses IP for delivery; however, unlike TCP, UDP provides for exchange of datagrams without acknowledgments or guaranteed delivery.

UNIX   The operating system originally designed by AT&T and enhanced by the University of California at Berkeley and others. Since it was powerful and essentially available for free, it became very popular at universities. Many vendors made their own versions of UNIX available—for example, IBM's AIX, based on OSF/1. The UNIX trademark and definition has since come under the control of X/Open, who will issue a unifying specification.

Upload   A term used to describe the transmission of a file from a PC to a mainframe or from a client to a server. See *Download*.

UPS   Uninterruptible Power Supply. A device that is used to provide temporary backup power to a computer system.

UTP   Unshielded Twisted-Pair cable used for LAN cabling.

V.22bis   The designation of the 2,400 bps (bits per second) modem standard.

V.32   The designation of the 9,600 bps (bits per second) modem standard.

V.32bis   The designation of the 14,400 bps (bits per second) modem standard.

V.34   The designation of the soon-to-be-released 28,800 bps (bits per second) modem standard. See V.FAST.

V.42   The designation of the error control standard for modems.

V.42.bis   The designation of the data compression standard for modems.

V.FAST   Prereleased name of the V.34 modem standard.

VGA   Vector Graphics Array. A standard for PC graphics, introduced by IBM with the PS/2 family in 1987. It provides for 640 by 480 pixels and up to 256 simultaneous colors.

VIM   Vendor Independent Messaging. A cross-platform messaging API for building message-enabled applications. VIM is supported by a number of companies including IBM, Apple, Lotus, Borland, and Novell.

Virtual circuit   A network service that provides connection-oriented service regardless of the underlying network structure. See *Connection-oriented*.

Virus   A program that replicates itself on computer systems by incorporating itself into other programs that are shared among computer systems.

Visualization   Applications that replace numerical tables and low-resolution graphics with images of high information content that enable users to see complex information and relationships quickly and easily.

VM   IBM's Virtual Machine operating system for mainframe computers.

Wabi   Windows Application Binary Interface. A product written by Sun Microsystems to let applications written for Microsoft's Windows to run unmodified on UNIX systems.

WAN   Wide Area Network. A long-distance network for the efficient transfer of voice, data, and/or video between local, metropolitan, campus, and site networks. WANs typically use lower transfer rates (64 Kbps) or high-speed services such as T1, which operates at 1.544M bps. WANs also typically use common-carrier services (communications services available to the general public) or private networking through satellite and microwave facilities [Van Norman, 1994].

Waterfall model   A method of software development in which each development phase cascades into the next. The typical phases from start to finish are requirements definition, specification, design, coding, testing, installation, maintenance.

Wide Area Network   See *WAN*.

Wiring Hub   See *Hub*.

Workflow application   An application that facilitates the flow of work among users on a network.

Workplace Shell   The name of an IBM software development project to create an operating system kernel with consistent APIs portable to high-performance RISC and CISC processors. Multiple operating system personalities, such as OS/2 and AIX, will be able to run on the kernel.

Workstation client   An engineering workstation, such as an RS/6000 system, or a PC used to do design or development activities.

WYSIWYG   What You See Is What You Get. A term used to describe a feature of some graphic applications that render text or graphics images such that the appearance on the display precisely matches a hardcopy image.

X.25   CCITT standard for data transmission over a public data network. It was designed originally for connection of terminals to host computers. X.25 transports packets from point-to-point (via virtual circuits) over a WAN.

X.400   CCITT standard for message-handling services. To conform to X.400, client e-mail applications maintain their user interfaces but would change the file format of each e-mail message produced to conform to the X.400 standard. Correspondingly, they would each accept the X.400 format for incoming e-mail messages. The X.400 server would then handle the messages from any number of unique e-mail applications transparently.

X.500   CCITT standard that defines a file organization and interface to distributed directory data for network users and resources.

XDR   EXternal Data Representation. A standard for machine-independent data structures developed by Sun Microsystems. Similar to ASN.1.

XDS   X/Open Directory Service. An API that provides full access to X.500 directories.

XGA   eXtended Graphics Array. A video graphics standard introduced by IBM in 1990 offering up to 1024 by 768 resolution with up to 65,000 simultaneous colors.

X/Open   A standards acceleration body, founded in 1984 by Bull, ICL, Olivetti, Nixdorf, and Siemens. IBM joined X/Open in 1988. X/Open does not normally define standards but chooses from existing standards. X/Open actively supports IEEE POSIX projects.

X Recommendations   The CCITT documents that describe data communication network standards. Well-known ones include X.25 Packet Switching standard, X.400 Message Handling System, and X.500 Directory Services.

X-station   A dependent display terminal client that uses X-Windows application support across a client/server network.

X-Windows   A network GUI, developed at MIT, that gives users "windows" into applications and processes not located on their system. A vehicle for distributed applications among users of heterogeneous networks.

Appendix C:

Pro Forma Client/Server Financial Spreadsheet

This appendix contains table formats that help organize the financial details and assumptions necessary to calculate the cost of a client/server computing investment. It can be easily turned into a spreadsheet by those skilled in the art to become a living model for financial estimates and projections. All values in this appendix are sample values only.

Client Analysis

Following are the spreadsheet tables required to estimate the client portion of expenses and capital outlays.

Client Software License + Maintenance

This table should be used to gather together the license fees and terms for all operating systems, software services, applications, and network-installed applications. Its values will be used by other tables to compute per client expenses.

	Fee	Terms
Operating System, Services	$100	12 months
Network Application Licenses	$50	12 months, per concurrent user
Total		

Client Installation, Setup, and Quarterly Maintenance

Estimate

This table should be used to gather together estimates of client installation, setup, and maintenance costs to be used by other tables for computing per client expenses. Values are per client system and can be estimated based on approximate hours required by a service provider for a typical client multiplied by a typical hourly rate. As an example: installation/setup, 4 hours/client annually; software maintenance/quarter, 2 hours; and hardware maintenance/quarter, 2 hours. A contractor performing these tasks might cost $25/hour.

Install/Setup (per client)	Quarterly Maintenance (SW) (per client)	Quarterly Maintenance (HW) (per client)
$100	$50	$50

Client Replacement Assumptions

This table's entries should be based on your client inventory results. The percentage mix will be used to produce an accurate capital expenditure estimate for client systems. The values in the table are sample percentages.

	% Power Users in Organization	% Office Workers in Organization	% Systems Requiring Memory Upgrade	% Systems Requiring Storage Upgrade	% Systems Requiring Monitor Upgrade
Org. 1-	0%	100%	10%	25%	100%
Org. 2-	50%	50%	10%	25%	30%
Org. 3-	50%	50%	10%	25%	30%

Client Capital Charge Assumptions

The following values should reflect actual purchase prices of client systems and optional upgrades for use in computing accumulated capital expenditures. For example:

Power User $xxxx PS/2 Premium   Includes: 486 33Mhz, 16 MB RAM, 256 MB Hard Drive OS/2 2.1 Preloaded

Office Worker $yyyy PS/ValuePoint   Includes: 486DX 33Mhz, 16 MB RAM, 256 MB Hard Drive OS/2 2.1 Preloaded

Optional Upgrades:

  Memory $xxxx 12 MB Memory Upgrade

  Storage $xxxx 400 MB Disk Upgrade

  Monitor $yyyy 15″ FST, Noninterlaced, Power Managed Monitor

Client Installs by Area by Quarter

This table should reflect a realistic assessment of the total number of individuals to receive new or upgraded client systems spread across the migration period, based on the number of individuals planned to perform the installations, assuming *n* installs/day/installer. See Chapter 4 for additional details. For example: 2 installs/day/installer with 10 installers, yields 100 installs/week = 1,200 installs/quarter, the following table lays out a possible installation schedule.

	Head-Count	Q1	Q2	Q3	Q4
Organization 1	800	800			
Organization 2	1,000	400	600		
Organization 3	1,500		600	900	
Total		1,200	1,200	900	

Client Capital by Area by Quarter

The previous table of installs should be used in combination with client mix and capital cost to complete estimated capital for client systems by quarter by organization. For example, if each client system cost $2,000, capital outlay required by quarter is as follows:

	Q1	Q2	Q3	Q4	Total
Organization 1	$16,000		$16,000		
Organization 2	$8,000	$12,000			$20,000
Organization 3		$12,000	$18,000		$30,000
Total	$24,000	$24,000	$18,000		$66,000

Client Expense by Area by Quarter

The combined depreciation charges (5-year straightline assumed), licensing, installation (one-time), and quarterly maintenance costs should be included in this table based upon the estimated rollout schedule—the Client Installs by Area by Quarter table.

	Q1	Q2	Q3	Q4	Total
Organization 1	$200K	$80K	$80K	$80K	$440K
Organization 2	$100K	$250K	$100K	$100K	$550K
Organization 3	$250K	$225K	$150K	$625K	
Total	$300K	$580K	$405K	$330K	$1615K

Server Analysis

Following are the spreadsheet tables required to estimate the server portion of expenses and capital outlays.

Servers by Type

This table should be used to gather together the capital cost of servers by type, estimated number of clients supported by each server given its application, software license and support charges, and server installation/setup/support charges. It will be used to compute capital and expense estimates in the following tables.

Server Type	Capital Cost	# Clients/ Server	Server Software License File	Support/ Quarter	Install/ Setup/ Quarter
Lotus Notes	$xxxx	150	$yyyy	$zzzz	$zzzz
TaP/2	$xxxx	200	$yyyy	$zzzz	$zzzz
CallUp C/S	$xxxx	800	$yyyy	$zzzz	$zzzz
NetDoor	$xxxx	70	$yyyy	$zzzz	$zzzz
Gateways	$xxxx	400	$yyyy	$zzzz	$zzzz
Misc/File	$xxxx	100	$yyyy	$zzzz	$zzzz

Assumptions: Hardware Configuration: PS/2 Model 195, 486/50, 32 MB RAM, 1 GB SCSI, Redundant Power Supply

Server Base Software

This table should be used to gather the software license fees for the base operating system, services, and network operating system installed on all servers. It will be used in conjunction with the previous table to compute the expense budget for the servers.

	License	Frequency
OS/2 2.1	$xxxx	One-Time
LAN Server	$xxxx	One-Time
NTS/2 (LAPS)	$xxxx	One-Time
TCP/IP	$xxxx	One-Time
ADSM (BACKUP)	$xxxx	Annual
Total	$xxxx	

Server Expense by Quarter

This table uses the client rollout schedule in combination with the number of users per server and the expense per server to sum up server expense by quarter. Don't forget to combine depreciation charges (5-year straightline assumed), installation/setup, support, and license fees in the total per server.

	Q1	Q2	Q3	Q4	Total
Lotus Notes					
TaP/2					
CallUp C/S					
NetDoor					
Gateways					
Misc/File					
Total					

Server Capital by Quarter

This table uses the server rollout schedule to sum the server capital to be expended by quarter by application.

	Q1	Q2	Q3	Q4	Total
Lotus Notes					
TaP/2					
CallUp C/S					
NetDoor					
Gateways					
Misc/File					
Total					

Infrastructure Analysis

Following are the spreadsheet tables required to estimate the infrastructure portion of expenses and capital outlays.

Infrastructure Capital by Quarter

This table should reflect the analysis of the network support team, estimating the network infrastructure upgrades needed to support the new environment.

	Q1	Q2	Q3	Q4	Total
Backbone Upgrade*					
Routers, Bridges*					
External Connectivity*					
Network Mgmt*					
Etc.					
Total					

*Examples

Infrastructure Expenses by Quarter

This table should reflect the depreciation charges, license fees, installation/setup, and support expenses expected for the network infrastructure based on current load plus any changes due to the migration. Don't forget to include charges incurred for site-to-site support!

	Q1	Q2	Q3	Q4	Total
Local					
Regional					
Total					
Assumptions					
$/Headcount	$xxxx				
Local Headcount	y				
Regional Headcount	z				

Information Technology

Capital Summary by Quarter

This table rolls up the total capital plan for each major area.

	Q1	Q2	Q3	Q4	Total
Clients					
Servers					
Infrastructure					
Total					

Expense Summary by Quarter

This table rolls up the total expenses for each major migration area, plus any ongoing mainframe charges, estimated software development, WAN charges, and network printer maintenance.

	Q1	Q2	Q3	Q4	Total
Clients					
Servers					
Infrastructure					
Mainframe Charges					
Software Development					
WAN Charges					
Printer Maintenance					
Total					

Some Useful Measurements

Here are a few measurements gleaned from trade press and consultant studies that you might find useful in gauging the accuracy of your client/server migration expense estimate.

The ratio of I/S expense per employee divided by revenue per employee, expressed as a percentage, is a measure of a company's efficiency in providing I/S tools. Based on a late 1992 study [*Infoweek*, Sept. 21, 1992], the most efficient companies were in the 2% range. The least efficient companies reported were over 7%.

Based on a recent Dataquest study [Dataquest, Inc., 1993], the average number of end users per support person for PC systems is 100 to 1, the average number of end users per workstation is 53 to 3, and the combined average is 85 to 5. They estimated that support costs, considering support staff and external services (hardware, software, systems integration, and application development), averages over $4,500 per user.

According to Vaskevitch [1993], companies that had been spending 1.5% of their corporate budgets on mainframe expenses during the 1980s, by 1990 were spending an additional 1.5% of their corporate budgets on personal computer expenses.

Appendix D:

Client Migration Questionnaire

The following questionnaire is completed interactively on Lotus Notes or VM by the user to be migrated. If Lotus Notes is used, the result is a new document in the Lotus Notes Client Migration database. If VM is used, the result is a file which is automatically transmitted to and imported as a new document into the Lotus Notes Client Migration database. In addition, the user transmits his OS/2 CONFIG.SYS and STARTUP.CMD files, which are appropriately renamed (i.e. Customer's_last_name.SYS and Customer's_last_name.CMD) and attached to the associated Lotus Notes document in the database, as well.

Please fill out the questionnaire as completely as you can. The completeness of this questionnaire is very important. Incomplete answers will delay the rollout of your new system or upgrade parts and software. If you do not know the answer to a question, try asking a member of your department who may know how to obtain the information needed.

1. When are you *not* available over the next 3 to 4 months (due to vacation or product commitments)?:
2. User last name:
3. First name:
4. Are you a secretary?:

5. Serial number:
6. VM user ID:
7. VM node:
8. Department:
9. Internal zip:
10. Office/Floor:
11. How many token-ring drops are in the office?:
12. Are any not being used?:
13. Building:
14. Tie-Line:
15. Manager's name:

Software Section

16. What is your primary Operating System?:
17. What version are you running?:
    (If you are running OS/2, type *VER* at an OS/2 prompt.)
18. If you get a new system, do you require DOS Dual Boot on your new system?:
19. If no, do you require High Performance File System (HPFS) on drive D:?
20. Are you running LAN Requester?:
    If you answered *No* to question 20 skip to question 41.
    If you are getting a new system, the following questions will help us understand your current LAN usage so that we can make sure your new system is capable of logging on to the same domains and servers that you have access to today.
21. What version of LAN Requester are you running?:
    (Type *SYSLEVEL* at an OS/2 prompt and look for the most recent version of LAN Requester.)
22. What is your primary LAN user ID?:
    (This ID will be used for all other domains.)
23. What is your workstation ID?:
    (Look in C:\IBMLAN\IBMLAN.INI file, on the line saying "COM PUTERNAME=")

24. What is your default domain?:
(Look in C:\IBMLAN\IBMLAN.INI file, on the line saying "DOMAIN=")

25. Do you currently log onto this domain?:
If you answered No to question 25 skip to question 29.

26. What are your other external domain names, if any?:

27. Who is/are the server administrator(s) for these domains? (if you know):

28. Please specify what applications and services these servers provide (for example, file storage, file access, access to network/shared/or department printers, applications, etc.). Please specify the names of the applications and printers you use:

29. Do you currently have, or have you ever had, NetDoor installed on your PC?:

30. Do you currently have, or have you ever had, CMVC installed on your PC?:
If you answered No to question 30 skip to question 36.

31. What is your primary CMVC family?:
(In your CONFIG.SYS file, look for "SET CMVC_FAMILY=")

32. What is your CMVC ID?:
(In your CONFIG.SYS file, look for "SET USER=")

33. What is your CMVC home directory?:
(In your CONFIG.SYS file, look for "SET CMVC_HOME=")

34. Please provide your CMVC login override (if one):
(In your CONFIG.SYS file, look for "SET CMVC_BECOME=")

35. Do you have a business need for CMVC?:

36. If you use NetDoor (CORE), what are the critical CoreAdd or Net Door applications you currently use?:
(Examples: Gopher, Newsreader, Lotus 1-2-3)

37. Do you currently have TCP/IP installed on your workstation?:
(Look for a TCP/IP subdirectory somewhere in one of the root directories on your drives.)
If you answered No to question 37 skip to question 41.

38. What is your TCP/IP ID?:
(Type *HOSTNAME* at an OS/2 prompt to find out your TCP/IP ID. It should be XXXXXX.bocaraton.ibm.com)

39. What is your TCP/IP address?:

> (Type *HOST hostname* at an OS/2 prompt, where *hostname* is your TCP/IP ID. Should be 9.83 . . .)

40. How was TCP/IP installed? Locally with diskettes or over a LAN, or using NetDoor (where TCP/IP code is shared from a server)?:

41. The following products are necessary for the client/server environment:

OS/2	Lotus Notes	FTP	NetView DM/2
LAN Req.	Time and Place/2	LSM	Comm.Mgr (optional)
LAPS	CallUp C/S	IBM	AV/2PCPRINT (optional)
TCP/IP	NetDoor	MMPM/2	
APCM (optional)	CMVC (optional)	Dual Boot	(optional)

> Other than these, what are the three most critical applications currently on your system that will require migration to your new or upgraded system? (do not include applications accessed through NetDoor):

42. Do you have the original diskettes for these applications?:

43. Do you currently have (or have you ever had) Lotus Notes installed?:

44. If Yes, what is your Lotus Notes ID?:
(This is likely to be the same as your VM ID. It is equivalent to your Lotus Notes' "shortname," which you can look up in the Lotus Notes Address Book database.)

45. Do you currently have (or have you ever had) Time and Place/2 installed here in Boca?:

46. If Yes, what is your Time and Place/2 user ID?:

47. Do you have any Multimedia applications installed?:

48. If yes, what are they?:

Existing Hardware Section

(Do not use this section to configure a new system.)

49. Do you have a modem installed?:

50. Baud rate?:

51. Do you currently have a business need for a modem?: 52. Do you have an office printer?:

53. If so, specify printer make and model?:
(Example: IBM 4019 LaserPrinter, IBM Proprinter II, . . .)

54. Do you have any other unique hardware installed?:
(such as a CD-ROM or external floppy drive)

55. Specify other hardware device types/model:
(Example: IBM SCSI-2 External CD-ROM, IBM 5¼″
floppy drive)

56. Is this hardware SCSI or IDE?:

57. Is your pointing device a mouse, trackball, touch screen, or other?:

58. If other, specify:

Education Requirements

59. OS/2 will be the operating system used on the new systems. Do you need education on OS/2?

60. Lotus Notes is one of the new client/server tools that will be installed. Do you need education on Lotus Notes?

61. Time and Place/2 (TaP/2) is one of the new client/server tools that will be installed. Do you need education on TaP/2?

62. Callup C/S is one of the new client/server tools that will be installed. Do you need education on Callup C/S?

63. NetDoor is one of the new client/server tools that will be installed. Do you need education on NetDoor?

64. TCP/IP is a communication product that will be installed to support some of the new client/server tools. Do you need education on TCP/IP?

65. If you require education on OS/2 2.1, do you prefer an overview or in-depth course?:

66. For the rest of the products, what is your learning preference?:

67. Would you attend an information session on our client/server migration?

68. Would you attend an overview of networking concepts?

Home Terminal Section

69. Are you currently a home terminal user?

70. If yes, specify system model and operating system used at home:

71. Specify modem and baud rate:

72. Specify processor type (i.e., 286, 386, 486, etc.):

73. Specify DASD capacity for all hard disks (e.g., C:100 MB):

74. Specify amount of system memory:

Completion

75. If an installer or interviewer helped you with this questionnaire, how much time was spent in customer's office for the interview?

Appendix E:

Service Level Agreements

This appendix is a sample set of service-level agreements (SLAs) that you can use as a reference to gauge the quality and completeness of service provided by your information technology supplier(s).

General Support Activities for Network Infrastructure

Prime Shift Time
- 8 a.m. to 5 p.m. Monday through Friday.

Maintenance Window Time
- Sunday 8 a.m. to 12 noon as needed for Operating System Support.
- Saturday midnight to 8 a.m. Sunday as needed for Network Support.

Weekend and Offshift Coverage
- Beeper and paging coverage, within 3 hours of notification

Network Support Coverage
- Prime shift

- On-site utilizing Cellular and Phone/Beeper coverage

Change Control Procedure
- Input on Thursdays to Central Database

Power Downs
- Prior negotiations with customer required

Disaster Recovery
- Mission critical systems and files as defined by customer

Remote LAN Access
- System availability 24 hours a day, 7 days a week, except during Main Service
- Maintenance window on Sundays 00:01 a.m. to noon as needed
- Change control notification will be one week in advance
- A report will be maintained monthly

Network Availability - Office LAN infrastructure
- 99.5% System Availability 24 hours a day, 7 days a week, except during Main Service
- Maintenance window on Sundays 00:01 a.m. to noon as needed
- Report outages monthly utilizing NetView/6000

Network Availability - Labs
- Bridge code installation is automated from site network to lab network installation
- Request processed within two business days of notification for lab connectivity to site network
- Monthly reporting utilizing NetView/6000

Internet
- Server and router availability
- 99.5% system availability 24 hours a day, 7 days a week, except during Main Service
- Maintenance Window on Sundays 00:01 a.m. to noon as needed
- Monthly reporting utilizing NetView/6000

WAN Router Availability
- 99.5% System Availability 24 hours a day, 7 days a week, except during Main Service Maintenance Window on Sundays 00:01 a.m. to noon as needed
- Outages reported monthly

Secure Connections to Remote Vendor
- Dependent upon availability of routers and lines
- Individual SLA per customer and vendor
- System or application SLA is exposed and no workaround exists.

Problem Management. The Problem Management Process is the detecting, reporting, and correcting problems that are impacting customer service. Following is a definition and target turnaround time for customer problems.

	Severity	Turnaround Time	Definition
A problem immediately resolved by the Help Desk.	0	NA	Information Only
Major outage with no alternatives.	1	24 hrs	Critical Impact
Major outage with no alternatives.	2	72 hrs	SLA Exposed
System or application SLA is exposed and a workaround exists, but the customer must have a correction within 7 days.	3	7 days	Functional impact
System or application SLA is exposed and a workaround exists.	4	30 days	Minor Impact

Server and Application Support SLAs

These SLAs include the server support and applications that run on the server. Server support includes server hardware planning, installation and configuration; customization; user ID administration; access control profiles and resource installations/assignments; security requirements and auditability.

Maintenance
- Server maintenance will include timely hardware upgrades as configuration and capacity measurements warrant. Software will be maintained at the current supported product level.
- Operating system upgrades will be provided within 30 days of availability except if software conflicts exist.

Availability
- Server availability will be targeted for 24 hours per day, 7 days per week. A maintenance window will be Sunday morning from 8 a.m. until 12 noon as required and with prior customer notifi-

cation. Emergency problem correction will occur with as minimal downtime to the customer as possible. Outages will be measured and documented, and will include customer notification.

Gateways
- All gateways will have the same support as indicated above for all servers. Measurements will be provided as required for performance tracking.

Server Backup/Recovery
- Daily backup of all customer data is currently provided via ADSM. Archiving of seven days of customer data will be provided. An off-site disaster recovery plan will be provided in conjunction with input provided by the customer for vital records.
- Default length of time to retain archive version = 365 days (archive files will be deleted after 365 days).
- Centrally scheduled archive window will be set up upon customer request only. This does not apply to client initiated archives.
- ADSM Server availability is 24 hours, 7 days a week, except for 8 a.m. - 12 a.m. maintenance window on Sunday.
- Vital records will be identified by the customer. They will be backed up weekly to an off-site location.

Server Coverage - Offshift and Weekends
- Coverage will be provided via a server monitoring paging system.
- Response time for second shift outages will be within 1 hour from pager notification.
- Response time for third shift outages will be within 1.5 hours of pager notification.

PC/Workstation Support SLAs

In-Office Support (Includes Installations)
- Initial request will be received via the current Help Desk support process (1st level support).
- Customer request requiring additional technical assistance may be forwarded to 2nd level support for resolution.
- Requests that require 'hands on' assistance will be forwarded from 2nd level to 3rd level (site) support.

- Customer contact will be initiated by Level 3 support within 3 hours of receiving notification, or by 10:00 a.m. the next business day if notification is after 4:00 p.m.
- Level 3 measurements: number of Level 3 calls and time to initial customer contact

Backup/Recovery

Customers are assigned a default management class that their files will be bound to upon registration. Additional management classes may be requested if the defaults do not meet the customer's need. The defaults in effect will be:

- Copy Frequency = 0 (Zero days allows clients to back up at will.)

- Number of backup versions

If client data exists = 2 (file still exists on workstation)

If client data is deleted = 1 (file has been deleted from workstation)

- Length of time to retain extra backup versions = 30 days (Oldest copy of backup deleted from ADSM after 30 days).

- Length of time to retain only backup version = 60 days (files deleted from workstation will be deleted from ADSM backup after 60 days).

- Copy mode = modified (only changed files will be backed up).

- Copy serialization = shared static (file must not be changing during backup. ADSM will try a number of times to back up the file. If the file is changing during each attempt this file will not be backed up.).

- Centrally scheduled backup window = 6:00 p.m. - 6:00 a.m. (Clients will be randomly selected by server to begin backup during this window. This window is for centrally scheduled backups only and does not apply to client initiated backups).

- Backup/recovery response time

File stored on on-line storage = immediate

File stored on off-line storage = 5 min. turnaround for tape mount

References

Adams, E. K. "Global Commonality in User Requirements (Network Management), Integrated Network Management, II," *Proceedings of the IFIP TC6/WG6.6, Second International Symposium 1991*, pp. 171–81.

Anderson, H. A. Jr. "Achieving the Intelligent Network Objectives of the 1990's by Integrating Heterogeneous Systems," Information Network and Data Communication III. *Proceedings of the IFIP TC6 International Conference 1990*, pp. 193–204.

Anonymous, *Client/Server Computing: Managing the Open Enterprise*, Faulkner Information Services CD-ROM, April, 1994.

Anonymous, *Client/Server Research Notes*, Gartner Group, October 25, 1993.

Anonymous. "Engineering Workstations and PCs," *IEEE Spectrum*, April 1994, p. 46.

Anonymous. "Planning for Network Management," *PC Week*, Networking Supplement, March 8, 1993, p. 49.

Anonymous, *Survey of MIS Professionals*, Sentry Market Research, Westboro, Massachusetts, 1992.

Barrett, R. "SNMP versus CMIP—Competitive or Complementary?" Networks 92. *Proceedings of the TC6 International Conference 1992*, pp. 91–100.

Anonymous, "Top 10 Barriers to Client/Server Implementation," *Computerworld*, May 23, 1994, p. 12.

Ben-Artzi, A. et al. "Network Management of TCP/IP Networks: Present and Future," *IEEE Network,* July 1990, pp. 35–43.

"BIG–LAN Frequently Asked Questions Memo," *BIG–LAN Digest, Vol. 4,* February 14, 1992, p. 18.

Boar, B. H. *Implementing Client/Server Computing: A Strategic Perspective,* McGraw–Hill, Inc., New York, 1993.

Borsook, P. "Data Communications," *IEEE Spectrum,* January 1994, pp. 27–28.

Bradner, S. "LAN Management Tips," *Infoworld,* December 13, 1993, p. 51.

Bryan, J. "IDE Takes Off," *Byte,* March 1994, p. 99.

Burns, N. and Chalstrom, B. "Just go with the (work)flow," *PC Week/Netweek,* November 29, 1993, pp. N/5–N/7.

Callahan, P. D. and Hyland, J. L. "The Bandwidth Bogeyman," *The Network Strategy Report,* Forrester Research, Inc., July 1993.

Carney and Gavurin. "Managing large Ethernet installations," *Business Communications Review (USA),* Vol. 23., No. 3, March 1993, pp. 21–26.

Carpenter, G. and Wijnen, B. "SNMP-DPI," *Network Working Group, Request for Comments: 1228,* May 1991.

Carr, J. "Backing Up the Enterprise," *Data Communications,* September 21, 1992, pp. 87–92.

Caruso, R. E. "Network Management: A tutorial overview," *IEEE Communications (USA),* Vol. 28, No. 3, March 1990, pp. 20–25.

Case, J. et. al. "A Simple Network Management Protocol," *Request for Comments: 1157,* MIT Laboratory for Computer Science, May, 1990.

Cerf, V. G. "Networks," *Scientific American,* Vol. 265, No. 1, September 1991, pp. 72–81.

Comer, D. *Internetworking with TCP/IP: Principles, Protocols and Architecture.* Prentice-Hall, Englewood Cliffs, New Jersey, 1988.

Cox, J. "Client/Server Apps are Gaining Ground," *Communications Week,* June 27, 1994, p. 70.

Coy, P. "Start with Some High-Tech Magic . . . ," *Business Week, Enterprise 1993,* pp. 24–25.

Davidson, R. P and Muller, N. J. *LANs to WANs: Network Management in the 90's: Operation, Design, and Management,* Artech House, Boston, 1990.

Day, B. "Rightsizing and C/S—Strategies, Trends, and the Customer Decision Process," *Dataquest.*

Deming, W. E. *Out of the Crisis.* Massachusetts Institute of Technology. 1982.

Derfler, F J. and Freed, L. *How Networks Work,* Ziff-Davis Press, Emeryville, CA, 1993.

Dix, H. S. and Woodring, S. D. "Client/Server Core Applications," *The Soft-*

ware Strategy Report Executive Summary, July 1993, Forrester Research, Inc., Cambridge, MA.

Embry, J. et. al. "An Open Network Management Architecture: OSI/NM Forum Architecture and Concepts," *IEEE Network Magazine,* July 1990, pp. 14–22.

Faul, B. M. "Using a CLIPS Expert System to Automatically Manage TCP/IP Networks and Their Components," *Second CLIPS Conference Proceedings,* September 1991, Vol. 1, pp. 41–51.

Flint, D. "Client Server Technology," Advanced Information Systems. *The New Technologies in Today's Business Environment Proceedings 1992,* pp. 41–48.

Francis, B. "Automate Your Asset Management," *Datamation,* June 1, 1993, pp. 47–50.

Freedman, A. *The Computer Glossary.* Amacom, New York, 1993.

Ga Cote, R. "Multiprocessor Horsepower," *Byte,* March 1994, pp. 129–134.

Gagliardi, *Client/Server Computing: Killing the Mainframe Dinosaur and Slashing Runaway MIS Costs*, Prentice-Hall, Englewood Cliffs, N.J., 1994.

Gasparro, D. M. and DeMartini, W. A. "Case Study: Booz, Allen Buys a Frame Relay Network," *Data Communications,* July 1993, pp. 70–84.

Gold, D. "Defining Network Management," *Network Management,* International Data Corporation, Framingham, Mass., No. 6304, Vol. 1.

Govoni, S. "The Birth of CDPD," Mobile Computing Supplement, *Communications Week,* March 7, 1994.

Hackathorn, D. "Client Server Database Networking," *Database Review,* Vol. 4, No. 1, February 1992, pp. 9–11.

Harper, L. and Bleakley, F. "An Era of Low Inflation Changes the Calculus for Buyers and Sellers," *The Wall Street Journal,* Vol. CCXXIII, January 14, 1994, p. 1.

Harrison, D. "File Servers," *Network Computing,* June 15, 1994, p. 20.

Herman, J. "Architectures and Standards for Multivendor Network Management," *Business Communications Review,* Vol. 21, No. 6, June 1991, pp. 79–80.

Hoffherr, G. D. et. al. *Breakthrough Thinking in Total Quality Management,* Prentice-Hall, Englewood Cliffs, NJ, 1994.

Infonetics Research Inc., "The High-Speed LAN Race: Winners and Losers," *PC Week,* January 10, 1994, p. 37.

IBM. *Image Plus—High Performance Transaction System,* GC31–2706–0, 1990.

IBM Networking Systems. *ATM Strategy, ATM System Management, Networking Systems,* Research Triangle Park, NC, July 13, 1993.

IBM. *Open Client/Server Computing,* June 1993.

IBM International Technical Support Organization, *Local Area Network Concepts and Products,* Document Number GG24–3178–03, Raleigh, NC, January 1994.

IBM Think Magazine, January/February 1993.

Jacobsen, O. and Lynch, D. *A Glossary of Networking Terms,* RFC 1208, March, 1991.

Jander, M. "Coming Soon to a Network Near You," *Data Communications International.* Vol. 21, No. 16, Nov. 1992.

Jander, M. "Proactive LAN Management" *Data Communications,* March 21, 1993, pp. 49–56.

Katz, R. H. "Network Attached Storage Systems," *Proceedings, Scalable High Performance Computing Conference* SHPCC 92, 1992, pp. 68–75.

Klerer, M. "The OSI Management Architecture: An Overview," *IEEE Network,* March 1988, pp. 13–19.

Kochmer, J. and NorthWestNet. "The Internet Passport: NorthWestNets Guide to Our World Online," NorthWestNet, Bellevue, WA, 1992.

Krol, E. *The Whole Internet.* O'Reilly and Associates, Inc., Sebastopol, CA. 1993.

Lazar, J. "The Cost of Wireless Data," Mobile Computing Supplement, *Communications Week,* March 7, 1994.

Lile, E. A. "Client/Server Architecture: A Brief Overview," *Journal of Systems Management,* December 1993, pp. 26–29.

Malamud, C. *Analyzing Sun Networks,* Van Nostrand Reinhold, New York, NY, 1992.

Malamud, C. *Stacks: Interoperability in Today's Computer Networks.* Prentice-Hall, Englewood Cliffs, NJ, 1992.

Mazda, F. "Conversion or Collision: SNMP and CMIP (Part I)", *Telecommunications,* September, 1991.

Mazda, F. "Conversion or Collision: SNMP and CMIP (Part II)", *Telecommunications,* November, 1991.

McCloghrie, K. et al. "Defining a Protocol Independent Management Information Base," *Proceedings of the IFIP TC6/WG6.6 Symposium on Integrated Network Management, 1989,* pp. 185–95.

McCusker, T. "LAN Hubs' Future Is in Switching," *Datamation,* January 7, 1994, pp. 55–58.

McFadden, C. "Client/Server Training," *Client/Server Computing: Managing the Open Enterprise,* CD–ROM,Faulkner Information Services, April, 1994.

Meir, E. E. "The Second Language of Networking," *Communications Week,* February 14, 1994, p. 55.

Meyer, M. "Rethinking Your Mainframe," *Newsweek,* June 6, 1994.

Modiri, N. "An Implementation of the Common Network Management Information Service Element Interfaces," *IEEE Communications Magazine,* July, 1991, pp. 29–38.

Morris, C. R and Ferguson, C. H. "How Architecture Wins Technology Wars," *Harvard Business Review,* March–April 1993, pp. 86–96.

Nolle, T. A. "Internetworking in the TCP/IP LAN Environment," *Datapro Communications Series: LAN Internetworking*, Delran, N.J., June 1992.

Patel, A. "Comprehensive network management issues, requirements and a model" Issues in LAN Management, II. *Proceedings of the IDIP TC6/WG6. 4a International Symposium 1991,* pp. 1–20.

Personick, S. D. "Towards Global Information Networking," *Proceedings of the IEEE,* Vol. 81, No. 11, November 1993, pp. 1549–1557.

Peters, T. *Liberation Management, A.A.* Knopf, New York, 1992, p. 108.

Pollack, A. "Now It's Japan's Time to Play Catch-up," *The New York Times,* Nov. 21, 1993. Presuhn, R. "Considering CMIP", *Data Communications,* Vol. 19, No. 4, March 1990, pp. 55–60.

Reinhardt, A. "Building the Data Highway," *Byte,* March 1994, pp. 46–74.

Rothfeder, J. "Is Big Iron Good for You?" *Beyond Computing,* May/June, 1993.

Sakata, S. "B-ISDN Multimedia Workstation Architecture," *IEEE Communications Magazine,* Vol. 31, No. 8, August 1993, pp. 64–67.

Scheier, R. L. "Put Your System to the Test—Early," *PC Week,* June 27, 1994, p. 26.

Schneider, J. "Shouldering the Burden of Support," *PC Week,* November 15, 1993, p. 123.

Schnurr, A. "Support is No. 1," *PC Week,* November 15, 1993, p. 126.

Semilof, M. "Expert Discusses Multimedia Implementations on Networks," *Communications Week,* September 13, 1993, pp. 23–24.

Shaw, L. "LAN Servers Won't Make the Mainframe Go Away," *PC Week,* Jan 31, 1994, p. 63.

Sinha, A. "Client Server Computing: Current Technology Review," *Communications of the ACM* Vol. 35, No. 7, July, 1992, pp. 77–98.

Sluman, C. "Architectures for Network and Systems Management," *IEEE Colloquium on Network Management,* London, October 1991, pp. 1–11.

Spicer, J. "Backing up the Network," *IEEE Spectrum,* April 1994, pp. 66–69.

Spragins, J. D. *Telecommunications: Protocols and Design ,* Addison-Wesley, Reading, MA, 1992, pp. 407, 416.

Stallings, W. *SNMP, SNMPv2, and CMIP, The Practical Guide to Network-Management Standards,* Addison-Wesley, Reading, MA, 1993.

Stallings, W. "SNMP-Based Network Management: Where Is It Headed?" *Telecommunications Magazine,* June 1993, pp. 87–92.

Stalvey, A. "The Value of Workgroup Computing," *IBM Workgroup Computing News,* September, 1993.

Stevenson, J. G. "Management of Multivendor Networks," *IBM System Journal,* Vol. 31, No. 2, 1992 pp. 189–205.

Tan, F. B. and King, P. G. "LAN Based Client Server System: A New Zealand Experience," IFIP TC8/WG8. 4, *Working Conference on the Open Systems Future: Leveraging the LAN,* Australia, September 1993. Tapscott, D. and Caston A. *Paradigm Shift,* McGraw-Hill, Inc., New York, 1993.

Terplan, K. "Standardized Multivendor Network Management," *NOMS '92. IEEE 1992 Network Operations and Management Symposium, 1992,* Vol. 2, pp. 457–467.

Van Kirk, D. "What Is Client/Server Computing Anyway?" *Infoworld,* November 15, 1993, p. 107.

Van Kirk, D. "Finding Network Bottlenecks Before They Find You," *Infoworld,* November 22, 1993, pp. 54–62.

Van Norman, H. "High-Speed LAN Technologies," Faulkner Information Services, Client/Server Computing: Managing the Open Enterprise, *CD-ROM,* April, 1994.

Van Norman, H. "LAN/WAN Internetworking Optimization Techniques," Faulkner Information Services, Client/Server Computing: Managing the Open Enterprise, *CD-ROM,* April, 1994.

Vaskevitch, D. *Client/Server Strategies—A Survival Guide for Corporate Reengineers.* IDG Books, San Mateo, CA, 1993.

Wallace, S. "Managing Mass Storage," *Byte,* March 1994, pp. 78–90.

Wilke, J. R. "Computer Links Erode Hierarchical Nature of Workplace Culture," *The Wall Street Journal,* December 9, 1993, p. 1.

Wrobel, L. A. "Write a Great Disaster Recovery Plan," *Network Computing,* March 1, 1994, pp. 96–97.

Epilogue

The IBM PC Company Moves to Raleigh, NC.

Announced in August 1994, this move appeared to threaten the success of the client/server migration. However, the PC Company strategy was to go client/server and make the Boca Raton environment and tools suite the standard for all employees. This meant that those PC Company users transferring to Raleigh would take their office client system with them. Therefore, a transition plan was developed with the new PC Company CIO in Raleigh and ISSC to plant the seeds of client/server productivity in North Carolina. It is turning out that the client/server environment is portable with careful planning, teamwork, and a little groupware. . . .

The Boca Rollout—December 1994

There have been many exciting accomplishments so far; there will be more to come in the months ahead. Critical mass in finances, infrastructure, teamwork, user support and management dedication has led Boca Raton to the threshold of IBM leadership in client/server computing.

There is now a large and growing user community, adapting to the new environment and enriching it as they go. It is only fitting that the original home of the IBM PC Company and OS/2 reach this pinnacle.

About the Author

Steve Krantz is a Senior Programmer with IBM in Boca Raton. He is the project leader responsible for the Boca Raton client/server migration in 1994. During his 26 years with IBM, Steve has held several management and technical positions. He has been the Boca Raton site Design Tools Manager, and, as Micro Channel Architecture Manager, he was part of the team responsible for the introduction of the IBM PS/2 family of systems in 1987. Steve has lectured internationally for IBM Marketing and has served as the announcement coordinator for IBM PC Company products. Steve occasionally teaches computer graphics at the graduate level at Nova Southeastern University in Ft. Lauderdale, Florida. He has a Bachelor of Arts in Mathematics from Queens College, an M.S. in Systems and Information Science from Syracuse University, and a Ph.D. in Computer Science from Nova Southeastern University. Material from his doctoral thesis was used in the creation of this book.

Steve is married with two children and lives in Coral Springs, Florida.

Index

Reader Feedback Sheet

Your comments and suggestions are very important in shaping future publications. Please jot down your thoughts here, photocopy this page, and
fax to (904) 934-9981 or mail it to:

Maximum Press
Attn: Jim Hoskins
605 Silverthorn Road
Gulf Breeze, FL 32561

MAXIMUM PRESS ORDER FORM

Quantity	Title	Price	ISBN	Total
	Marketing on the Internet / Mathiesen (5/95)	$39.95	1-885068-01-8	
	The IBM PowerPC Series / Hoskins, Bradley (5/95)	$29.95	0-9633214-5-5	
	Exploring the PowerPC Revolution! / 2nd ed. / Hoskins (4/95)	$22.95	1-885068-02-6	
	IBM Personal Computers, 8th ed. / A Business Perspective / Hoskins (4/95)	$27.95	0471-04795-3	
	Exploring the IBM AS/400 Advanced 36 / Hoskins, Dimmick	$19.95	1-885068-00-X	
	Exploring the IBM RISC System/6000 Model 41 / MaxFacts Special Report / Hoskins	$19.95	0-9633214-8-X	
	IBM RISC System/6000, 5th ed. / A Business Perspective / Hoskins	$27.95	0471-04809-7	
	IBM AS/400, 5th ed. / A Business Perspective / Hoskins	$25.95	0471-59934-4	
	IBM System/390, 3rd ed. / A Business Perspective / Hoskins	$29.95	0471-04805-4	
	What About ProductManager? / Curtis	$34.95	0-9633214-4-7	

Subtotal

Shipping/Handling: First book $3.75 ($5 Canada); Each additional book, $1.75 ($2 Canada)

OVERSEAS SHIPPING/HANDLING
$18 (delivery in 4-6 weeks) or
$27 (delivery in 3-5 working days)

Florida and Tennessee customers add appropriate sales tax

TOTAL

☐ Visa   ☐ Check enclosed
☐ Mastercard ☐ Bill me (U.S. customers only)

Card # ☐☐☐☐☐☐☐☐☐☐☐☐☐☐☐☐

Exp. Date ☐☐☐☐

Signature _____

Phone orders: (800) 989-6733 code 391
Fax orders: (615) 254-2408
Mail orders: Maximum Press
1501 County Hospital Rd.
Nashville, TN 37218

NAME _____
TITLE _____
COMPANY _____
ADDRESS _____
CITY _____
STATE/ZIP _____
PHONE _____
SIGNATURE _____

(ORDER IS INVALID WITHOUT SIGNATURE AND PHONE NUMBER)

TAPE BUSINESS CARD HERE

**Satisfaction
Guaranteed
or Your
Money Back!**